Carol Ankney's

HeartLines

Heartlines

ISBN: 978-0-9787472-8-2
Printed in the United States of America
©2010 by Carol Ankney

Cover and interior design by Isaac Publishing, Inc.

Library of Congress Cataloging-in-Publication Data

IPI
Isaac Publishing, Inc.
P.O. 342
Three Rivers, MI 49093
www.isaacpublishing.com

Please direct your inquiries to admin@isaacpublishing.com

Carol Ankney's

HeartLines

Isaac Publishing, Inc.
P.O. Box 342
Three Rivers, MI 49093
www.isaacpublishing.com
1.866.273.4569

Endorsements

"As a young reporter beginning my career, I learned valuable lessons from the work of Carol Ankney. She was raised and lived among the people she interviewed and wrote about. She understood them and loved who they where and what they did. She understood where they came from and what they wanted. Everyday she shared their stories with her readers. She made us all laugh and cry because the stories she found and wrote were about everyone. I watched her interview people and respect each of them, whether it was a gardener with a huge vegetable or a parent whose child had a life threatening disease. Reporters tells us of the unusual but Carol's best work was to tell stories common to all of us, to tell us about our-selves, and she made us want to read them to the end."

Trace Christenson

"Carol Ankney was a chronicler of small town life in Southwest Michigan. She tapped into the core of people's feelings and thoughts in a way that made her articles and columns folksy and relevant. We haven't seen the likes of Carol's talent since her passing and we probably never will."

Cameron S. Brown
State Senator, Michigan District 16

"Carol Ankney was what newspapers need today more than ever — a voice for the guy next door, the neighbor around the corner, the kids down the street. She won more awards than any newspaperwoman I've had the privilege of know-ing during my own 31-year career, and yet for Carol, it was never about the accolades. She was always too preoccupied with what she'd write next. Who could she help? How could she be an advocate? How many people will this benefit? I'm convinced that there are two kinds of people in this world, the kind who enter a room and say, 'Here I am,' and then the kind who enter the room and say, 'Ah, there you are.' Carol was indeed a 'There you are' person. And her reading should be mandatory for anyone trying to become a better friend, confidant, human..."

Tom Rademacher
Author, Award Winning 31 year Columnist for The Grand Rapids Press

In Memoriam

Carol J. Ankney was born December 25, 1930, lived in Sidnaw, Michigan, until the age of ten, when her family moved to Branch County, MI. She moved to Burr Oak in 1944 and married Charles H. Ankney in 1949.

Carol served eighteen years on the Board of Education in Burr Oak, serving as president several terms. She was instrumental in obtaining a Federal Economic Development Grant for the school, the funding of which was later withdrawn. She fought the battle up to the General Accounting Office, which order the Commerce Department to return the funds. A new educational complex was then built at the school.

She had been a member of the Burr Oak Village Council since 1990, and had previously served on the council for three terms in the 1960s. She served as street administrator the entirety of her Council career, helping to obtain a State and Federal Grant for a new bridge over Prairie River.

She also had served a short time on the ARCH board, and the Michigan Governor's Council for the Aging.

She had been employed at the Bronson Journal a short time before her marriage, and at the Sturgis Journal 23 years, retiring as executive editor in 1989.

She was a longtime member of the Michigan Women's Press Club and the National Federation of Press Women. She had earned over 570 writing, editing and photography awards, and had twice been named Sweepstakes winner in National Federation of Press Women competition. She had been Sweepstakes winner in the Michigan unit for 17 consecutive years. Many of her awards were earned in Associated Press and United Press International competition.

Her hobbies included reading, history and genealogy. She also held a lifetime interest in environmental issues.

Fondly remembered by readers as the author of "Heartlines," Carol Ankney died November 14, 2001 in Sturgis, MI.

Dedications

"I would like to dedicate this book to my wife, Carol. I found these articles under the bed and I thought they were Christmas wrapping paper. When I realized what they were, I decided to save them before the dog wrecked them. I think perhaps, a book was Carol's plan all along. So here you go, Babe."

Charles Ankney, husband

"Mom's "words of silver" were meant to be enjoyed by this generation and future ones. She truly left us her 'Heartlines.'"

Barbara Rosales, daughter

"Mom was lovingly referred to as "Nose for News." If there was a story out there, she would find it. I miss her each and every day."

Kathy Wall, daughter

"Mom's legacy was to leave her soul in her writings to her family, friends and even strangers. But in the end there were no friends or strangers, as she had the uncompromised ability to make all who read her stories, feel like part of the family."

Mark Ankney, son

"In memory of my mother...honoring the gifts she gave us all."

Tim Ankney, son

Thank you to the Sturgis Journal for providing photos and giving Carol a platform to tell her stories.

Awards

Carol Ankney was a longtime member of the Michigan Women's Press Club and the National Federation of Press Women. She had earned over 570 writing, editing and photography awards, and had twice been named Sweepstakes winner in National Federation of Press Women competition. She had been Sweepstakes winner in the Michigan unit for 17 consecutive years. Many of her awards were earned in Associated Press and United Press International competition.

Carol was senior editor of the Sturgis Journal when she was presented with the 1988 NFPW Sweepstakes award at the Little Rock, Arkansas, conference. In her acceptance speech she said:

"I've always believed that words are like silver. Left stored away and unused, they become tarnished. Brought to the surface and polished, they remain bright forever.

"Maybe I'm still hungry. I started out late in life as a journalist. I took care of my parents, who died young and there was no chance for a career. But the words were always there, prodding and accusing me. I knew that someday I would have to write.

"At 40, I got my first job in the journalism world as a proofreader. That job taught me to understand the accuracy of words and their importance. When a reporter position opened up, I had the gall to ask for it. To prove I could do it, I worked for two weeks at no pay, the same time as doing my regular job.

"I've never used a tape recorder in my life. I think reporters become complacent and don't pay enough attention when they use one. I watch for the signs of the person I am interviewing...the twist of the fingers, the sighs, the pain in their voices. I want to tell the readers about the smell, the taste, the feeling of the moment.

"I don't want to be a publisher. Starting out so late, I still want to write, to create, to have a hands-on position. And in coming to this editor post I am proud of something else: I have walked on no one's body, nor walked over it. I earned it honestly.

"I've had my indiscretions. One male boss treated women like second class reporters, if that. He said we should write society news and make coffee. He also thought that we should make chocolate cupcakes. And so I made them. The rest of the staff got plain ones; he got the X-Lax ones. He was busy all day as I recall. And he never asked me to do that again.

"So here I am at 57, still chasing the fires, writing editorials, doing features. I've had a lot of help from members of Michigan Press Women and NFPW. I've picked their brains, read their best stories, studied their best photos. And learned.

"Young people starting out should disregard about half of what they learned in journalism school. Go out after those stories with an open mind. Don't decide first on how you'll write the story. You'll fail. You'll also rob yourself of the necessary learning step: to tell the story in their words. People don't give a damn about how you write a story if it touches them, if it portrays a true picture of that person.

"And another important thing. LISTEN. LISTEN. LISTEN. God, but it's paid dividends for me. Not just awards, but being able to share people's lives and to tell their stories." (As quoted in *Michigan Press Women today and yesterday*, by Willah Weddon)

Contents

Contents

Contents

Heartlines

He Seasoned Life

March 27, 1982

He died in the spring. I am not a creature of habit, but sometimes at this time of year I go to the small cemetery. I never find him there.

If there are individuals who question that statement, let them. That priority is mine. Some answers in life are owed to no man, only God.

A bitter wind sweeps under the tall pine trees in the tiny burial plot in Branch County. Standing there, in the raw bone-chill of a Spring day, I find it fitting. It is exactly my sentiments as I look at the gravestone above his sleep.

He was my father. He was no saint. He had no special title, position in the community.

I recall hearing he had a roving eye in the early days of my parents' marriage. I dislike hearing that, but he drummed the virtue of honesty in me as a young child. He would chide me now for not admitting family faults.

He was, mostly, a man of his word – and it was good. He did not desert friends – nor enemies. Rather, he searched for a compromise, even if he swallowed some pride in the yielding. He figured an angry friend was better than none.

Outside his family, education was the one thing he wanted in life.

He was denied it. In youth, it was lost because his father needed him on the farm. In adulthood there was no chance. Family responsibilities, poverty and poor health claimed his time.

He left high school in the 10th grade. It was a silent grievance that continued to the day he died.

I doubt if he ever spoke about it to his father, but there was an underlying bitterness. I know my father had one failing. Although he loved his father and did his duty, he never quite forgot the loss of his high school learning.

He fled the farm as soon as he could, but came to realize his roots were with the land. It was just that as a youth the land was his bindings, at a time he didn't want them.

His mind was quick. He absorbed books and magazines as a sponge soaks water. It was an unquenched thirst that never left him.

I suppose some could say he was a loser. He owned no property, stocks, bank account, car.

But he was rich. He had a wife who loved him and children who believed in him. Perhaps life puts blinders on people. Perhaps not. One searches for a true soul – and sometimes finds it.

He was a man who left his sickbed to help a child fly a kite. He was a man who could sell a treasured harmonica to purchase a pair of hip boots for a youngster who helped him on his trapping run.

I've told the story before that he sometimes forgot the Bible teachings of his mother. He admonished me once when I got in a scuffle. He remarked that I should "turn the other cheek." And then wryly added "and when you've turned both cheeks and get kicked in the other two, you come out fighting for what you believe!"

He was not a fellow given to temper, but the authority was there and the counsel. I guess I can blame him a bit for the fact I refuse to take an easy way out of a problem.

I've always faced it head on – sometimes foolishly. It's like I feel his finger tapping my shoulder and saying you can't compromise conscience and integrity. I wish he'd hadn't taught that lesson quite so well; there's hurt from some encounters.

He died young, the third – and last – son his parents would bury. But he was old in the knowledge of what life meant and how to accept it.

During his last illness he came home to the farm. He died there, quietly, in his parent's bed. There was dignity and a measure of peace on his face.

I remember the Spring day he was buried. The country road to the cemetery was impassable. His casket had to be carried on the back of a pickup truck to the burial plot. As the pallbearers struggled to make their way along a hedgerow, I smiled.

My dad would have loved it. In life he was forced to do the conventional, to abide by society's rules. Once in a while, however, he jumped the barrier and was free. In death he had done it again.

So, when velvet lilacs waft their heady fragrance to greet a new season, I remember a man who enriched all of mine.

I won't apologize for saying I don't find him in that small cemetery. Spirits aren't conquered. His is free.

Some Good, Bad Times

November 6, 1982

It's been an interesting month. First of all, the yearly vacation was nice. Traveled to the east and particularly enjoyed the fall colors. New Hampshire, Vermont and Maine were delightful, although you can't beat Michigan.

One of the things I like most about traveling is reading other newspapers. Newspapers are a mirror of their communities, its industry, its mores, its endeavors. Mostly, newspaper pages explain the people. People, of course, are a community's most valuable resource.

It seems the smaller a community, the more homier the articles. Big paper staffers sometimes cringe, and laugh about those items, but what serves the community best is what it's all about. Who's to judge – except those communities?

Newspapers try to print what's essential and interesting in their locale. And, it's the same all over, from what I gathered from reading other papers. The readers don't always like what they'd read.

The elections Tuesday went reasonably well. The campaigns were decent. We didn't have the usual candidate slaps at each other, and at least some of them didn't promise us the world on a platter. An honest promise to attempt to alleviate some of our problems usually gets a hopeful officeholder the most votes. Voters aren't stupid.

Notices, too, that campaign mugs weren't illegally plastered as much on private property as they've been in the past. Folks get upset with that kind of thing. Wrote a couple editorials about this practice a year or so ago (without giving names) and the fact that it's illegal to post signs on right-of-ways and private property unless owners give consent.

Got a phone call from a candidate, asking who set me up as judge. Explained to the candidate that folks had called the Journal saying they didn't appreciate the placards and signs coloring up their yards and property without being asked.

The caller's conversation got colorful. (P.S. The candidate didn't win). No comment.

Kids. You hope your own will always do the right thing. Sadly, you learn they sometimes don't. That doesn't mean they're less good human beings. Just a bit imperfect – like most of us.

There was an incident that affected me deeply a couple of weeks ago – and renewed my faith in the belief that good parents make their kids face up to their mistakes. Several youngsters committed wrongdoings in my town. Their folks are to be commended for explaining the consequences of characters being blemished by such doings.

What's outstanding about these parents is that they didn't turn the other cheek. Their kids will be making amends for some time to right their misdeeds. The most notable thing about these parents – and the kids – is that the youngsters appeared in person to make apologizes. There's a lot of good in people out there, if we only look for it – and acknowledge it. Hope this does.

I think a lot about times changing, especially this time of year.

Used to be the worst thing a kid could do on Halloween was tip over the outside privy. Few left to tip over now. I recall I was errant myself one Halloween and assisted some pals in tipping over a shanty. Thing was, the owner was inside, waiting for us. Best thing that happened was the owner kept his seat, so to speak. Worst thing was, one of the kids fell into the open pit. Took a lot of washing off while sitting under an old pump. Come to think of it, the pumps have pretty well disappeared too. Maybe the two went together.

On a serious note, this Halloween was pretty pathetic in some parts of the nation. However, the needles, razor blades and such that we heard were put into treats for the kids always seemed to happen somewhere else. We were immune. Who would do that kind of thing in our communities? We might argue among ourselves, but certainly not harm a child. Sadly enough, it happened in three nearby communities. A pity. Trust is so easily given – and so easily taken away.

Which reminds me. Some trickster bequeathed the Journal an item (for Halloween, I presume). Hoisted ladies apparel to the top of our flagpole. Interesting enough, the gift wasn't discovered until Thursday afternoon.

Anyone missing anything?

I'm glad I live in a small town. So many bigger cities have banned leaf burning in the fall. I realize it's necessary, but part of my best memories are childhood days when we romped through huge piles of patchwork-colored leaves. I can bring to mind that pungent odor of leaves burning just thinking about it.

What do folks do without marshmallow roasts, with the neighborhood invited? There was a closeness in sharing the end of a season and the hint of a new one. Even when individuals outgrew (if one could) the marshmallows, there were always grandchildren – or borrow a friend's kid.

They call it progress, conservation, and environment protection, and who knows what all.

I don't like it. They can bag 'em – I'll burn 'em.

And, that'll bring more irate phone calls.

Ode to a Woodpile

November 13, 1982

I guess, if you live long enough, things come full circle. Things like fashion, trends and that long ago love, wood stoves. Well, love might be tempered to like, depending on your experiences.

I hear they now have log splitters, fancy electric saws and other modern tools to make it easier to warm a home.

Back in my young years, things were different – a lot different. For instance, I recall walking a few miles from my Branch County home to the farm of D.B. Royer near the Silver Creek area. He had a woodlot and my family was welcome to take what was needed. I loved those outings, and especially loved D.B. Didn't matter that I was a kid, he always had time for me. Could be some of the reason I went to the Royer home was because the youngest in the family was a kid named Dick. I was jealous of Dick. D.B. was a frequent North Country deer hunter and stayed at our home in the Upper Peninsula. Having never met Dick until we moved down here, I was prepared to dislike this kid D.B. was so fond of.

After I met Dick, I didn't just help load wood onto the truck, but tormented and provoked fights with him. I wonder how we ever managed to become such good friends. Could be a few shoves into frigid creek waters sobered our priorities.

Anyway, wood cutting was a time in itself those days. The all-day outing included neighbors sharing a noon, and sometimes supper meal. We'd usually end the day playing cards, games and sharing neighborhood news. (When did you last get together and make popcorn and candy, topping it off with a juicy apple from your own orchard?)

Wood cutting was a back-breaking chore. The dropping of trees and cutting wood logs by hand saw was only the beginning. You loaded it onto a wagon or truck, and then unloaded it. To add it that, my Dad believed a woodpile should be neat. He insisted, for some reason, that it should be separated into piles of about five cords each. Ever do that? And, the darned chunks had to be stacked carefully (we eventually used that woodpile for a playground and ruined Dad's plans for neatness).

Then, having nothing fancy to cover up the wood that wasn't put in the woodhouse, we spent the last part of the cold weather season digging chucks of wood from frozen ice and snow.

One also had the duty of lugging the wood into the house and putting it in the wood box. Needless to say, that meant snow melting and dripping all over the floor. Guess how much fun it is scrubbing floors on one's hands and knees. It was Mother's turn to insist on the work being done properly.

Now in those times, one used mostly round stoves. Not just trade names. Round stoves. Wood chunks, however, weren't always round. One had the lousy chore of fitting a chunk into the stove. Invariably, it didn't fit. I recall my Dad once solved the problem by giving the chunk a healthy kick. It worked. Thing was, the jolt knocked the stovepipe loose. Did you ever clean soot and steam from furniture, floors, walls and curtains? Talk about unhealthy looks Mother gave Dad!

Had a neighbor who didn't worry about that problem. He cut a piece of log and inserted one end into the open stove door. When it burned down, he simply shoved it in further. I didn't like staying overnight at that house. When I did, I planned an escape route in case of fire.

Those old wood stoves sure warmed the place up – at least close to them. You roasted on one side and froze on the other. I remember hurrying downstairs on wintry mornings and literally thawing out by the stove. That old soapstone we took to bed to keep warm held up only so long, you know (I imagine I'll get a call from someone in the younger generation, asking what a soapstone is).

Now, if you think that ended the chores of using wood, be advised that there were ashes to haul. I hate to think of all the buckets I carted outside. Then, in Spring, I had the job of working the ashes into the soil.

I guess it wasn't so bad. Seeing as how we got drinking water from the pump out by the barn, used the outside privy and all those handy things, wood cutting wasn't so bad.

If I ever doubted that fact in the Spring, I knew the whole process would start all over again in a couple of months.

Of Food and Such

November 27, 1982

I know I've always had a lot of things wrong about me (some of our readers point that out), but I've come to the conclusion that I ought to add another fault to the long list.

How come I'm the only one in my family of six who likes the food others hate? They don't like rhubarb, mincemeat, parsnips, elderberries, dewberries, cranberries.

A couple of them like nuts, but not mixed into baked food. A couple can't stand onions (that's inconceivable to me), and several won't touch anything with salad dressing in it. Another puts salad dressing on potatoes and everything else that sits still on his plate. He even dips potato chips into it.

One child ignores escalloped potatoes like they're kin to the plague. One of the girls retches when I hint of making escalloped corn.

The same guy who won't eat anything with nuts in it also won't consider tasting cookies or breads with raisins. Oddly enough, he'll eat raisins by the pound from the box.

All the kids are crazy about catsup, but the man of the family says we're just covering up the taste of food. Maybe he's trying to say something about my cooking.

I've got one kid who believes dates (I use a lot of them in fruit-cakes and anything else I can dream up) are identified with some-thing you'd throw out with the garbage. But then, he's the kid who mixes catsup and salad dressing together and claims it's delicious.

I will say the family is universal in loving peanut butter, ham, apple pie, sugar and molasses cookies and things in that category. I can't say they feel the same for boiled dinners. Father and I pig out on boiled dinner. It lasts through a couple of meals, even if the cab-bage looks like something from last's year's Thanksgiving fare.

Speaking of parsnips, what's the matter with folks who don't like such goodies? I recall my dad going out to the garden, shoveling away snow, and digging some of those tasty morsels out for dinner. Those little items, slowly simmered in butter, melt in one's mouth.

And rhubarb. Why, you can mix it with strawberries, dewberries, raspberries, even mulberries, and make delicious pies. No luck. They still won't touch it. I'll eat it raw, dipping it into sugar. Puckers up the mouth a bit, but sufficient.

My kids also think I'm a bit wacko when I make potato soup. So, what's wrong with tossing in leftover peas, carrots, onions, noodles and anything else that looks edible? I do notice they manage to slup it down.

I enjoy making fruitcakes. Any kind of fruitcake, light, dark, you name it. A couple of folks will eat a piece or two and then it's all left there for me to finish. (Don't they realize that's the general idea?) I've been able to locate fruitcake in March and April after making it in early December. Lovely.

I probably shouldn't be telling this secret, but the guy I married hates jello. Hates it in any shape, manner or form. Way back before they put all those pudding mixes into cakes to make the cake more moist, I had my own remedy. I always put half a box of jello into my cakes. The fella ate 'em, too – and never knew why they were so good!

I wish my family loved pasties, those delicacies from my childhood in the Upper Peninsula. A homemade pastie is something again. I took those tasty items to school with me for years.

Just thought of something. My mother always made pasties with turnips, or rutabagas – whatever proper name they go by. I dislike turnips. I managed to enjoy those pasties – after I picked out the turnips and threw them away.

I must confess I have a major food fault. I detest lima beans. Can't stand to even look at them. I learned early on how to stuff them in the side of my mouth, and spit them out after dinner.

I'll tell you one thing. There hasn't been a lima bean on the table of my home since the day I got married. Never will.

The Meaning of Christmas

December 24, 1982

Sometimes during the Christmas season, as it always has, my mood will change. It always has. Nothing my family does will deter it. My children don't understand, but learned long ago to tolerate my moment.

It's not easy to explain one's yesterdays. Not easy, when today's lifestyle has little comparison.

Christmas is special to me, and I don't apologize for saying I can't explain. How do you explain memories reserved from childhood? Especially when its heartbreak mixed with happiness?

This time of year, I remember other Christmases, when hope was all we had in my parents' home. Sometimes, hope was a lot to expect. Reality tempered it.

Christmas meant a lot to my dad. I didn't understand too well then, seeing as how we were so poor, but time has a way of helping sort priorities.

There wasn't money for toys and new clothes. We learned early those things weren't important. Good health and a family were treasures. My folks had much of the latter, and little of the former. Their health failed early in their lives. Their biggest struggle was not for worldly goods, but just to stay in the world.

I recall that one of my parent's most important aims in life was to live long enough to instill in their children a will to look beyond adversity. I'm not sure how well they succeeded, but I didn't know the meaning of defeat until I found it in the dictionary.

My parents also understood that friends shouldn't be judged only by their status. They picked friends for the meaning they brought to their lives, or how they treated others.

One of my folk's best friends was a tavern owner named Mike. I knew some neighbors didn't approve of Mike. After all, he sold spirits. Many a husband and father had to be helped home after an evening at Mike's establishment. Mike was the helper home many times, and usually faced the lady of the house's nagging.

A lot of folks didn't know Mike's story. They couldn't see beyond the tavern door and into Mike's heart. Mike was more forgiving of the townspeople than those who frowned disapprovingly from behind lace curtains.

The good citizens in that small Upper Peninsula town didn't know Mike was the guy who chucked a hundred dollars into the church envelope at Christmas to buy gifts for poor kids during the Depression years – and swore the priest to silence.

I learned it by accident, while changing my choir robe. I overheard the priest and Mike talking. When they saw me, I was sworn to secrecy. I never broke the vow until now. It doesn't matter if I tell. Many of the people who were around then have died. Besides, Mike wasn't one to hold grudges.

Mike was a big fellow, unpolished and loud. He had a hand that covered my whole face when he tried to pat my cheek. Having no children of his own, he considered the town kids his. He watched us like a hawk, reprimanding when we'd done wrong.

But he was putty in the hands of a kid who took him a bouquet of wild arbutus. He'd make me wait while he went to the store down the way and fetched root beer. The root beer was usually shared with Tim Sullivan, my next door neighbor.

Tim and Mike made an odd pair. A Catholic and an Episcopalian. No matter, friendship had little to do with one's religion.

Tim and Mike would sit and talk about their childhood days – and sing. I'd be included for one reason: I had to sing Tim's favorite song, "Beautiful Brown Eyes." I never learned why Tim loved that song – or who it was with brown eyes he had loved so much. I never knew any woman in his life. He'd had a wife, but she was long gone from my earliest remembrance. Mike apparently knew who brown eyes was – and wasn't telling.

The Christmas I remember most from our family friendship with Mike was one when my mother was hospitalized. Christmas wasn't the same without her. No mincemeat pie in the oven, no cinnamon-perfumed apron hanging on the pantry door hook.

Dad tried to keep our minds off mom's absence. He ran our legs off doing chores. Then, for a treat, we scooped clean snow, mixed it with vanilla, sugar and canned milk, and called it ice cream. We thought it was wonderful.

On the afternoon of Christmas Eve, we walked deep into the woods and cut a tree. We might not have many presents under it, but that tree was equal to any in town. We used cranberries and popcorn to decorate it, along with old trinkets mother had carefully packed away. We strung garlands throughout the house. We didn't spare a doorway.

That left the goodies. We four girls baked cookies. Mine were flat and lopsided as I recall, but dad said they'd do.

We knew there'd be handmade presents of some kind, but that we wouldn't open them in the morning. We never knew a Christmas morning. Dad couldn't wait. He always woke us up before dawn to see what Santa had brought.

It still was going to be a sad Christmas. The hospital was too far away to visit mom, and we had no car. It was going to be Christmas with just dad.

Not quite. Along about 11 p.m., there was a loud thump on the door. Mike's booming voice was heard, there he was, arms loaded with bags. There was fruitcake, groceries and the trimmings, and a present for everyone. Before he left, Mike thrust a five-pound box of chocolates into my hands.

That night we turned off the house lamps and turned on the tree lights. We threw another chunk of wood into the stove and gathered near the Airline radio to listen to Christmas carols. And thought a lot about our mother, who must have been pretty lonesome in that hospital room.

I don't remember the presents I got that long ago Christmas. I do remember a sick mother, a father who cared about his kids, and a special man named Mike who knew the real meaning of Christmas.

Today, when I walk by a tavern, I don't cast judgment. A soul's pureness and charity shouldn't be measured by mere humans.

Besides, the owner might be a guy like Mike.

Let's Remember the Lesson Well

December 11, 1982

Overheard an interesting conversation the other morning, during breakfast in a downtown Sturgis restaurant. At the table opposite me, some fellows were discussing the wars they had served in.

It was strange, having the Vietnam controversial war focused in the media recently, to listen to the veterans talk about older wars and battles. Represented, from what I could tell, were World War I and II. The men spoke of registration for the draft, how and where they had been inducted, and some of their experiences.

It was a sobering conversation. I knew the talk would lead to another subject, simply because the anniversary was coming up early the next week.

Pearl Harbor. The name alone, for those of us who remember that day, recalls shock, terror, bewilderment and anxiety.

Can you remember that day? Most folks can, but whether their thoughts return on the anniversary each year I don't know. I hope so.

I remember that day well. My dad had been closely following the political climate of those days, reading everything he could concerning the world situation. I recall him, saying to himself, "It's going to come. I know it." I didn't really understand it all; being just a kid, but his somberness concerned me. But still, in the innocence childhood, my world seemed secure.

That terrible Dec. 7, 1941 brought reality and understanding of his words home. The radio was on. I remember hearing the words drift through the doorway from the living room.

Pearl Harbor had been attacked by the Japanese. Our lives never would be the same. The next few years would be lived amid reports of rare heroism and terrible losses. We would learn of Bataan, the Solomons, Philippines, and many other places on the map that meant little to school children until that December day.

It's strange, but I still recall the early war years and their battles far better than later ones. Maybe something indelible lingers on in one's memories when such a thing happens as that sneak attack on Pearl.

Whatever the reason, that attack drew forth the beginning of a rare unified front in this nation. From that day came enlistments of boys who would never return, bond sales (we bought stamps each week in school) to finance the war effort. Ration cards came. Who can forget that we wore our shoes out long before we were issued a new stamp to buy new ones?

I remember my mother canned food each year. Friends who didn't have gardens would give her their stamps so she could buy sugar, which was high on the ration list.

School kids collected scrap metal and paper. We even collected milkweed pods. We were told they used the fluff as insulation to line pilot's flight jackets. I know each time I gathered some; I wondered what young fellow would be 'wearing' my contribution.

The war years dragged on. We were never far from its headlines. We began to see the stars in the windows, with the dreaded gold star always drawing an aura of sorrow and respect from all who passed by.

I recall when we heard about the nation's Sullivan family, whose five sailor sons died together when their ship was torpedoed. Can you imagine that loss? Closer to home there were many servicemen who gave their lives to preserve America's freedom.

That was when the reality of war came hard to our towns and villages. It didn't end with the news. It was relived long afterwards, when the bodies of the boys were returned home after the war's end.

But there was a pride in this nation during that war, a closeness and determination that we would survive its harsh cost. We did. But the cost was dear, and the price we paid is one of the reasons that makes that war unforgettable.

There are many Americans who remembered last Tuesday, on the anniversary of the attack on Pearl 41 years ago. It's true that we shouldn't blame all Japanese for that terrible act of infamy. But, for all those young men and women who suffered and died to keep the cause of America's freedom alive, we should never forget.

That's one of the reasons so many Americans will always remember Pearl Harbor. We dare not forget.

A Cry from the Darkness

December 18, 1982

Christmas for me this year will be a joyous one. My family will be home, they are all well, and that is what's important. I've always felt a bit sentimental at Christmas, maybe because it's also my birthday and I cherish the memories of other holidays. My parents died when I was a young girl and I know what it's like not to have them at Christmastime.

In the newspaper business, Christmas is a time for reflection, and sometimes of sorting priorities. There are many priorities we don't like, but the simple truth is that's the kind of job it is.

Reporters and editors learn from necessity to prepare for the worst. However, one never really adjusts to the sight of mangled bodies in accidents, the terror of nature's disasters and horror of man's inhumanity.

I've seen a lot of tragedy. The bad news, unfortunately, many times crowds out the good news. News develops that way throughout the world. The Journal isn't an exception.

There are many events that have touched me since I've worked as a reporter. There was the call from a distraught parent whose child never saw another birthday. A death on a highway that left children parentless. The young father, entering the golden days of his life, who fell victim to an incurable disease. The parents who endured a lonely, hopeless wait of watching their youngster die slowly, unknowingly of their vigil.

Maybe I should be calloused by now. I know it's easier to live out the drama of the newspaper business if one becomes hardened to the miseries of the world. But I made a promise to myself a long time ago: If I ever think I've reached that stage where I don't care about others, I'll get out of this line of work.

Even if it may be easier not to have empathy, to build up a barrier where the hurt of the world won't creep in, I still maintain its worse not to allow oneself to care.

I don't know why a particular letter sent to the Journal the other day got to me. I've had worse things come across my desk and worse tragedies to write about. I've had to intrude on people's grief. I've listened to heartbroken people who lost their home and cherished belongings in a fire. I've interviewed a young fellow who used to be a runner, but now can't walk.

Don't think it doesn't bother a reporter. I've gone back to work worn with the pain, and felt guilty that my own life is blessed.

It isn't that I'm not conditioned to tragedy. I've known that intrusion. But in this business one learns there are others far worse off. One's own misfortune is miniscule in comparison.

But this one letter, at a time of year when there should be only happiness and appreciation, I find myself wrapped up in another person's anguish.

The letter came in a batch of children's letters to Santa, which the Journal publishes each year. It was immediately noticed. For one thing, it wasn't written by a youngster, and couldn't be added to the others.

The letter was placed on my desk, gently, by the managing editor, Frank Keegan. A gruff, supposedly tough character, this man also was moved by its contents. I laid the letter down after I read it, and attempted to complete my day's work. The letter, however, seemed unwilling to be brushed aside. I couldn't ignore it.

In that hand printed letter, its message simple and to the point, was a desperate plea for love. The particulars aren't clear. Reading between the lines, one surmises that the person who wrote it has a family that's divided. Taking the liberty of assuming that point, I also realize that Christmas this year may be bleak for the author of the missive.

For whatever reasons that left the letter-writer alone this time of year when love is shared so abundantly, the author feels only abandonment and despair.

He (or she) who wrote it only asked for one thing this Christmas: "Santa: Could you touch the hearts of my far away family so they may see it clear to come and see me this year? Could you leave a little love under each of my children's pillows?" That was enough to unnerve me, but what really touched me was the line "You see, Santa, I may not be here next year to see the joy in their eyes on Christmas morning. I have cancer."

I don't have the answer for something I know little about. I do know that family problems should be settled within families, if at all possible. But, I can't help feeling involved, if only because I chanced to read the letter.

I don't know who sent the letter. No name was included. But, if there are folks out there who may be alienated from their families, or hurt feelings prevent apology or reconciliation, maybe it's time to check priorities. Life is too short to waste on unforgiveness.

I hope the letter-writer gets the wish he or she wants so badly. I also hope that person's world is turned around by love. That's what Christmas is all about.

I know I can't bring about a miracle or change that letter-writer's predicament, but I can care about that person's plight. I also know that in the midst of my own special Christmas gathering, I'll be thinking of the soul who wrote that letter. And wondering – and hoping.

A Matter of Friendship

December 31, 1982

Time doesn't stretch out before the old man. It is more private than that, a holding on and enduring of each day, seeking out happenings in a life that has no future.

In his mind, now cluttered with aimless thoughts and memories too scattered and difficult to put in order, the dog is the one thing that holds him to reality.

They are an odd pair. That old man came to his son's home in the fall, in the winter of his life, to live out his allotted days. He had not wanted to come. It was not because of a lack of love, only that he did not want to be a burden, to have someone attend to his daily needs. But the simple fact was, when the decision was reached, he knew it was the right thing to do.

The family gathered love around him and made an easier acceptance of what his life had come to be.

Still, the old man felt the loneliness and despair of not being the one in charge, of being needed. Being in charge was something he had taken pride in all his life.

In his more lucid moments, the old man was able to handle the day's events, but the debilitating illness, hardening of the arteries to the brain, was robbing him of memory. His awareness was being reduced to bits and pieces. Many days he was confused and his mind refused to center on where he was and why. There were times he felt alone in a place where he had no ties. The son and daughter – in – law, the grandbabies, would lead him back to his chair and gently hug him. That settled him, but the family had other events and duties. The old man felt disorganized, with no sure reason for his existence and no firm link to his place in life.

For the old man, life dragged on. He needed something more to cling to, so he could free his thoughts from their bindings. Mostly, he needed something to sustain him while he was lost and confused on his last journey. Someone or something that needed him alone.

In the beginning, the old man was able to walk around the house with help. He spent his days in an easy chair in the living room. He wanted more. Somewhere, in the dark recesses of a mind trapped within a mind, he instinctively was aware of that need – and silently cried out for release.

Duffy came. He, too, was trapped in his own world. Abandoned by a family who didn't know – nor didn't care about honest love and concern - Duffy wandered until he found a temporary home at Pet Haven, a place where unwanted animals are taken. It is a haven from starvation, abuse, neglect, and early death.

Here, Duffy was treated kindly for the first time in his life. He received his shots, was neutered and fed. The first meaning of love stirred in the dog's conscious. He began to respond to the kindness extended at the shelter. But Duffy couldn't stay at Pet Haven forever. There were other animals that needed a home.

Duffy was taken to the home where the old man lived. It also would be temporary. The family would provide foster care until Pet

Haven officials found a permanent home for the dog.

There was another dog at the home, but it spent its days playing with the kids. The old man was acknowledged, but only that.

Duffy and the old man began a strange relationship. The dog sat a long time, sizing up the grandfather. Duffy was wary of strangers – too many had abused him. But there was something about the old man that drew the dog's attention. Maybe, Duffy reasoned, it wouldn't hurt to try and make friends with the man.

The dog hesitantly approached the old man. A hand was extended. The trembling dog cringed. When the soft pat came, and a gentle touching to his head, the dog threw caution aside. He pushed his nose closer and laid his head on the old man's lap. The hand patted again.

It was done. The friendship, freely given, was freely accepted.

The dog spent his hours by the chair, where the grandfather had only to reach down. A pat brought a gentle lick on the fingers and an eager head in the man's lap. Only mealtime and an occasional romp with the children and the other dog drew Duffy from the old man's side.

The relationship was never questioned. The unloved, unwanted creature had found someone who accepted his love gratefully, and returned it quietly.

The old man's condition deteriorated. He became bedridden, unable to talk. The disease was taking its toll. Confined to a hospital bed in the home, he was no longer accessible to the dog's touch. No matter. The dog remained at the bedside. Occasionally, the dog was rewarded with a lift to the bed, where the old man got a free face washing. The face brightened, and broke into one of the now infrequent smiles.

So it goes. Though it is now difficult for the old man to move, when the dog comes, he manages to touch him. The dog lies quietly on the bed, sensing how difficult it is for the grandfather to reach out for anything.

Their days are unhurried. Duffy, with the wisdom animals seem to have, knows there will be time later for romps, running and frisks through the cold weather. Time now must be spent with the person for whom time will soon be gone.

The last days of the old man are shared in quiet times with the dog from the street. They are two of God's creatures who found each other. They are content.

For the old man, whenever clear moments come – they are fewer each day – there is assurance that the dog is there, waiting. A love shared without reservations.

There will be no Pet Haven again for Duffy. Some other lucky dog will be able to stay there until the Haven's caring individuals find it a home.

When the old man dies, the family will keep Duffy. Duffy took the time to enrich the last moments of a man who needed a special friend. The dog's love is too valuable to give away to someone else. Duffy's loving heart found the dog a home.

Beginnings - and Endings

January 8, 1983

It is the New Year. Hopefully, it will be a good one and our hopes and dreams will become reality. A new year offers us something tangible, a new time, a new beginning.

Perhaps it's also the time to review happenings that interweave one's life. Time for reflection of what has taken place.

I've written about gallant people the last couple of years. Every now and then someone asks for an update on those folks.

Let's start with Skip Dinger. You'll recall he was the young man in his early 20's who suffered a broken neck in a diving accident. A quadriplegic, he has accepted the fact he will use a wheelchair the rest of his life. Only sitting in one; Skip doesn't intend to let life pass him by.

There are Janet Brubaker and Angela Stukey, who were under-going kidney dialysis several times a week. Janet and Angela have received kidney transplants, Janet's from her brother, and Angela's from her mother. They're doing fine.

In the midst of this happiness and triumph, there is sadness. Two of the people I wrote about, Shawn Courtney of Howe and Nikki Bieber of Wolcottville, are not among us. Both youngsters, suffering from brain tumors, died last year. But from those tragedies came forth a fund drive in LaGrange County that aids other children and families who experience disabling illnesses. If one looks at it another way, something of Nikki and Shawn lives on.

There also have been inquiries about a column written during Christmas Week, concerning the person who wrote a letter to Santa Claus. The unfortunate writer felt her family wouldn't care to be with her at Christmas. To make it worse, the letter writer has cancer and may not be around another Christmas.

I still don't know who wrote the letter. Perhaps I never will. There was much discussion about that column and that person. I continue to hope her family will rally to help.

I've received a lot of calls from people who are concerned about the person who wrote that letter. For reasons of their own, whether they felt the same hopelessness or a loved one has chosen to leave the warmth of the family circle and they are powerless to change the situation, they have empathy with the individual. Some simply said they would pray for that lonely human being.

From that column came another letter, a deeply moving letter from a close friend. She wrote to tell me the words had touched her. I know the woman well. I know the kind of Christian lady she is, how she has always gone out of her way to help others. She's always been a cheerful, hopeful person, appreciating the rich life God gave her. I have long known that her family idolizes her, that her friends and neighbors cherish the fact they know her.

She explained the concern she has for the person who wrote the Santa letter. She went on to describe how her family gave up their own schedules and plans to be with her this Christmas. Her church, her friends and neighbors have gathered around her. She is thankful she doesn't have the kind of situation the first letter writer has.

And then, the words of her letter brought shock. My friend said that just before Christmas she was told she has inoperable lung cancer. It is a fast-growing malignancy. She knows she will not live long. She has accepted that, and is appreciative of the loving life she has known. She said she has accepted God's will and knows a measure of peace.

I hadn't known about her illness. She hadn't stopped in the Journal lately to see me, but I still didn't know. She isn't the kind of person to burden others with her problems. I assumed she was busy with holiday preparations, brightening the lives of others.

What makes her situation different from my former letter-writer is that her brothers, her children, her sister, everyone she knows, have extended special help. And yet, in the midst of her own trouble, she is concerned about another soul who searches in the darkness of her own misery.

My friend asked, in her letter, that I not mention her name. I will respect that. But her friends know who she is, as does her family – and so do I.

I have been blessed in my lifetime with friends of great value. I also have learned that without friends one is poor.

Sometimes, when writing articles about success and happiness, sadness intrudes in this drama called life. This is one of those times.

A Sharing of Life

January 15, 1983

Mary (Johnson) Sargent, Sturgis, picked up the telephone directory the other day to locate a hairdresser. The listing of Midge's Beauty Shop caught her eye. She smiled. She remembered a friend from childhood, Marjorie ("Midge" Mosier) Parker, had owned a beauty shop many years in Sturgis.

"Couldn't be Midge," Mary thought. "She certainly gave up the business years ago. Someone else probably continued the firm's name."

Mary dialed the number. Midge's voice answered.

That conversation rekindled a school friendship of over 58 years ago – a friendship that never waned, even if the participant's hadn't seen each other since ninth grade – since 1925.

The women had lived in Ontario, Ind., when they were youngsters, attended the same school several years, but separated when they reached high school and Mary moved away. Although they knew some details about each other through the years, thanks to mutual friends, they never managed to see one another.

Mary, a widow, moved back to Sturgis recently from Ohio, after a 44 – year absence from the area. Her children reside there, and she wanted to live close to them.

Reminiscing in Midge's shop the other day, the women recalled their adventures – and misadventures – as youngsters. There were many smiles, and a few warm tears.

It seems as children, they were sharers – even had the same boyfriend. They wrote him letters – enclosing them in the same envelope. He wrote back to the girls, sending both letters in one envelope. "Guess he was community property," Midge said, laughing.

"I saw him down in the Ontario area the other day," Mary remarked. "I'd have known him anywhere. Saw him walking across the yard at his farm. Guess I should have stopped and said hello."

The girls were together in their freshman year at Lima High School, and their talk centered on the school and their happy experiences there. The school has been remodeled into an apartment building. The church they loved was destroyed by fire. Those memories saddened the women a bit, as they recalled happier times.

They talked of marriages (Marge has a husband, but no children), what they've been doing the past century ("I'm still a hairdresser – since 1929" Midge added), the childhood picnics and "snitching watermelons from a farmer's patch."

"We used to climb up into my uncle's ice house," Midge added. "And then used it as a playhouse in the summer months."

The women grew pensive when they recalled picnics at the Ontario Dam. Both have traveled back to the location to visit.

Did the women recognize each other at their first meeting in 55 years?

"I'd have known Mary anywhere," Midge said.

"I wouldn't have known Midge if I'd passed her on the street," Mary said. "Her face is so thin – it used to be much rounder."

What are their plans, now that they've been reunited?

"Well, we'll surely get along well," Midge said. "Did over 50 years ago. Can't see why that kind of friendship can't continue."

"Except for one thing, Mary added. "We aren't going to be able to share an envelope to write the same fella."

"Some things change," Midge said, with a warm smile.

A Time of Caring

January 22, 1983

She's petite, dark-haired and pretty. And busy. A sophomore at Centreville High School, Brenda Halsey figures the good life stretches out before her – waiting. Waiting to offer her whatever she figures she can handle.

She's handled a lot. Like suffering from cerebral palsy since the age of six months and being confined to a wheelchair. But don't count her out. Brenda doesn't intend to be left behind.

Besides school studies, Brenda worked part-time at the Pathfinder Center during her second semester last year. She says the work was "exciting and rewarding."

She has a tough load each day, but Brenda finds time to help others. Like working with the White Pigeon Boy Scout Troop 419 and Brownie Troop 530 to raise money. Money to help others. They raised $2,000 for the national telethon that television personality John Ritter will host this weekend.

The money was raised in a bowl-a-thon in Mendon a while back. Brenda will turn the proceeds in during a televised program in Fort Wayne (Channel 21) on Sunday.

The daughter of LeRoy and Sharlene Halsey, Sturgis, Brenda finds life "interesting and good." She doesn't quibble about the problems of being in a wheelchair. Those who know her say her personality is bright and she's usually cheerful.

The wheelchair is merely an inconvenience, Brenda says. Traveling the road of life in it will be a challenge that won't be ignored.

Brenda is 18. She admits life hasn't been easy, but "why worry about it – I'd rather concentrate on attempting to do more things." And, she adds, "a lot of folks are worse off. Why should I complain?"

Maybe that explains why Brenda Halsey tries to be where she's needed, even though it costs her time and a lot of effort.

"I just want to help to help other people," she says.

She's doing just that – and doing it pretty well.

Some Kind of Newspaperman

January 29, 1983

A fellow I know observed his 80th birthday the other day. That got me to thinking about unsaid words that should have been spoken long ago. This column offers a splendid opportunity.

Knowing the guy, it's the only way I can get away with publishing words of praise about him.

Harold Pringle came to the Sturgis Journal from the western side of the state, over in the Grand Haven –South Haven area. The move to Sturgis was carefully planned and one he couldn't refuse. Not with the chance of working with Mark Haines, one of the most respected publishers in the Midwest and beyond. Haines was highly regarded and his friendship and counsel cherished.

It was a chance Pringle grabbed with glee. And never regretted it. To this day he extols Haines' memory.

One of the first promises Pringle made to himself in that early time was to closely follow in Haines' footsteps. He succeeded.

There's a lot one can say about Pringle's long career in the newspaper field. Respected by his peers, he earned posts on newspaper boards and several leadership appointments. Those are the public things.

There's folks around – our numbers are getting smaller each

day - who remember the days of working for Pringle when he either managed the Journal or was the owner-editor-publisher.

He hired me, and I didn't have an ounce of journalism training – neither in school nor college. I had no background in newspapers, no degree beyond my high school diploma. There were no references, summaries or resumes filed with him.

It was a simple matter. The Journal needed a proofreader. My one question from Pringle was a blunt one: "You a good speller?" he bellowed from his office doorway.

To be honest, I never wanted to be a proofreader, though I think they do one of the most important jobs on a newspaper. Simply put, I wanted to write.

That chance came six months later, when a desk opened up in the newspaper. Being rather brave, I asked to be considered. The boss approved, although he haunted my desk for several days.

Anyone who knows Harold Pringle knows he's a man of many moods. A bluff exterior, but all softness inside. I remember when there was a family crisis in a staff member's life; Pringle was quietly there, to offer support and friendship.

I remember other things. As a newspaperman, Pringle was blunt and to the point. There was little polish in his delivery. When he believed in something and took a stand, dogged determination kept him on it.

As I recall, there was one thing Pringle expected – and demanded – if need be. He expected good writing, reasonable well-constructed sentences – and professionalism. And to reporter' dismay, at arm's reach was our arch enemy, that hated, red editing pencil. He loved that red pencil.

Pringle also didn't like to be corrected. I found that out early on. He wrote editorials. Darned good ones, many unmatched today in newspapers around the state and nation. He said it like it was and neither subscription holder nor advertiser compromised him. The smart ones knew better than to try.

He was – and is – a man of opinions. As I said, I quickly learned that. He asked me to proof his editorials. I did. Then one day, he asked me to give my opinion on a controversial issue he had written about, to be published on the editorial page. Without thinking (I'm known for that) I told him he was telling one side – his.

The newsroom grew silent. His face darkened. He grabbed the copy from my hand and tore it in half- about two inches from my face. He never said a word.

I mentally wondered why my mouth had opened before my mind did, but the damage was done. I expected a yellow slip in that week's paycheck, seeing as how he avoided me like the plague.

Several days later, he strode into the newsroom and tossed a piece of copy paper in front of me.

"Read it," Pringle directed, "and tell me what you think of it."

He'd rewritten – and edited – the editorial quite a bit.

I learned from that incident. I realized that you didn't coddle up to Harold Pringle if you wanted respect. He spotted phonies a mile back. I did have enough brains to continue giving him an honest answer. Our relationship was based on that to the day he retired.

I learned more from that man. Like the importance of a newspaper and the criteria in choosing news. Like trying to show two sides of an issue, even when one has a personal opinion. Like treating the public as important people, that their opinions and concerns matter.

And he taught me there is a joy in putting words down, especially in writing features. He always maintained the guts of a newspaper, after you publish the hard news, comes down to a unbending fact: stories about the community – its shortcomings, its pride, its mistakes and its triumphs – are the "starch" of a small newspaper. Mostly, Pringle asserted, people make a newspaper, because newspapers are people.

I asked him something once, in those days when I felt insecure and unsure of what kind of copy I was turning out. I knew he considered everyday events in people's lives of interest, and that he believed most people have something important about them that a reporter can search out by simply listening.

"Features!" he'd bark at the staff. "This paper wants to know about people! Features!"

I asked Pringle (innocently enough), what feature stories were and how I could learn to write them. He stared at me with a withering look and I suspected he knew he had an idiot on his hands. Finally, he looked out the big windows of the old Journal building overlooking Chicago Road and the town he loved. He watched the traffic pass and people walking by.

He turned back to me. He said, smiling, "well kiddo, you've been writing them all along."

It's a compliment I cherish to this day – more than award plaques and certificates of merit. Those items brighten walls, but words warm the soul.

So, while I can still say it, the world should know I consider it a privilege to have worked for Harold Pringle. And, keeping up my record of being honest with him, I'll say something else: anything I may be today in this profession called journalism, I owe to him. All of it.

Kinda tickles me, though, that I can say all this without him editing it out with that lousy, slashing red pencil – and hearing him say "that's how you learn!"

I'm sure the years haven't tempered Harold Pringle one bit. It's nice to know some good things don't change.

Happy 80th, Harold!

Politics From Another View

February 5, 1983

A former resident from Sturgis claims he was afforded a unique look at the political scene. Turns out it was a pretty perceptive one, even if he's blind.

Folks who remember former Sturgis resident Don McLaughlin say it's no surprise. They always thought he had a pretty good outlook on life.

Eunice Nelson, a city resident, remembers the young man just out the State School for the Blind, who came here to work at Marvel Industries. She said McLaughlin was known as an excellent worker. He stayed in Sturgis 15 years, until Marvel closed. McLaughlin then landed a job in Lansing.

His knowledge of politicians came pretty easy: McLaughlin operated one of the busy concession stands at the capitol building.

He and his wife, Revena, worked a decade in Lansing and got to know the political scene and the people who shaped it. Don, blind since the age of 15 when nerves in his eyes "dried up," and Revena, also blind, met at the school for the blind. They married after Don established his position at Marvel.

It's no surprise to Nelson what the McLaughlin's made of the Lansing business. An assistant from the school for the blind had spent only two days in Sturgis helping McLaughlin get settled "before he was on his own," Nelson said.

Nelson got to know the young couple well. She owned a restaurant and the McLaughlin's spent a lot of time at her establishment. "They were a friendly couple," she said, and added that she treasures their friendship, which continued through letters after the McLaughlin's moved away.

The McLaughlins retired a year ago, observing their 33rd wedding anniversary the same day. Though the couple worked at the capitol site 14 years, McLaughlin operated concession stands for the State Department of Labor since 1961 through a special program for the blind.

To cap off the retirement festivities, Don and Revena received a standing ovation in the Michigan House of Representatives. The couple was called to the speaker's platform to accept a resolution of tribute saluting their work.

While the McLaughlin's have told Mrs. Nelson they enjoyed their years at the stand, getting to know so many legislators, they claim their happiest moments were talking to young children who came to visit them while on field trips to the capitol.

The McLaughlins raised two children and have three grandchildren, Nelson said. In a letter last year, the couple wrote Nelson to say they don't have specific plans in their retirement. They admit they miss the capitol rush.

To help them along on retirement plans, the couple got an additional bonus: On the day they retired, McLaughlin cashed in a $25,000 Lottery ticket he sold himself the year before.

"Nice present for a nice couple," Nelson said.

A Kid's Best Friend

February 12, 1983

I knew there'd come a time I'd write about that dog. I refused to do it for years, but her memory crept into my thoughts at odd moments, nudging at my conscience, begging for remembrance.

It's time.

I've loved several dogs in my lifetime, but only two captured my heart. There was no sharing of my love between them, because one dog was gone from my life when the other entered it.

One loves animals in different ways, for reasons that sometimes can't be explained. The dog I loved as a child had no comparison to the one I lost a short time ago.

I've written about the last dog, but never the first. Maybe the joy of having that dog—and then losing her—closed off a feeling I felt too personal to relate. I don't have the answer to why that is, only that it is something that bothers me at moments when I am unprepared for such thoughts.

To begin with, she wasn't even my dog. We couldn't have a dog when we lived up North, because my father suffered from asthma. That didn't stop me from borrowing my aunt's dog, or a neighbor's pet to love. But it wasn't the same as having one's own dog. Not the least.

She became my dog the winter day we drove into the yard at the farm in Branch County, when my father moved the family back to the homestead in Branch County.

I was nine and so was she. When she heard the car, she lumbered out from her sleep among the straw bales underneath the back porch. She was a big dog, part shepherd and part collie, with luminous eyes. When she crawled from under the porch, she met only strangers—except for one she chose to know. She ignored everyone else and unhesitantly came to me.

It was settled as simply as that. I had a dog—and she had me. She would never again be my grandparents' cherished friend. She may have selfishly turned away in a moment from their love, which had sustained her so many years, but without reservations she gave it all to me. And never gave it away again.

I hated the farm when I first moved there. I was used to forests and a lot of wild animals. I lit out a couple to times (actually it was about five) for the North—and the dog went with me. Got as far as Burr Oak one time before my grandfather caught up with us. He never said a word, just opened the car door and we climbed in. And ran away again in a couple of months.

After I adjusted to my new home a bit, the dog and I became the kind of pals that happens on farms. We chased squirrels, went swimming in the creek, fetched the cow's home, went hunting in the fall. She was allowed to accompany me everywhere, except two places: the house and school. She accepted the school banishment, but would lie near the road where she could hear me coming before she spotted me. That dog running to meet me after school is a memory I hold dear.

The house problem was another thing. She was supposed to be a farm dog, but I couldn't bear to be parted from her. Mostly, I felt she needed me when storms came. She had been underneath a grainery when lightning struck it early in her life and she was terrified of storms.

If I didn't sneak her into the house, she'd go through whatever screen door barred her way—to the dismay and disgust of my dad, who had the task of replacing the screen.

That dog and I rollicked through life without needing much of anyone or anything. She was the dearest thing I owned.

Then, one day, she chased a delivery van and was run over by the wheels. When I got home from school, Doc Dauber, the veterinarian, was there. He knew my family, all the way down from my grandparents, and he knew me. Always called me "kid" or "hard-boiled." Never did call me by my name, even though I accompanied him many times of his visits to neighboring farms.

Doc owned the next farm up from ours and I enjoyed tormenting him. He had a slight speech impediment and when I got under his skin a bit, he'd let loose with some words that only scrambled in his mouth. I howled with glee and he'd cuff me lightly back of the head. Doc liked me. I knew that.

The day the dog was hit; Doc put it bluntly to me. "Her back's hurt bad. She'll never walk. She's in misery. If you love her, you'll know that putting her to sleep is the kindest thing you can do for her."

The decision was mine. I looked at that dog and her eyes were begging me—but for what? I stood there shaking, and then shook my head. "No way," I told Doc. He exploded. His wrath wasn't nice to hear, but when he got done, he said he'd return in the morning and if the dog wasn't better, he was going to put her to sleep.

I put the dog in my wagon, pulled her up to the next farmhouse and hid her. I think my folks knew, but I also believe my Dad found the hiding place and checked her out, although he never told me. I suppose he felt that a decision to put the dog away would have to come from me and he was trusting my judgment.

I worked with that dog for days, massaging her, coaxing her to eat, pleading with her to walk. I even cursed her one time when she wouldn't move her legs. And then one day, when I returned home from school and told her I was going to take a walk North again, she moved a bit. In the next days and weeks, with me lifting her and moving her legs, she finally attempted to walk.

The day I came home from school and saw her slowly hunch to her feet and stumble towards me was one I'll never forget. She cried in pain and happiness. I cried in thankfulness.

I knew then that sometimes stubbornness, faith and love has a lot to do with recovery. I learned it from that dog.

The dog regained all her mobility and zest for life and lived several years after the accident.

One summer, I got a chance to take the train back to the Upper Peninsula. With some misgivings and a sorrowful look from the dog, I left. I missed the dog those months up North. I missed her a lot. Through letters, I'd asked about her. For some reason no one said much. When my parents drove North to pick me up, my mother told me the dog became sick and Doc had to put her to sleep. Their words were kind, saying the dog was old, she had a stroke or something of that nature, and her heart gave out.

I still wonder what she thought about me going North without her. I hope she understood. I'm not sure I do.

Stryker Never Struck Out in Medicine

February 19, 1983

If you're an arthritis sufferer, or had a hip or knee artificial implant, you can thank a gentleman from the area, who founded a company years ago to help such folks.

It started with a guy named Homer Stryker, who lost the soft part of his palm from a rope burn when he was a youth.

Stryker didn't let the injury keep him on the sidelines, he worked around his handicap. After graduating from Western State Normal College (now WMU), Stryker coached baseball at Grand Ledge and Keweenaw Bay.

After that, Stryker served in the European Theater during World War I and later studied medicine at the University of Michigan. He even pitched for the college baseball team, using a special hold he fashioned with his hand to throw the ball. He got so good, he received an offer from the Detroit Tigers to join their team, but turned it down to practice medicine in Kalamazoo.

According to most reports, Stryker studied orthopedic surgery and set up a workshop in the hospital basement. Knowing how injuries can affect the lives and livelihood of persons crippled through accidents or birth defects, Stryker worked most of his spare time at inventions, eventually earning 30 patents.

They say Stryker, utilizing his small town rural beginnings, learned something important early in life and made it his motto: Never make a product whose only purpose it is to make money, and to "make a product simple enough that any dumb orderly on his worst day won't have any problem with."

That motto apparently served Stryker well. Among his inventions was a stretcher, rigged with traction, used to immobilize injured patients and prevent further damage.

The frames became popular on battlefields during World War II. Doctors returning from the war began ordering the Stryker frames from the inventor.

The business flourished. Eventually, Stryker turned the operation over to his son, Lee. Lee is credited with steering the firm to rapid sales growth.

Unfortunately, Lee, his wife and two other family members died in an airplane crash in 1976. Some months after Lee's death, the firm's board of directors hired John Brown, who had worked for a company which manufactured surgical instruments.

Homer Stryker died three years after his son, but the company is going strong. The Kalamazoo firm has added joint and other implants to its inventory. The implants are widely used in orthopedic surgery.

And, if you've always wondered where the name Stryker came from, you can tell everyone the founder of the Stryker frame - the company – came from the little town of Athens.

An Enduring Kind of Flower

February 26, 1983

They call her "Mrs. B." Not to keep her name secret, or anything like that. It is simply that time has brought it to this in the small town of Burr Oak, where things are open and down-to-earth.

She does have an appropriate name, Thelma, and for matters of a more personal nature, she is Mrs. Clesson Burnsides. But it is Mrs. B that most folks call her – and it is stated with love.

Mrs. B belongs to Burr Oak – and you might say Burr Oak belongs to her. It came about, simply enough, from the years she spent caring about people.

She was a local girl who went into teaching as a young woman. It was the only choice she considered, friends say. A host of families and several generations of children are grateful for that.

Mrs. B wasn't your ordinary teacher. She put something extra into it, and her peers were motivated to pattern themselves after her. Unfortunately, the character mold of Mrs. B can't be found easily, so it's doubtful she can be duplicated.

She taught a strict class, tempered with love. A kid who misbehaved soon earned her attention – and the kid usually got smart enough to devote time to the books. Mrs. B would appear out of nowhere, some said, when students acted up. A sharp word put things back to normal. There was no time in Mrs. B's teaching day to coddle kids. Pupils were in school to learn and she intended to bring out the best in them.

In the midst of Mrs. B's career, she took time to help folks in town, especially the kids. She won't say, but there's been talk for years about many gifts and donations for causes big and small. Doesn't matter whether it's for church, school or community. She just does the unexpected.

Things like a couple dollars for a kid with his first car, to help pay the gas bill. A bit of coin for a long-planned trip. Talking to parents when a kid errs and needs a buffer to help explain it to the folks.

Many other stories are known of her concern for youths. Some parents regrettably sigh and say they wish she was still teaching.

She taught school longer than she had to, simply because she loved it. Besides, there were kids who needed her. She had the knack of knowing which kid needed something extra. Folks remember Mrs. B would pick out students who didn't feel they belonged, who wouldn't take responsibility and join in. It's been said "You're the ones who can do this job best!" Strange thing was, she was right. Most kids just needed to be trusted and treated as individuals – with a little love thrown in.

It's common knowledge that Mrs. B turned many headstrong kids onto the right path.

She said she didn't have favorites – and she didn't. She does admit several students became special to her. One such boy, whose unpredictable nature masked insecurity and love, never forget her kindness. He sent her a violet plant one day. The message on the card, according to those who know the story, went something like this, in the teenager's heartfelt, unpolished words: "Roses are supposed to be sent to great ladies, but roses bloom quickly, fade and are gone. You're like violets, strong, enduring and lovely, and bloom brightly forever."

After Mrs. B retired, her home became the stopping off place for the kids, including those who married, moved away and started families. Mrs. B didn't forget them. She made sure she knew how they were doing by asking their relatives about her former students.

The other day, the young man she did so much for years ago stopped off at her home with his small son in tow. As unpredictable as ever, he didn't call. There is no such need in Mrs. B's home.

The fellow's little boy will never know the privilege of having Mrs. B as his teacher, but he knows where her house is and that its door is open to him. Already, her attention is sought, and the toddler says "My Mrs. B! Mine!" No one questions.

The boy left a plant for Mrs. B when he stopped by. When he is older, he will fully understand the message on the card. A card which said, in part, "... *you're like violets, strong, enduring and lovely* ..."

You Think that this Winter's Strange...

March 5, 1983

I'm the one who loves winter and snow – lots of snow. But this winter has been the strangest one I remember, at least from the point of warmer temperatures and abrupt weather changes.

The weather this year has been a topic of many conversations, and a lot of comparisons of other years.

Apparently Mrs. Ora Clark of Shimmel Road has been keeping a close watch on the weather. She sent along a clipping from a 1973 Sturgis Journal, which was a reprint of a story that appeared about 1930 in the Journal. The original article was the possession of John Huntress of Sturgis. The story is worth repeating in its entirety:

The year 1816 was known throughout the United States and Europe as the coldest ever experienced by any person then living. January was so mild that most persons allowed their fires to go out, and did not burn wood except for cooking. February was not cold.

March, from the first to the sixth, was inclined to be windy. It came in like a small lion and went out like a lamb.

April came in warm, but as the days grew longer, the air became colder. By the first of May it was like winter, with plenty of snow and ice.

In May young buds were frozen dead. Cornfields were planted again and again until it became too late to raise corn. When the last of May arrived everything had been killed by the cold.

Mothers knitted socks of double thickness for their children and made thick mittens.

On June 17, there was a heavy fall of snow. A Vermont farmer sent a flock of sheep to pasture on June 16. That morning of the 17th dawned with the thermometer below the freezing point. At about 9 a.m., the owner of the sheep started to look up his flock. Before leaving home he turned to his wife and said, jokingly, "Better start to the neighbors soon. It's the middle of June and I may get lost in the snow."

A terrible storm came up after he had left home. Not returning home that evening his wife alarmed the neighbors. He was found on the third day, both feet frozen, half covered with snow, but alive. Most of the sheep were lost.

July came in with ice and snow. To the surprise of everyone, August proved the worst month of all. Almost every green thing in this country and Europe was blasted with frost.

Newspapers from England stated that 1816 would be remembered by the existing generation as the year in which there was no summer. Thousands of persons would have perished had it not been for the abundance of fish and wild game."

It's nice that folks like Mrs. Clark hang on to clippings such as this one. Maybe reading them will keep us from griping about the weather and give thanks for what we have.

FDR, The Depression and Matters of Pride

March 12, 1983

The Franklin D. Roosevelt memories that flooded the media last week drew some thoughts- memories of times and places etched in my mind like indelible tracings. And I've thought a lot about it the past week.

That other time should be remembered, not because it was the "good old days," but for a simple reason: If nothing else, it taught a valuable lesson. The lesson came hard, but much of the learning remains. I wonder, sometimes, if I should remember so well, seeing as how it took some of the laughter out of my life and afterwards I wasn't quite as open with the world.

Anyone who lived the Depression years knows what I mean. After that time, we were never quite as young, as carefree as succeeding generations would be.

We had reason not to be. We'd experienced a portion of life forever ingrained in our minds.

I know many folks who'd rather forget or hide a truth from their past: that they were poor and were forced to be on relief. The evolution of that word has come to be known as welfare. Aid to Dependent Children and Public Assistance. None of the titles change the fact: Your daily needs are being paid by someone else, from someone else's pocketbook.

I've never forgotten that my family had to accept help. I hope I don't. I don't ever want to be in the position where I take a good job, good fortune for granted. The measure of doing for oneself remains unchanged, a simple matter: pride.

It was a long time ago. I was nearly six. I didn't know it then, but the shadow of adult reality was to steal early into my life like an unwanted, unasked thief.

It came with shattering impact. Jobs, already scarce in that Upper Peninsula town, suddenly were gone.

My family had another problem. When the jobs with the county, or WPA (Works Progress Administration) finally opened up, my dad could only work part-time. Asthma and a bad heart forced him to his bed. He was only a young man, but already old in the knowledge and despair of not being able to fully support his family.

My dad eeked out earnings by putting in a large garden, and trapping when he could make the river runs.

My mother took in washings, at 25 cents per week. Water was heated in boilers on the cook-stove.

Those washings were for CCC (Civilian Conservation Corps) officers at the Sidnaw Camp at the edge of town. The work was completed by scrubbing clothes on a board, rinsing in a tub, and running them through an old crank wringer.

I can still see my mother's stiff, blue fingers as she wrestled frozen clothing from the clothesline in below-zero weather.

I remember my dad looking at her out the window. I watched

him lay his head against the window frame and cry, not knowing I witnessed his anguish.

I remember, too, that my mother saved a nickel a week to buy her kids a wagon. I was nearly grown before I realized the double intent behind that purchase. We used the wagon in summer to haul water from the village pump to our home.

Small wonder that we kids ever found time to laugh and play, but we did. We learned not to waste precious moments, to make a game of what life had to offer.

Little things from those long-ago days keep creeping into my thoughts. There was the day my sister and I were sent to the corner where a truck was delivering baskets of food for families (they weren't called needy in those days). Words were more blunt. Feelings weren't considered.

My sister and I watched with wonder as the basket was handed down to us. There were bananas in it. I'd never tasted a banana. Then I looked around and caught the eye of my best friend's father, who had stopped to watch. He owned several stores. There was a look of pity in his eyes.

I didn't touch those bananas, in fact, wouldn't eat bananas for years – not until I learned to sort my priorities and better understand my feelings.

I've never forgotten my mother's look when my grandfather bought me a pair of oxfords. They cost $4.95 and I ran into the house to show her. The visiting caseworker was there. He asked what they cost, and deducted that figure from our monthly check. I know now what that amount of money meant to our family.

I'm not embarrassed to say I was on public welfare. I know it was a necessary thing my parents had to do. I know my mother had eight major operations before her untimely death; my father had two. I realize the depth of their concern when they had to accept public assistance. The least I can do is not desecrate their memory by refusing to acknowledge something that cost them a measure of pride.

Last week, when I listened to the talk and watched the programs about Roosevelt and the New Deal, I remembered. Maybe FDR wasn't perfect, maybe much of what he did was wrong. I don't judge too harshly, because I know that at least he opened the door for many families by establishing job programs. He also gave us something to hope for, a means to rekindle pride in ourselves.

Sometimes, things like that are worth remembering.

A Gift from a Passing Stranger

March 19, 1983

She was driving by an Oshtemo Township home on her way to work recently. Her mind was filled with thoughts of her day ahead at a physician's office where she is a registered practical nurse.

In the next few minutes, however, she would play an important role – she would breathe life into a stranger.

Connie (Tuttle) Dideriksen, Lawrence, Mich., former Sturgis resident, and daughter of Doris Besser, Sturgis, and Don Tuttle, Kalamazoo, remembers only that she saw the man, later identified as Charles Bushman, collapse in his yard.

As her mother said, "she recalls being frightened, but didn't hesitate to stop and help."

That simple act saved the life of Bushman, who had suffered a severe heart attack. A fireman who arrived later on the scene credited Dideriksen with being "the most important link within the first vital three of four minutes – that saved Bushman's life." The crucial time element in such cases is when the victim has stopped breathing. Medical personnel say that time frame is not more than four minutes before brain damage occurs.

Dideriksen, after seeing the man fall to the ground, stopped her car and rushed to the Bushman home and pounded on the door.

When Bushman's wife appeared, not realizing her husband was ill, Dideriksen told her to call paramedics.

But Dideriksen knew that she couldn't wait until the ambulance arrived. Weeping, the women ran back to Bushman, who was not breathing and had begun to lose normal color. Dideriksen told Mrs. Bushman to elevate her husband's feet and Dideriksen began breathing into Bushman, alternating with chest compressions.

Dideriksen had received cardiopulmonary resuscitation training (CPR) 12 years ago – but the recent incident was the first time she had used it.

After Oshtemo Township fireman and paramedics arrived at the scene, Dideriksen left – without telling anyone her name.

After Bushman's hospitalization, his family began to wonder who the brave woman was who had taken the time to stop and help. When the Kalamazoo Gazette staff learned about the incident, a story was published. Even then Dideriksen did not reveal her identity. The Bushman family learned who she was when her mother-in-law's pastor called the family.

The Bushman family and Dideriksen met in the hospital, where Bushman is listed in critical condition.

Mrs. Bushman summed up Dideriksen's heroics with a simple statement: "She was like an angel."

A Man of History

March 26, 1983

Leland (Lee) Thornton of Centreville is a man in love with history. He studies it, teaches it and stands in awe of it. He admits his life revolves around it, "especially when I hear about some new diary, pictures or day books."

Mostly, Thornton is entranced with the Civil War years, although he confesses that the Spanish-American War and other conflicts draw his interest.

He speaks at many meetings concerning his hobby, but never fails to reveal some aspect about history when involved in conversation.

He's a busy man, serving as Nottawa Township clerk and chairman of the Humanities and Social Sciences Department at Glen Oak Community College. The college is his reason for coming to the area and he's been with it since it was opened.

But history is his love. He doesn't deny it. "It's been a compelling interest for years," he says. He has a master's degree, but is working on another – writing a thesis on the Michigan 11th Volunteer Infantry, a unit he says "certainly deserves writing a book about."

The book on the 11th Infantry (the unit was comprised mainly of county soldiers) is his immediate goal, but he also hopes to complete a history concerning "the patriotism of St. Joseph County," which will involve other early wars.

He says the "whole 19ᵗʰ Century war history of this area demands to be told in its entirety, including the stories of soldiers in the Mexican War."

In his quest to learn more about the Civil War, Thornton not only went back to college, he also spends many days searching archives, court records, libraries and reading "anything I can get my hands on concerning the war," Thornton said.

In his quest for more information, Thornton has asked for help. He needs more material to read, especially family records and letters of the Civil War period. He notes that there are few letters available that were written home from the soldiers. "They're few and far between. I especially would like to read some of those, as well as letters of family members to relatives which might add information about the homelife during that time."

Thornton doesn't know when his information will be gathered and the book started, but "I'm going to keep working."

For those of you who might have old letters or diaries packed away, Thornton would be pleased to read them. He'll copy any he's allowed to, and will return them as soon as possible. Any material given to Thornton to keep is being turned over to Western Michigan University's regional archives, to allow others to have the chance Thornton has had in reading the material.

I hope there are folks who can help Thornton in his labor of love. History isn't much use to us if we don't know all the particulars. Thornton would like to help that effort along. His project is surely worthwhile and one area residents could make more interesting.

Monitor to Life

April 2, 1983

A cry in the night from a baby might disturb some parents, but others are only thankful their baby doesn't sleep deep and not cry out. Some tots simply stop breathing – and die -their death sounds unheard and unknown by their caring parents.

If you're the parent of a youngster with Apnea or Sudden Infant Death Syndrome (SID), there's help for you – not only life support assistance, but that necessary ingredient, moral support.

Ask Connie Wells, Burr Oak, and Susie Fry, Sturgis. Their children suddenly stop breathing.

Connie has two youngsters who have been placed on monitors to alert the parents when the babies cease breathing. Suzie has one.

Connie's daughter, Janell, now two, and son, B.J., are accustomed to being hooked up to monitors. Janell has been on a monitor since the age of seven weeks, and B.J. since his birth 10 months ago.

While neither of the Wells children was born prematurely, the Fry triplets were. One died shortly after birth. One of the surviving girls, Cheryl, was placed on a monitor. Casey was fortunate and breathes well on her own.

Connie says a support group is essential because once a youngster is taken home from the hospital, someone close by is needed, preferably someone who has undergone, or who understands the SID of Apnea problem.

The women's – and others – concern is the reason for founding the non-profit Apnea Support Group of Southwestern Michigan, organized a year ago. Connie, Nina Steele of Paw Paw and Val Boosi of Kalamazoo, serve on the board.

They are holding the meeting at the Sturgis Church of Christ at 7 p.m., Tuesday, March 5. They already have 21 persons who plan to attend.

At the meeting, three crucial issues will be explained, with professional persons present to offer advice:

- How to stimulate an infant or child when they have stopped breathing.
- How to do infant cardiopulmonary resuscitation.
- How to work with monitors.

Connie says no youngster suffering from Apnea or SID symptoms is released from the hospital until the parents can handle monitor chores, but it helps to have support persons, especially friends and family members, learn to how to handle emergencies of this kind.

"It will be a teaching class Tuesday," Connie explained, "a kind of babysitting class to teach other individuals how to cope with children suffering from breathing problems. Many people are afraid to babysit with these children."

As a result, parents spend most of their time near the children, very often not getting a break or an evening out.

"It's pretty hard for parents to leave a child under these circumstances," Connie said, "but with training, it will allow families to live as normally as possible until the breathing crisis is past."

When she brought her daughter home from the hospital, Connie knew only one other family who had the same problem. In the past year, she has gathered names of 15 families in St. Joseph and Branch counties.

"Our main concern is to focus on helping others," Connie added. If the number of persons exceeds a good teaching class size, Connie will schedule another class. She urges those interested to call her (489-5385) to allow for scheduling. There is no cost for the meeting.

But cost also raises another problem. Connie said she publishes a newsletter for parents. Cost of printing and mailing are high. Borgess and Bronson Hospitals have helped with the cost, but holding meetings and paying for rental buildings adds burden to the families. Being a non-profit organization, donations are tax deductible. Connie hopes this will help in the groups' continuation to help other families.

"I know what it's like to have a support person to call when I was confused, when the monitor frightened me, or the baby had stopped breathing," Connie said. "I now do the same for other parents. You have to realize some of these parents can be awakened by the monitor alarm as often as 20 times a night, from midnight on, usually. A simple call to another person who understands and knows what to do, helps in those frightening moments."

"And, sometimes, it's more than just a simple shaking the child. It could be CPR or other means to save a child's life."

"This support group provides the extra strength and concern that is so desperately needed."

And what's more precious than a child's life?

Smoking Them Out

April 9, 1983

Some folks love to smoke. Robert Ritzenthaler wants to "smoke them out." And he has plenty of support.

Ritzenthaler, director of the cardio-respiratory department at Sturgis Hospital, has long known the dangers of smoking. Some of his patients are testimony to smoking histories.

Ritzenthaler also is associated with the five-day smoking clinic. It's a program to help people stop smoking – and not start again.

Ritzenthaler's chief helpers through the years have been Rev. Byron Churchill and Dr. Vincente Cabansag, who have donated time, support and effort to the project.

They'll be at it again five nights April 24-28, from 7-9 p.m. They will teach the clinics at Sturgis Hospital and hope a large crowd will join their crusade.

The stop smoking program is copyrighted and endorsed by the Seventh Day Adventist Church and the American Cancer Society. Both groups and the hospital assist in providing speakers from its medical staff, and a place to hold the clinics. The hospital auxiliary helps with registration.

Dr. Randy Wood of the Department of Health will speak this year. Professionals and laymen also will offer their words of wisdom and experience at the clinics.

This is the 10th clinic. Classes are held twice a year. The sessions began in 1978, Ritzenthaler said.

At least 187 persons have attended the clinic. Ritzenthaler said the success rate of those who stopped smoking at least a year ranges in the 50 percent. Nationally, that figure stands about 30 percent, Ritzenthaler added.

Follow-up help after the clinics is available, in that many of the speakers will talk to persons who feel they need moral support and advice.

This, year, Ritzenthaler started a new program. He asked principals of Wall, Congress and Wenzel schools if they would like him to speak to students on the no-smoking subject.

"The response was great," Ritzenthaler said.

Students in fifth grade, some eight classes in all, were chosen because of their age level. Ritzenthaler said he was surprised at questions the children asked and their interest in learning about smoking habits and their dangers.

"Students had been studying about lungs and hearts in their health classes. The talks and visual aids fit right into their classroom studies," Ritzenthaler added.

To enlarge the program, because the students seemed eager to express their feelings, posters were made by pupils. "Some students have deep feelings about smoking. They don't want their parents or loved ones to smoke. But, how could they tell adults what to do? This is their way of expressing their thoughts," Ritzenthaler said.

Ritzenthaler is enthused at the addition to the no smoking program. He says that might be where discussions about smoking problems should start, when youngsters are at an impressionable age.

"I had fantastic cooperation from the schools. It was also an excellent learning experience for me, because I also came to see the dangers of smoking from children's views.

"And the posters – they are quality materials," Ritzenthaler said. The posters will be put in factories, businesses and other sites in the community.

"I don't want to force myself on school children's training," Ritzenthaler said. "The subject fit into what they were studying and they expressed interest."

If asked, Ritzenthaler said he will return to classrooms next year.

Right now, his attention is focused on the April 24-28 stop smoking sessions. He hopes he's swamped with questions and registration. For those who want to sign-up, call him at Sturgis Hospital. He'll be glad to hear from you.

Perryville, Kentucky Revisited

April 16, 1983

They will do it right, these members of the "Michigan at Perryville Society." Not only will they revive memories of the brave Michigan regiments and two field artillery batteries who fought in the Battle of Perryville, Ky., Oct. 8, 1862, but they will do it at the site of that skirmish.

Civil War buffs founded the society to keep alive the deeds of those heroic men from the Wolverine State.

The Michigan units under General Don Carlos Buell were part of the army that stopped Confederate General Braxton Bragg's thrust to bring Kentucky into the Confederacy and invade the Midwest.

Of prime interest will be the unveiling of a Michigan historic marker at the battlefield. It will be only the second marker erected outside the state for a Michigan unit which fought in the Civil War. The other marker is at Stone's River National Battlefield in Tennessee, where many St. Joseph County soldiers fought and died.

The honored units from Michigan who fought at Perryville were the 13th Michigan Volunteer Infantry, 2nd Michigan Volunteer Cavalry, 1st Michigan Engineers and Mechanics Regiment, Battery A (Loomis') 1st Michigan Light Artillery and Battery D (Church's

1ˢᵗ Michigan Light Artillery. Battery A and B were organized in Coldwater and Branch County.

The society is endorsed by every major historical group in Michigan, including the Michigan Historical Commission, all the Civil War Round Tables and several civic organizations.

The Kentucky Heritage Commission and other Bluegrass organizations are taking part in festivities.

According to John J. Collins, the group's press secretary, more than 100 Michigan Civil War enthusiasts and historians will travel by bus to the Bluegrass States to participate in a two-day program.

Events will be held in Perryville, with side trips to the battlefield site and historical points of interest.

Co-chairman are Jerry D. Roe of Lansing and James S. Brady II of Kalamazoo.

It's a great chance to take part in a great revival of Civil War history. The bus trip, which includes full membership in the society, cost $100. The cost includes the round trip on the bus, all meals, receptions, souvenirs, publications, piece of the marker, etc.

The two-day expedition will be held Sept. 10-11, 1983. It is expected one bus will originate in Detroit and another will cover Lansing and Kalamazoo regions.

Members will stay at a hotel, which will be the only outside cost to participants.

It sounds like a great weekend trip, and an important one. Besides, the Blue and the Gray will be together again – this time in peace.

Call It Family Tradition

April 23, 1983

Reunions are events that bring families together. Some are haphazard occasions, with no specific dates set to observe family traditions.

Others, like the Yunker reunion, are important times. Plans through the year usually center around the reunion.

This year, the Yunkers are going to do it up right, according to Inez Warmbread of Sturgis. There's reason to celebrate: the family will observe its 100-year mark of the Yunker family arriving in America.

"We had a special 50-year observance in 1933, but this one will really be something for the family to remember," Inez said.

It's being held today, April 23, at the UAW Union Hall in Sturgis. Those attending are expected to number in the hundreds.

Maybe having a reunion doesn't mean much to some families, but to the Yunker descendants it's a time to remember the spirit and courage of their ancestors, who left Yegenstorf, Switzerland, a century ago. Inez says the family homestead was about nine miles from Bern, a village of around 1,100 persons.

The patriarch of the family was Jacob Yunker, who had four children. One son, also named Jacob (Jake), always wanted to come to the United States, so the family had the children study American maps and histories of people of the United States. They learned to write the American ABCs.

At the age of 21, Jack Yunker announced that he was going to America. The family wrote to Uncle Jake Abbey, who lived in America. They asked him to come over and cross the ocean with them. After sending him money three times, he finally sailed to Switzerland to accompany them, Inez said.

The family sold their farm in Switzerland. On March 28, 1883, the entire family, along with cousin Jake, Fred Peiffer, and another (unrelated) man named John Yunker, took the train from Bern to France. They set sail from Harve, France on the French Steamer Mamia Leone. The ship was 365 feet long and carried 1,000 passengers. After suffering seasickness during a severe storm, the ship docked in New York Harbor after 12 days on the ocean. A train was taken to Sturgis, where the family would live.

Arriving here April 15, some family members spent the night in the hay loft because there wasn't room in the uncle's house. A neighbor took in several of the family.

The Yunkers purchased 67 acres of land for $500. They still had $500 left to build a house. While the home was being built, a tornado swept through the area, but family members remained unhurt.

Soon after, the family "accepted a call from God and became members of the Evangelical Church, "walking two miles to prayer meetings, Inez said.

The next winter, a nearby farm was to be sold at auction in front of the National Bank. Jake Yunker made the high bid of $5,555. A lawyer who attended asked: "Say, you want to bid – if you want that place," Jake's reply, according to family lore, was "do you think I am fool enough to raise my bid."

The lawyer said: "Well, that little Dutchman isn't as dumb as I thought!"

Some neighbors thought the farm would never be paid for, but the Yunkers fooled them. It was free of debt in five years and the family had 12 horses, 25 cattle, and sheep, hogs, chickens and geese. They also owned two binders, two mowers and tools. They harvested 3,000 bushels of wheat and 2,000 of oats, which were sold for $1.01 a bushel.

As Inez said, "maybe our family doesn't have such a dramatic past, but it's typical of the hard-working, church-going folks who gave up established roots in other countries to make their way in America."

And so, today, the Yunker descendants will recall old Jacob's words and remember that he forged the way for them in a new world. If Jake were alive today, he'd be mighty proud of his descendants.

Warren Miller, Journal Standby

April 30, 1983

He's full of grit and vigor and one of the nicest people to have around. He's in and out of the Journal at odd hours, sometimes here in the wee hours of the Saturday morning press runs and always here to greet the first arriver for the day's business.

He's witty, quick to enjoy a joke and doesn't let a minute pass to level a feisty remark.

He's also 84 and without him the Journal wouldn't be the same. In fact, the word has been passed around that if Warren Miller is ever let go from employment here, "there will be a mutiny."

That's because we love him.

Warren has been with the Journal a long time, years before I came here. But his face, was the first I saw the day I joined the staff. His gruff, blunt greeting was typical of the man: "Hi. I'm Warren Miller. Who are you?"

And our friendship was begun as simply as that. We even have nicknames for each other, but I'm not going to publicize them, but they're names of mutual admiration – I hope.

Warren's been around the Journal some 25 years, coming first to set up tubes and posts for the first motor route the Journal established. He's been a janitor, he handles bundles of newspapers for circulation, he rakes leaves. He even shovels snow (I'm forever hollering at him about that, to no avail.)

He does a lot of other things for the Journal, but mostly, he does a lot for us by just being there.

He's stability, a starchy fellow who is old only in terms of years. Certainly his attitude doesn't portray his age.

He's concerned about his fellow workers, and gets upset if someone doesn't show up when they are suppose to. He worries until they come in the door.

He's always worked hard. He lived on a farm near Bronson as a youngster and before his marriage was employed at the White Pigeon paper mill. He moved to Sturgis after his marriage and had remained here since.

Before coming to the Journal he worked at a furniture factory in the city until the Depression. He then joined Harvey Paper Products and remained there 28 years until the firm moved. He worked odd jobs around town until hired by the Journal.

He worked for six Journal publishers: Mark Haines, Harold Pringle, Douglas Bullock, James Gunderson, Jo-Ann Huff Ablers and Roanne Fry.

He manages to keep busy at home. Says he watches television some, although trying to get him to buy a color television is "pure nonsense," he says. "Old one works fine."

He admits he misses the pretty girl he married so many years ago, but doesn't dwell on the sadness of losing her through death. He has other family members to help keep him happy and busy.

Warren is the kind of guy you can tell your troubles to, and he'll keep family confidences.

I don't know what life would be like without Warren Miller. I hope I don't ever learn. Right now, the Journal employees are grateful for the time we've shared with him and hope it continues a long time.

Besides, we owe him a couple of practical jokes.

Fragrance of Another Time

May 7, 1983

It is nearly time again. I would not deny it even if I could. The season of awakening bids. The land—and emotions—stir anew.

The sweet smell of spring means many things. To me, as it has since the days of my first remembrance, it means arbutus. Just the word draws strong memories.

Life's happenings have a way of drawing questions from the recess of the mind. The primary question is, why do I remember arbutus so well when I have not gathered its lovely blossoms nor smelled its heady fragrance since I was a child of 10?

Arbutus. They say the trailing arbutus, at least the particular strain that grows in the Upper Peninsula, cannot be transplanted. I should grieve for that, but a measure of my yesterdays takes satisfaction that it cannot be moved at whim by possibly uncaring hands. I think a lot about that this time of year.

I went back one time to that scene of early years. I was grown, searching for unanswered questions from my childhood. Maybe it was because I wanted to reconcile the child within me who refused to leave when the adult came unbidden to stay.

It was not spring when I went back; it was a cool fall day. I had prepared myself. I would not be so foolish as to visit my childhood home. I knew the house had changed and bore no resemblance to the one where I was born and remained for 10 years. My aunts, who had remained in the small town, had wrote and told me that much.

But there I was, rounding the turn in the dusty road, and confronted my past. Gone was the house as I had remembered it. The blunt, square lines of the dwelling horrified me. Where was the bay window that used to be my favorite niche for reading? Bile rose in my throat.

And then, for a reason I have never been able to explain, the heady, rich perfume of arbutus filled my nostrils. It could not be, of course, but there it was. Why was the fragrance so powerful it burned my eyes? Or was it tears that came?

Arbutus comes early in the northlands, usually around May Day. I had no means to buy my mother a present in those days, so a May Day basket was the epitome of what I could offer. She always welcomed the gift, especially the arbutus. I don't know why. Perhaps it was because the arbutus grew free, unshackled and could not be kept in the confines of a yard.

Maybe it was because she knew, as mothers always do, that no ordinary patch of arbutus was chosen to make the selection for a bouquet. Always it came from far across the creek, close in the shadow of the pine trees, where the warm spring sun crept to coax the flowers' brilliant blooms.

Maybe, that fall day as I retraced my life's steps, my journey made little sense to the outsider. I only know there was a silent cry for a mother lost much too young, much too soon.

There is another puzzle that comes at odd moments to haunt my thoughts. Why is it that if I love the arbutus so much, I have not returned when it comes to color and warm the bleak, reawakening soil?

I suspect some memories are too private, too unwilling to be shared, and I am afraid they will be tarnished by allowing their beauty to be diluted by other's eyes—and questions too difficult to answer.

Sometimes, the path to yesterday and childhood is a difficult one I think a bit about that, too, although I wish I could place a bouquet or arbutus on my mother's grave. Especially when Mother's Day comes.

I know one simple fact: The arbutus—and its memories tied always to a mother I loved—seem best left with the past and my own recollections. It is a selfish thought, but at least the memories remain mine.

A Vigil Known as Love

May 21, 1983

Spent some time in the hospital recently. As always, a hospital is the mirror of life—or death. It is a stage where, many times, the drama of life's destiny is decided.

I re-found old friends, people who work at the hospital. They are folks who in small, unasked ways, made my stay easier.

I also met again, friends I know have walked hospital and nursing hallways a long time. They have been in the hospitals in the brightness of day and during the long, shadows of night, when loneliness seems the hardest to bear.

They are the Lees, Bonnie and Larry. Their young son, Chris, was grievously hurt in a swimming accident two years ago this July.

To date, no reason for Chris' accident or resulting problems is known. Chris had surfaced from the waters of a friend's pool, cried out that something was wrong, and he needed help. That cry for help still comes from the youth, although he has uttered few words since that day.

Chris has been in several hospitals and nursing homes since the accident. So have his devoted parents, brother, Jeff, and other family members.

One wonders about the Lees' kind of faith, their courage and the love that sustains them through this terrible ordeal. They are at Chris' side every possible moment, attending to his needs, bathing him, massaging his limbs. Offering always, the knowledge to their son that they are there, even if they are unsure how much he understands.

I didn't ask to see Chris. There was a sign on the door to his room that said no visitors. I understood why. There are always the gawkers, the curious, the morbid onlookers who never fail to appear at difficult moments. It is a fact one cannot deny.

I did ask about Chris. One does not dismiss a human being even if he or she cannot converse with the world. His mother unhesitantly motioned me into Chris' room. She knows, instinctively I suspect, who cares about Chris. She and Larry probably have learned that fact the hard way during the long months of their vigil.

There may be individuals who question if it would be better for the Lees to institutionalize Chris—to go on with their lives. The important thing is—and what those people fail to realize—is that Chris IS their life, as surely as his healthy brother is.

There is another reason why they maintain their hope so keenly— one that was evident to me at my first sight of Chris in that hospital room.

He recognizes his parents, or "recognizes I am someone he knows," the soft-spoken Bonnie said. And he responds to commands, such as when Bonnie told him to "look at Carol." He did—with a questioning look—and then quickly looked back at his mother and smiled in recognition.

There was a plea in Chris' eyes when he looked at me. I don't profess to know what it was, but he knew I was unfamiliar, and he was uneasy. Yet there was alertness in his gaze.

Chris enjoys television and laughs when something on the screen seems to please him, Bonnie said. The Lees know Chris still has touch with the world.

It is difficult for the Lees. Especially difficult for Larry, whose memories of his son are stirred by thoughts of other times. Of a vibrant boy who loved baseball, whose strong young body was a personal pride to the teen-ager.

The Lees are not giving up their lives for Chris, as some would assume. It is simply that he is part of them, and they of him. Part of their future is in this hurt, suffering young man. Their tomorrows—whatever fate decrees—are invested in this son who for now is enveloped in his own world.

But one thing is evident—Chris Lee is not a human being who has retreated completely into a twilight world that holds no reality for him. Even the layman recognizes that.

He struggles to talk. There is desperation in his desire to communicate. This is no passive, unresponsive boy. Somewhere , in that web of the unknowns of the mind, the youth who is Chris Lee attempts to return.

That is what turns Bonnie and Larry Lee's days and nights into a continued vigilance. It is the simple hope that spurs their everyday existence.

"As long as there is breath in my body, I will continue to hope, because I see how hard Chris is trying," Bonnie said.

Watching Chris, seeing those eyes, alert in a mind trapped by merciless captors, one cannot question the Lees' quest.

This year will be poignant one for the Lees—Chris would have joined his classmates in graduation ceremonies. In their openness, the Lees are happy for the other youths, and wish them well. Chris' friends still ask about him, still attempt to help his parents in their long struggle with Chris, Bonnie added.

And the Lees continue to seek new means to help their ailing son. This month, they took him to Mary Free Bed Hospital in Grand Rapids, where the staff will attempt new ways to evaluate Chris' status and to set new goals for him.

The Lees try not to think about what Chris has lost, but as his friends go on to new beginnings and happenings in a future that is bright and beckoning, it is only understandable that the Lees' thoughts turn to what might have been.

"But that, in our case, serves no purpose, and wastes precious time," Bonnie said.

"We search for little things, small steps. Small, but significant signs of progress," Bonnie added. "We could not, in any measure of conscience, turn away from Chris. We will keep trying, trying to bring him back to us."

As Larry Lee said, a year into their vigil—and repeats today— "Chris is worth it."

Change of Time, Not Place

June 4, 1983

Wallace "Wally" Bowman Sr., "semi-retired" from operating the B&W Bar in downtown Sturgis five years ago. "Retired, but didn't stay out of the business completely," Wally said. But now he's decided to turn over ownership reins to his only son, Wally, "Butch" Jr., and his wife, Kathy.

It's not an easy move for Wally to make. After all, he's been in the same location since June of 1941. "I've been told I've operated a bar in the same building in Michigan longer than anyone else," he said.

So, Wally's family and friends are hosting an open house for him on June 10-12 and "it looks like it's going to be some party," Wally said.

A lot of folks wonder what the initials in the firm's name means. They stand for Bowman and Ware. Seems Ernest "Slim" Ware Sr., and Wally bought the business from Rosina Sgambellure when it was known as the Green Lantern Cafe.

Changing it to a bar wasn't difficult. Although the cafe served meals and was known for its soda fountain, it also served beer to the many patrons who stopped by.

Wally and Slim bought the establishment for a pretty good price – about $1,500 as Wally recalls. He left the business for a year while serving in the Army during World War II, but he and Slim had an agreement that he could come back after his tour of duty.

In those days, the building had a marble floor and 12-foot ceilings. The walls were brick. But the men realized that renovations were necessary to conserve energy and cut down on noise.

In 1943, Slim decided to sell his interest to Wally. Times were hard. It was wartime. Rationing was in effect and beer deliveries were few.

"We were lucky to get five or six cases of beer. When the beer came in, we'd open up early and stay open only until the beer was gone," Wally said.

"Of course, the factories here were working around the clock," Wally said, so "employees who got off at 7 a.m got first chance."

Reminiscing about the war years, Wally chuckled. It seems obtaining meat for lunches also was a problem. "There was this fellow who offered to supply me with enough meat – no questions asked," Wally said. As he remembers, the meat was clean and good - "customers said we served great hamburgers."

Several years after the war, the guy told Wally what kind of meat it was – goat. "Seemed he had a big herd of goats. He brought us about 39 pounds of hamburg at a time." Wally said. "All those war years, I never caught on."

"Bottle beer in those days sold at 10 cents a glass; draft beer (the bar got a keg once in a while during the war) was a nickel. And that," Wally added, "was for a 14-ounce glass." It is now served in eight or nine ounce glasses and costs 50 cents.

"Sold hamburgers for 10 cents," Wally said.

Cigarettes were a luxury. At one time Wally used them as

drawing cards. "We'd save them up until Sunday and each person coming in was allowed one pack. Didn't have machines in those days. Turned out it was a losing cause; older people came in just to buy a pack for friends and relatives, and didn't buy anything else."

Business hours were the same then, 7 a.m to 2:30 p.m.

Wally added that running a bar hasn't changed much, either. "We know most of our crowd. We know what time to expect different folks to come in. Problems, if any, are about the same. A few rowdy individuals, sometimes a loudmouth. But overall, it's a pretty good group."

The B&W's appearance has changed. The floor is carpeted and the walls paneled.

"We have to keep the place clean. We undergo inspections. Proper sanitation is especially important."

The menu is standard: "We serve sandwiches, pizza, soup and chili. About the same as others bars," Wally said.

Wally has made many friends through the years and "heard a lot of good and bad news from customers. You get to know family histories and learn to keep your mouth shut when they tell you their problems. They trust you, have confidence they can tell you their troubles. You don't abuse that privilege," Wally added.

Wally doesn't worry about folks saying anything about him earning a living running a bar. "It was a livelihood," he said. "I figure I conducted my life as well as anybody. A lot of good folks came in the bar – and still do. They contribute to this city. They're good citizens.

"Why should anyone point a finger at another person's business if you keep your house in order?"

Next week at the open house, Wally will share many memories

with his family and customers. He'll recall friends from those years. He'll also remember his hard-working wife, Marion, who helped him with the firm's operations. He lost Marion to cancer several years ago.

He's especially proud of Butch and his grandchildren. He says he knows, "Butch'll do a good job. Has done pretty well the past five years."

So, Wally will spend his time with the grandchildren and friends. He also will travel and enjoy fishing and hunting trips.

"Don't expect to sit still a minute," he said. "Stood still 42 years in the B&W and that's long enough. Time to make a change."

"But the change is only in me. The B&W will go on. It's that kind of place."

The Measure of a Good Man

June 11, 1983

He died the other day, in his own home as he had wished it. As quietly as he had made his mark on this mortal world, he left it.

He was a gentle man, a man whose feelings ran deep, whose eyes could fill easily at the sight of wrongdoing.

I called him friend. But that was not the real treasure; I knew he also called me friend. I cherished that thought.

I knew this man since the days of high school, though we lived in different towns. I recall the wiry young boy who loved sports, whose shy smile was always there to greet me.

It was odd. I can't remember what stood out about him. Maybe it was his unquestioning love of life and what it had to offer. I suppose I will never know the answer to that.

Our friendship was not the dating kind. The kind of friendship you are blessed with sometimes only once in life. It was a common caring that allowed for mistakes and errors on our characters—with understanding always there. There may have been questions about actions we made, but we overcame them.

He went away to college and for awhile I didn't see much of him. He married the girl he always had wanted to wed and settled down into a promising career. Only one thing marred their happiness:

no child came to their household. But then, with the openness the couple had, they adopted a small boy. And, as God does sometimes for those who share their love, a son of their union came to bless their home.

Through the years, the awkwardness of the young man disappeared and the gracefulness that was to be part of his character emerged. He drew respect, not only in his profession, but in his civic endeavors. And those endeavors were many.

We became close again when he began to referee athletic events at which my children participated. I recall him calling a foul on one of my sons during a basketball game and a bit of devilment crept out from his official duties. His eyes sought mine in the crowd and he winked. The kid, of course, was headstrong like me and had deserved the foul. The message was understood.

He wasn't perfect. I'd never say that, nor would he have wanted me to. I do know he faced his problems head on and agonized over them.

I remember how near to tears he was one day when he asked me to have coffee with him. He had made a business decision and personalities were involved. He also knew, without discussing it, that I saw another side to the problem. He knew my loyalties were divided and that I was concerned.

He said something that day, something that speaks of his kind of honor. His decision was unpopular to many, but he felt he had to make it. And, talking about it that day, he said, "Well, if I am wrong, then it will be on my conscience. It is my problem. I'll pay the price." He reached out and touched my hand. "Don't take sides; don't make a choice," he added. He refused to burden me with the problem.

My opinion was never compromised. He asked no quarter, no sympathy. Only understanding.

I could say a lot about his public life and his work in the community. But that has been said. The eulogies with all the proper, deserving words have been said. I cannot add to them. His deeds have been well chronicled.

I prefer to remember the man who added richness to my life. The man who understood that for the first time in my life I chose the coward's way out. I could not watch him die. Though I sensed he welcomed and needed some of his friends to be at his side through his terminal illness with cancer, there were unspoken words between us: I would not take away his final dignity by watching that spirit and body diminish.

And so I stayed away, but kept in contact with him. I kept the memories of the strong man I had known and he was content to know I had no other sight to haunt me. The thing I am forever grateful for is that he understood.

Sometimes I wonder about friendships and what makes them. And why one loves friends so dearly when it hurts so much to lose them. I know one thing: when friends die, part of you goes with them.

I will remember the man named Bob Hackman for many reasons, for the talks we shared over our common school board duties, for the moments over coffee, for a lot of things. Mostly I remember that whatever mood I was in, his smile warmed my days.

I miss him already.

A Guy Who Looks Forward

June 18, 1983

It's a long way up the ladder from janitor to plant manager. Not many individuals reach that goal. And only a few attain that position of responsibility while fighting blindness.

Harry Adamson, Bronson, did. He's plant manager at Douglas Manufacturer Co., in Bronson. He knows what adversity is, but doesn't speak of it often. He's not that kind of man.

Adamson started work at Douglas in 1967. He needed work to support his growing family. The only position open was for a second shift janitor. Adamson openly says "I wasn't too proud to accept it. Work was work. I never wanted handouts and prided myself on doing for my family."

But landing a job wasn't Adamson's only concern. He had a goal in mind: he wanted to earn a college education.

But first things first. His job needed his attention. He soon worked his way up to foreman. That spurred him on and he signed up for evening classes at a community college. It took him five years, but he graduated with an associate degree in business.

It wasn't enough for the ambitious Adamson. He decided to enroll at Western Michigan University, taking nine credits a semester.

That meant two to three classes a week.

Adamson recalls the tough times, how he'd leave work at the end of his shift, drive to Kalamazoo and after classes have only time to return home, grab a bite to eat and fall into bed.

His determination impressed his bosses. They also saw the potential in the motivated young man. Adamson was moved up the ladder to assistant plant superintendent. Then came a special assignment in manufacturing systems. Finally, the coveted post of plant manager was offered to him.

During that time, Adamson had enrolled in more college courses, commuting to school three times a week.

But something was wrong. Terribly wrong. Adamson discovered he was going blind. He lost the sight in one eye and was told that his only option was a cornea transplant. Adamson was frightened. "I'd come that far, going to school nine years; I sure was scared of losing all that."

His father-in-law, Walter Wohlers of Bronson, recalls how determined Adamson was. "He'd leave for college at night and we knew he couldn't see well. It worried us a lot, but he insisted on continuing. Many times the kids would read his assignments to him because he couldn't see good the copy. But he was persistent; he wouldn't give up. He's some guy."

A cornea transplant was made. With contact lenses, Adamson's vision was 20/20. Things were looking up.

And then, Adamson learned he was going blind in the other eye. That brought another cornea transplant last year. This time Adamson wasn't worried. "I just knew I had to get on with my career—and my life," he said.

He credits his family, the Douglas personnel and his friends for helping reach his goal, downplaying his part in his business success.

"Couldn't have done it without everyone's support," he added.

He gets a bit emotional explaining his last degree. Being older than most students, he thought it was best to have his diploma mailed to him. Nothing doing. The family wouldn't hear of it. When he walked up to receive the diploma he remembers he could hear cheers of "Yeah, Dad!"

So what's next on this genial fellow's schedule? Simple enough. He wants to continue his education, something he feels is the most important thing an individual can do. "You never stop learning," he said." So he plans to study basic programming for microcomputers.

I never knew about Adamson's long struggle for his degrees. He never talked about it. What's more, I had no inkling of his blindness—and I've known him several years.

Some men go their way quietly, overcoming obstacles and inconveniences, building careers. Men who ask no favors and expect none. Men who are thankful for the opportunity to better themselves. Men like Harry Adamson.

A Column – Between the Lines

June 25, 1983

This column is a year old. A year of trial, a year of testing. A year of error and uncertainties. A beginning in which I was unsure of the ending. And I am still learning.

I explained early on in this column that I don't consider myself a columnist. Then why is this column on the editorial page?

Simple enough: It is a commentary. And, with a smaller paper and less room for local news, it is the one place available.

One discovers much about human nature when writing a personal column. I learned quickly from people who commented on the column that many want something down-to-earth, something they can relate to, such as childhood memories or an article about their neighbor.

In this age of sophistication, I am amazed to learn that folks many times look for something besides the 'hard news.' They tell me they want articles about people and events.

Sometimes it's difficult to come up with a new subject each week, but eventually something turns up, or someone calls.

As far the column contents, I look for different ideas: historical, personal relationships, sometimes a pat on the back for an area person or group.

The most rewarding column to write, at least for me, is about individuals. Maybe it's a housewife who has a gift for being the town's shoulder to cry on; or the fellow who volunteers much of his time to help others. Or there's someone out there who has an interesting hobby.

As in life, there are columns about the sad happenings: A sick child who cannot be saved, or the close friend who put her own problems in the background to make her dying easier for her family.

The writing isn't great (and now and then I hear from someone who expresses that sentiment—and their criticism is proper), but the people whose lives have graced this column certainly are at the top of the honors list. They make things work in this world, usually by contributing their own goodness.

It isn't often these kind of people get their name in the paper. Too often it is the bad news that floods the pages. I figure this column is a way to tell the other side of the coin and give these folks the praise they deserve.

Along the way, the column has drawn many phone calls, some of them to my home. And the letters and notes along the way fortify my decision to keep trying.

I enjoy people. I've always maintained that you can go into any house on any street and find something about a person noteworthy to write about.

Experiences are to be shared, and I've been privileged to share them with many people. It's a rare gift, being allowed to intrude into their lives.

I enjoy doing it for many reasons. You can say just so much in the journalism world in a news or feature story. In a column, you can comment on something or someone—good or bad.

And I have come to know wonderful people who have enriched my life. People who offer ideas for me to investigate, or folks like elder citizen Lou Moon, late of Sturgis and now of Kalamazoo. I have never met this charming man, but it matters not; we are friends through this column. I eagerly await his short notes. He has much to offer in words of encouragement, advice and just plain talk about how to sort out what's important in life.

I gave the column a year. A year to see if there was response for or against it. And the response has been such that the column will continue.

So, for those who don't like the column, I apologize. I cannot please all of you and some of your suggestions for its contents may never come to reality. But this column will continue to be a mirror of life, as it has since the beginning. I believe such communication is a necessary ingredient in these times.

I hope you share the same thought.

Schools Out For This Lady

July 2, 1983

Come fall, Thelma Brenneman knows she'll miss them. But, she tells herself, her days will be quieter. Maybe too quiet. She's not sure how she will adjust to all that.

Brenneman retired in June after 17 years as a Sturgis school playground, kindergarten, grade school and library aide.

She figures it was time to stop her school work. Husband Earl had retired and the couple want to spend more time together. Raising two boys, Earl , Jr., and Carl, was a rewarding experience, but Thelma and Earl wanted to do some traveling, just the two of them. Get back into the routine of the old days.

Still, Brenneman wonders if she'll be satisfied when school begins again. "I loved it, even the times when the kids bothered me; when they fought or got hurt. It was a big responsibility. I learned a lot from those kids."

She especially loved working with the kindergarteners."Oh, to see how they came along in those first days and to watch them develop and adjust to new routines," she said. "I just loved them."

Brenneman started work at Wenzel School in February of 1966 as a kindergarten aide. She moved around, working at Congress School, finally spending most of her time at Wall School.

"In the beginning it was only noon hours, but later, aides took over the duties such as playground, recess and noon hour supervision," she said.

Brenneman, who lives on West Lafayette Street in the city, still figures it was the best of two worlds. "I could work while my kids were in school and be home when they got there. Besides, I had my summers off and could spend time with them."

Brenneman learned early on that sometimes it was the kid who acts up, who seems to be a problem child, who was the one she should spend extra time with. "And I sure found some of those kids," she added. "But how gratifying it was to see them reach their potential, to adjust, to learn to accept their playmates and to begin studying."

She remembers many youngsters came from broken homes. She reached out to them: I guess it's the mother in me, although I always told them that I couldn't be their mom. I could be a foster grandma, though."

Brenneman said there haven't been many changes in playground duties over the years, although she remembers that students used to have organized, supervised "snowball throwing" at Wall School.

That was where a piece of material resembling whatever a child wanted to throw at, be it a supervisor on the playground, a teacher, a principal, was put up on the playground. "We let them exercise their frustration by throwing at the figure," Brenneman said. "They also had a lot of fun. Problem was, when there were too many kids, it was hard to control. So we had to stop.

Through the years, Brenneman kept track of many youngsters, watching "them graduate and start out on life." Many still keep in touch with her and she hears from them on a regular basis.

So, just before school let out this year, the kids threw a party for their special friend. The kids wrote Brenneman special notes and other goodies were given.

The clincher for Brenneman – and the most emotional for her – was a huge poster with all the kids' names on it.

"It's special to me," she said. "I had it framed and hung on a wall in my house. I love it. A special gift from special kids."

So, come fall, she thinks she'll miss the special times. But, after all, she lives close to the school and maybe, just maybe, someone will ask her to help our now and then at the school. Perhaps she can volunteer to help in the library.

And too, the kids might stop in and say hello. That will make next fall a lot easier for the lady named Thelma Brenneman, who happens to love kids. Hers and everyone else's.

A Cooperative Kind of Girl

July 9, 1983

A cold wind makes me remember. So does the stillness of
the night when I awake quickly, my mind uncluttered of dreams.
Wondering. Listening for something in the blackness when sleep
won't return.

The call does not come, but in the shadows that surround me like
a cocoon, I am afraid.

It happens less often now, but occasionally, for reasons I don't
understand, the feeling comes again.

She was a shy, beautiful child. An elfin toddler with luminous
brown eyes and a sweet smile.

As with her character later in life, the child we loved was un-
demanding. Even as a youngster she carried an air of gentleness, of
grace. She would not tolerate arguments, nor join in them. It was as if
she found only lightness and good in people.

I recall things about her early years. That she upchucked whenever she ate cherry pie – her favorite food. That she loved bright
ribbons in her hair.

She loved solitude, times when she could be alone with a special
book or doll, but unhesitantly sought a lap when she felt the world
had deserted her.

Her shyness continued through elementary and high school. But she excelled in her studies, graduating near the top of her class at Bronson High School. And always, from teachers, friends and the public, there was the word "cooperative" spoken about her.

When she was younger, she spoke of being a nun. She was a good Catholic girl, and her religion meant a great deal to her. But for reasons known only to her, she turned her thoughts to business college and again graduated with honors. She landed a job as a legal secretary and her employers praised her loyalty and dedication to her work. A bright future beckoned. She was full of excitement, zest.

But something sinister lurked deep within her. It was there, unknown, awaiting its time to strike. The unknown came in tormenting, puzzling moments; double vision and headaches. New glasses didn't help. A specialist discounted any problem. And then, she tried to chew food one day and couldn't swallow. She knew something was wrong. Within hours she was hospitalized.

The terrible diagnosis came shortly afterwards. She had myasthenia gravis, a neuro-muscular disease. It is, simply stated, an incurable disease whereby "messages" from the brain to the muscles are short-circuited.

MG is a devastating disease that can take a victim from a normal day's activity to a life support system within hours. Breathing sometimes stops without respiratory machines to sustain it. It is an illness that humiliates, immobilizes its victims.

There were crises. Hospitalizations. She "turned sour" one night when a nurse ignored her pleas to help her swallow a pill that was necessary to keep her alive. Her heart and breathing stopped. Only heroic measures by interns saved her life.

When she struggled back to consciousness, unable to speak, she took her mother's hands and formed the letters to the words "I died" on them. The inevitable loomed.

But like the fighter she always was, she fought back. She took up the reins of life and went back to work for as long as she could. She did volunteer work at a local hospital.

And she changed. The shy, solemn girl was gone. As if she knew she could count on no sure tomorrows, she made each day count. She bought a house and redecorated it. She took up new hobbies, new experiences.

More crises came as expected, but she cooperated. Cooperation seemed to be her main trait in life and it emerged as a paramount help in her illness. Only once, however, did she go freely to the hospital. Only once – and hospital personnel told her parents she only had a cold. Her frantic family knew better. They rushed her to their doctor's office. Horrified, he ordered her admitted.

It was obvious to those in the intensive care unit that her illness was critical. When they brought the dreaded tube apparatus – her last chance to talk coming with it – she told the doctors, "I'll cooperate with you."

That tube proved the turning point, as her parents would later learn. While hospital personnel were inserting it, she vomited and some of the material went into her lungs. Shortly afterwards, she lapsed into unconsciousness.

The call came in the night. The words from a relative only said she was failing.

I was there when the doctors said her brain function had ceased. But her heart – that valiant heart – beat on, unwilling to give up life.

I sensed the anguish and knew what the decision was going to be – to say when to disconnect the life support system. It would be her parents' final agony.

When the Catholic sister came quietly into the waiting room and said her heart had failed and the struggle was over, I felt a sense of thankfulness that her parents had being spared that last ordeal.

The nun spoke softly . . . "she was such a nice girl . . . so cooperative."

That is why, sometimes, I wake in the night and think about the young girl who fought so hard to live and whose battle with death was as difficult as her life struggle.

I remember the courage of that young woman, the girl named Sherry Bogucki, my firstborn niece. I recall her dignity and spirit – a spirit that remains. And I am grateful for the richness she brought to all of us in the few short years she graced this earth and our lives.

The Perils of Press Conventions

July 16, 1983

Spent four lively days in Colorado last week. I always heard Colorado was Rocky Mountain High, ski slopes, lovely streams, and blah, blah. For a gal who loves Michigan, tolerates (but hates) its humid, hot summer weather, I figured Colorado, at least from all the hype and advertising, must have it all.

At Vail, they do; the rich ones, that is. They sleep late, party late and the stores open late. Just as well. I wandered into a kid's clothing store for something to do and discovered a boy's polo shirt was priced at $42.

My kids were deprived, I tell you. For $42, I could have bought all four a shirt, thrown in a pair of jeans and outfitted them in underwear. If I could have afforded that shirt for one of my grandchildren, I think his or her mom would have been afraid to let 'em wear it. She'd probably have framed it.

Many of the stores in Vail opened at 11 a.m. (I'd been up since 5:30) and they had this chaff, seeds or whatever blowing off aspen trees into the stores. Ever try and eat a hamburg (it cost $5.49) with that stuff floating on top? A bit like chewing dental floss.

It isn't that the trip to Vail wasn't stimulating. I attended the National Federation of Press Women's annual convention. To begin with, Ann Burford of the Environmental Protection Agency in Washington was scheduled to speak. I was eager to hear her. We were told her attorney had advised her not to speak because "you'll all find out later." Still waiting to know.

Did hear Betty Ford, President Ford's wife. She's nice enough, but the Secret Service fellows were more interesting. Their comments under their breath were just as appealing.

Betty Ford autographed her book for me. She couldn't begin to pronounce my name. Talk about deflating my ego.

I attended a management meeting and learned I'm doing everything wrong, but then the speaker was some bigwig who doesn't know what it's like to vacuum a floor. I've even done that on my job. Couldn't really relate too much to the speaker. Wonder if she knows what real workstyles are all about – heard someone say her workday starts at 9 a.m.

Then, at the business meeting, run similar to the national Republican and Democratic conventions, I found Michigan in hot water. Seems our delegation had introduced an amendment to the by-laws – simple thing like not wanting a president-elect in addition to a first vice-president. Now that proposal drew the wrath of half a dozen members. I considered removing my nametag to protect myself.

One lady (I think she was a lady; at least I'm giving her the benefit of the notion) asked for the floor and announced that Michigan had done the group a disservice for bringing the motion to the floor.

Mercy, but that proposal was the liveliest thing during that afternoon session. At least the couple dozen people who had slept through most of it stayed awake to hear the rumble. (Our proposal lost).

As most everyone knows, Colorado had raft runs on its rivers. I didn't go. After all, going from Denver up the mountain in an old bus, creeping along at 20 miles an hour and taking nearly four hours to get there was enough excitement. The bus' fuel pump broke halfway up the mountain and we had to stop.

And, if that wasn't enough to get my temper stewing, we were scheduled to go higher up the mountain one evening, via gondola. Just before one of the meetings ended, the announcement was made that we should begin boarding the gondolas "before 5:30 p.m. They're going to run a safety check at 6:30."

I should have known better. You guessed it. I went anyway, and guess when the gondola broke down? Right – just after we were halfway up. I'll tell you this much, the conversation in that swinging gondola was interesting. Five of us had plenty to say. A sixth said nothing. I still wonder if she was praying.

My trip wasn't all bad. I learned a lot from some of the sessions. I'm always learning – usually the hard way.

To make the trip one to remember, my roommate, a lady from Traverse City, got hustled the whole convention time by a fellow from Arkansas.

Now, if you're wondering what a fellow from Arkansas was doing at the convention, I should tell you he's a bonafide member of the National Press Women. Oh well, to each his own.

So, when I got off the plane at South Bend, leaving behind the cool Colorado temperatures for Michigan's miserable 90 degree-plus, humid weather, I smiled. Can't say I like this Michigan summer one bit, but at least I pretty well know what's going to happen around here.

I might just decide, though, to go to Arkansas if they ever hold a convention there. I still haven't figured that fellow out . . .

Spreuer: On Fire to the End

July 23, 1983

The call came 43 years ago. Mort Spreuer, busy in his White Pigeon garage, asked his friend if he had car trouble. "Well, yes and no," the fellow said. "Come on down when you have a minute." Mort ambled down a bit later, "looking like the mechanic I was," and found the town board and firemen gathered around a table laden with food.

After the meal, Mort casually asked: "What's the occasion?"

"Well, you're our new fire chief," he was told.

That was 1940, a long time ago. Mort retired as chief July 11, after 53 years tenure with the department.

He admits he'll miss the department and the men. He points out that "it's the department – the guys – that have made it outstanding. And it's the best department, second to none."

Mort remembers the department he joined in 1930. The fire engine was an old Ford Roadster with two chemical tanks. "We had eight firemen, as I recall," Mort said. "As business grew, the need for more equipment came. We added a Model A Ford front pumper."

The unit now has 16 volunteer firefighters and five trucks. There are two tankers with 2,000 gallon tanks, a smaller 265-gallon truck to fight grass fires, a pumper with a 750-gallon tank and another with a 500-gallon capacity.

A mechanic all his life, Mort insisted that trucks and equipment remain in top condition. "Never changed my mind on that," he drawled.

He said his town board has "been real supportive through the years. They recognize the need for good equipment and good men."

The department serves White Pigeon and Mottville Townships. Mottville is billed for cost of the runs, he said.

Several large fires stand out in Mort's memories, one of them the Sturgis Masonic Building. "That was a big one," he said.

Born in Sturgis Township, Mort has lived in White Pigeon 54 years, operating a garage there and also working at several other businesses.

Firefighting has been his "major interest." Mort admits he "never stopped being a fireman." He credits his first interest in the department to the earlier chief, Ernest Wilke.

In the early days, the fire department didn't have a siren. "We had this old bell up on a derrick. The fireman who got there first yanked the rope attached to the bell to sound the alarm." The department now had pagers each fireman carries, to alert them of fires.

Mort is proud of his years as a fireman, and touts the fact that in all those years, no fireman was seriously hurt. "It can be a dangerous job, but we lucked out," he said.

His worst memories of fires are a couple he was called to when someone burned to death. "You never forget it," he said quietly. "You never forget it . . ."

Mort was honored three years ago on his 50th anniversary with the department. "They gave me quite a party. I treasure the gifts and the memories. It was sure nice."

He feels fire departments must be "a team. Your life depends on the others many times. And they've been a great bunch of guys. I couldn't have managed without them."

Mort downplays his role as chief. "I never got any self-glory as chief. I've always been glad to do it. I never felt I should get a lot of attention. A fire department is a business; it has to be. A fireman's main concern is to help others. That's the reason we've got such a great department in White Pigeon."

So why'd he retire?

"Myrtle, my wife, has been wanting me to get out for some time. I'm getting up there in years, you know. Besides, it's time for new blood. The new chief, my assistant chief, is Ralph Ballinger. He'll do a good job. I take stock in that."

So, what will Mort do when he hears the sirens wail and the engines roar past?

"I guess I'll miss it . . . sure I'll miss it." He thought a moment and then quietly said "but I've got memories . . . all those memories of a good department and good men."

Ed Doty: Goodbyes Aren't Easy

July 30, 1983

He's been known to his fellow workers as the "Sturgis Journal gentleman." And gentleman he is.

None dispute his title. None come close to filling it. Only the quiet man named Ed Doty.

It is his manner that first strikes you, always the respectful tone, the willingness to listen, the eagerness to please.

He retires from the Journal today and I am not sure how well this paper will do without him. He is a man of punctuality, dedication, preciseness and a perfectionist.

He is not a man of many moods; only one paramount trait, that of the old school. Honor and tradition mean much to him, although he does not speak often of them. He displays them.

More than that, he is my friend. And I seem to have lost so many of them through the years. Some went by retirement, some by death. Each took a bit of me with them, whether they know or knew it.

Ed is an individual who values trust, responsibility and the knowledge of doing a good job. Funny about that; sometimes you wonder how well someone does a job when they are in another department of your business. With Ed, you know. There is never doubt.

He isn't a cut-up kind of fellow, but his wry humor sometimes breaks the gloom of the day when weariness intrudes.

Ed remains interested in his co-workers and their families. He knows who your spouse and kids are. He makes a point of knowing the whole you – and we know he cares about what happens in our lives.

He is a family man, immensely proud of his wife and sons. He is a man secure in the knowledge of what is right for his children. I have never heard him compare them. Each, he feels, is important and valued in their own right. It is an attitude more parents would be wise to hold.

His grandchildren are treasures to gladden his later years. Talking about them is one time Ed throws caution and reserve away. He basks in the knowledge that he is a beloved grandfather.

There's another trait about Ed one learns in small moments, in quiet conversations with him. He is very close and fond of his father-in-law, a fellow getting up there in years, but on whom Ed dotes. There is an unquestioned assumption when Ed considers older people. He knows their experiences and opinions still have value.

To those of us at the Journal, Ed is an integral part of this newspaper. It will be difficult to come in Monday morning and not see him here before 6:30 a.m. I know it will be hard to pass the ad department and not hear his cheery "good morning." And it won't get easier. I know that from experience: I still miss those friends who have moved on.

I wonder how we choose acquaintances, and how we choose

friends. There is a difference. Only a select few acquaintances are considered friends, regardless of how many times we refer to them as such.

Ed Doty had been our balance here at the Journal. He has maintained a respectability, a confidence, a continuance of the hometown flavor so necessary to a small newspaper.

We will try to overcome that loss, at least outwardly. But I'm not sure of the personal loss. People like Ed Doty don't come along that often. The mold that formed his basic character usually is lost in the shuffle of competitive business.

Ed Doty's character always emerged as one of stability, honor and understanding. A rare recipe of ingredients, one that will not come often again in my lifetime. And that is the reason I value Ed Doty's friendship and why its daily existence here at the Journal will be missed.

Life moves on, sometimes without those we care about. We at the Journal hope Ed has half as good memories of us as we have of him. Knowing him as been a rare privilege.

Kevin: A Life to Grow From

August 6, 1983

Kevin Kleitsch is eight years old and growing – finally. But Kevin won't grow much more unless someone dies. The trouble is, Kevin's body doesn't produce enough of a chemical called human growth hormone. He needs hormones from cadaver pituitary glands.

Kevin is the son of Karl and Sally Kleitsch, Ann Arbor, and grandson of Walter and Lorene Mayer, Burr Oak. The Mayers and Kleitschs are well-known in Sturgis. The Mayers formerly owned and operated Mayer's Card and Gift Shop, and Sally graduated from high school here.

Kevin was a small baby, Mrs. Mayer said, but his mother always thought something else was wrong. "He didn't grow much. His growth pattern was nothing like his older sister's," Mrs. Mayer added.

Though small in size, Kevin "has always been energetic and as bright as any other youngster," Mrs. Mayer said.

When Kevin began treatment at the age of six, he was about 38 inches tall, the size of a normal three-year-old. His weight corresponded with that of a two-year-old and his bone development that of a four-year-old.

A third grader this fall, Kevin is 44 inches tall, weighs 40 pounds and grew 2 ½ inches the past year. He has grown six inches since treatments started.

Kevin's treatments began in 1981. Before treatments, he grew about an inch and a half a year, compared to a normal youngster's growth of about six inches. Without treatment he probably wouldn't have reached five feet in height.

Kevin grew four inches the first year he took treatments. The HGH is injected three times a week into his buttocks or thighs. His mother, a registered nurse, administers the shots.

Kevin's growth is slowed because he has a deficiency of the human growth hormone (HGH), also known as somatotropin. HGH is one of several hormones which affect development produced by the front portion of the pituitary gland, located in the middle of the skull. The pituitary is an endocrine gland. The hormones it produces direct function of other glands: adrenal, thyroid, ovaries and testes.

Kevin has a partial HGH deficiency, doctors say, believed to the result from problems in the "messenger" system between the pituitary and hypothalamus, the lower portion of the brain which signals the pituitary to release HGH.

Kevin is one of the reported 15,000 children in the nation who has the problem.

Kevin can't receive synthetic HGH because youngsters who are started on the human hormone don't do well on the other. Kevin was started on human HGH hormones because specialists decided he shouldn't wait until the synthetic HGH was tested and available.

And that brings up the immediate problem. Kevin's parents received a letter this month from Mott's Children Hospital in Ann Arbor, stating that the National Pituitary Program has been forced to cut back allotments of the cadaver hormones necessary for Kevin's growth. The cutback means Kevin will receive four months' less treatment this year.

Kevin must receive the hormones before he is much older. Best results occur when a child's problem is diagnosed early and hormone treatments are begun before the child reaches puberty. Kevin will be on the hormones through his late teen years. That is, if the hormone is available.

The main concern is that more donors are needed to sign cards authorizing removal of their pituitary glands after death. Other than release forms, the only means to obtain the human hormone is through bodies released for medical research, Mrs. Mayer said.

The removal of the gland can be handled the same way corneas and other body organs are donated. But the public is not well enough informed about the pituitary gland donations, Mrs. Mayer said, or how desperately they are needed.

While it is expected there is enough HGH to take care of the needs of children who have total pituitary deficiency, youngsters or teens having partial deficiency are suffering cutbacks in treatment.

Parents of these children hope to alert and inform the public of the need for pituitary gland donations after death. Pathologists and funeral directors are being advised to check donation cards carefully to see if such a request has been made.

Until the supply of cadaver hormones is at the level where Kevin can receive the treatments he needs, his chances to grow into a normal-sized adult remain in doubt.

Yard Sale: Diary to History

August 13, 1983

Brad J. Bogart, Montague, wants to know about yard sales held in Sturgis on Saturday, July 9. He wants to meet a lady from this city. Good intentions, mind you. He doesn't want to be forward. He wants to go backward.

A Sturgis resident held the yard sale, "somewhere in the city," Bogart said in a letter to the Journal. She was selling her home and furnishings to relocate into a senior citizen center, as best as Bogart can determine.

Among the woman's items for sale that day, was a "desk diary," from the Crane Co., dated 1913. The diary belonged to G.E. Lark, an inquiry clerk for Crane.

Lark didn't use the diary for that purpose; he used it for a photo album.

The buyer of the diary was Sharon Briggs, owner of the "Hump-T-Dump" flea market near Montague. She was looking for items for her business.

As this long-winded story goes, Bogart wandered into Briggs; flea market recently and spied the diary.

He was fascinated by it. A lover of history, it sparked an interest that Bogart couldn't ignore. He purchased the diary.

It seems that within the leaves of the diary are 61 photographs taken of Lark's "Mississippi, Ohio and Tennessee River Trip in June of 1914."

As Bogart puts it, the pictures are "61 pieces of American history, people who lived, worked and loved, and from the nature of some of the photos, partied quite a bit."

Bogart by admittance, is "a photographer of the arts" and "obsessed" with the people in the photographs.

He intends to find out what happened to all of them, what they did in life and where they are buried. He also wants to learn what happened to the Steamship *St. Louis* on which the travelers took their trip. The paddle wheeler fascinates Bogart, who added that some of the names in the diary are Adele Moylan, Helen Buckley, Robert Clark, E. Frederickson, H.A. Schmidt and "an interesting Jewish fellow named Blomgren."

Bogart is on a mission of history. He wants to travel the rivers and , if possible, locate the places the photos were taken and re-photograph them. Some of the cities he will be visiting include Cairo, Ill., Chester, Kalkaska and Paducah, Ky., Savannah and Johnsonville, Tenn., and the last stop, the Battlefield at Shiloh. He "intends to take the same route the early travelers followed."

Incidentally, Bogart has done some research. He figures the people probably all worked for Crane. He also located the Crane Co., a New York-based firm. Company officials are excited about Bogart's task and have offered any help they can in determining who the people in the pictures are. The Crane firm, at the time the pictures were taken, manufactured the valves for paddle wheelers. Now a firm with holdings throughout the world, they made the valves for our

U.S. lunar modules. That also fascinates Bogart.

So because he is a lover of history and because he wants to venture back to a time when this nation was one of "steam and strong people," Bogart needs help. In order to step back into history, he needs to know who had the yard sale and sold the diary to Briggs.

If anyone out there knows the lady, or perhaps she may read this, please contact me at the Journal. I'll pass the information on to Bogart.

I'll have to admit: I'm envious of the project Bogart has set out to do, but I appreciate his mission. History is a great love of mine. I understand where Bogart's coming from. He knows where he's going.

The Porch: Window to Life

August 20, 1983

We've been discussing porches at our house. We've got this old one, and its not in the best of shape. We'd like to change its design, because it isn't doing us much good the way it is.

But then I think of other days, when we still had two large maple trees in the front of the house. They shaded the porch and we used to spend a lot of time there. Those were the struggling days when money for air conditioners wasn't possible. The porch was the only cool spot.

But that porch meant more. I rocked the babies there when teething pains wouldn't let them sleep. I can still find the broken end of a board where one of the more rambunctious kids tripped and split a lip.

Marks on the floor remain where the old chairs were, a sign of another era.

That porch was my window to the world.

Those were the days when you knew nearly everything about your neighborhood. In the summer you could listen to household arguments and grin a bit at how the humidity was warming up tempers.

There's the porch area where we cranked the ice cream freezer. Started out that only the family was going to eat it, and eventually half the block came over. What fun.

The smells from porches can be good and bad, but the aroma of warm sweetrolls wafting through backyards was an open invitation to join a neighbor.

And other things. The hook on the porch ceiling still remains. I always hung my plants (I'm a plant freak) there. I recall the time a water meter reader cracked his head on a plant pot and said some colorful words.

I can't forget the edge of the porch overhang where my husband tarred the roof to patch a leak and dumb me decided to weed the flowerbed. The tar warmed up and before I could move away, it dripped onto my hair.

There's the spot where our hoot owl perched to greet passersby. We raised him from a baby and he refused to leave. I still smile remembering all the people who passed by and wished him a good day or said hello. They talked to him as if he was a human being. He loved it.

There were the hours spent on that old porch watching the kids in the neighborhood grow up. It was a happy and sad privilege to be so close to other people. Close enough to share their joys and sorrows if they needed and wanted you to, and far enough away if they didn't.

That porch draws other memories. We moved the steps to the side one year. A friend came calling one evening, forgot about it and fell on his face. (I forgot myself, and walked off the side where the steps used to be).

I recall many steps on that porch. One of our tots took his first hesitant steps there. In the corner is the place the playpen always set and the youngest child made his first acquaintance with the neighborhood, chewing on the playpen top and gazing out at the world.

Then came steps of others, teenage boys who came to call on my daughters on their first date. Those feet sometimes traced a path a couple of times before courage came to knock on the door.

And there are many other recollections. Summer nights when fireflies danced in the glowing splendor across the yards. The sounds of a neighbor playing organ music. The tolling of church bells from nearby churches. Watching the endless parade of characters that moved through one's life. Discovering sometimes that a stranger walked by, something that doesn't happen often in a small town.

The porch was the place to crochet or solve crossword puzzles, read books or write letters. Sometimes it was pea-shelling time or the favorite spot to peel apples for pies.

One could even share floor space with a lazy beetle ambling by, unconcerned about my presence. And there were butterflies, humming birds and inquisitive squirrels who shared a moment of time.

Life in the fast lane is probably for some folks. Mine is a bit that way now, but I still think of other times.

You miss a lot in this world of fast-moving things. You miss the quiet coffee time shared on porches with a friend, exchanging snapshots of grandbabies, hearing of personal problems when your comfort is asked.

I suppose what I'm doing is talking myself into keeping that porch. I know that with my asthma I should have it glassed in and cooled. It doesn't do me much good the way it is. But glassing it in would shut me away from the sounds and happenings that keep me close to friends. It would take away some of the openness I enjoy.

That's why I think of other times, days when life was quieter and slower, when I looked at life differently from that old porch.

Maybe that's the simple answer. I need the porch for that reason, the richness of its memories.

Honeywells: Yesterday Relived

August 27, 1983

Each August the Honeywell sisters and brother invite friends to a party. Some party. Last year 3,000 people showed up.

That's how the Honeywells like it. "I guess we want to remember our ties with the land and our past," Mable, one of the three surviving Honeywell children says.

Mable, her sister, Mildred, and brother Glenn carry on a tradition steeped in historical bent. Each year for the past seven years the trio has opened their farmland on Cranson Road near Bronson for an old-times party.

The Honeywell farm is Centennial acreage, land purchased in 1853 by the Honeywell's grandfather and his wife, Erastus and Caroline Honeywell. Erastus died in the Mexican War, never seeing his infant son. But the line continued, with Frank Sr., and Nettie Honeywell eventually owning the property. The couple had five children. Besides Mable, Mildred and Glenn, there were Frank Jr., and Maurice. Only one child married.

Initially, Frank worked on plans for the huge farm celebration, held in August each year. He died the month before the first event. But his brother and sisters continued the dream.

In the first years, mostly threshing events were held, with old time machinery and antiques handling the work in a field set aside each year for the harvesting.

It's more than threshing now, with three days necessary to handle all the activities. Included during the event are displays, exhibits, crafts and hobbies, demonstrations, flea markets and music. Special programs are held each afternoon. Friday is a stage show; Saturday a fiddler's contest, and Sunday a fife and drum corps.

A parade takes place each day, and worship services are scheduled on Sunday. Special music is planned for Friday and Saturday evenings. Volunteers who like plain (no electric) instruments are welcomed.

In addition, the state Centennial Farm Association meets at the Honeywell farm. Members hold a dinner, conduct business meeting and visit. Mable said the group also hopes to organized a county association.

"Actually, the celebration kicks off on Thursday evening when we gather for a potluck dinner," Mable said. "We only ask for a $2 donation from anyone attending during the day. If you want to come for one of the two evening events, we only ask $1. Youngsters under 12 are admitted free."

Mable admits she and her siblings get "a bit uptight" sometimes. "It's a lot of work, but my, what a lot of fun."

The brothers used to attend threshing shows in other areas. "They commented time and again that we had a better place to hold an event," Mable said. "That's how this whole thing was started. We just set aside a field for threshing and held a public gathering in 1977. We didn't realize it would be so popular."

The brother and sisters, now in their 60s and 70s, find the

homespun festival stimulating and admit that "It's been worth all the work. We've met so many new acquaintances and renewed friendships."

Since Thursday and continuing through Sunday, the Honeywells will welcome folks to their annual farm fling and marvel again at "the folks who want to show crafts and items they make. Folks who mostly want to spend a wholesome time with friends, remembering other times."

Mable pretty well says it all. You'll find out if you drive out Cranson Road tomorrow – where yesterday is today.

The Church in the Wildwood

September 3, 1983

It's a church in the wildwood, this worship place at Steinke's Resort in Colon Township. It's in the woods, on the shores of Long Lake. No established complex, mind you, just a place where those who vacation at the lake each summer can come together with their Lord.

There are no stained glass windows, no church pews. The congregation sits on picnic table benches. It's not unusual for the Sunday morning service to be interrupted – but not halted – by a fisherman coming into the building and purchasing bait.

The church, named the Long Lake Christian Fellowship by its parishioners, is in its first year. Gatherings are held in the recreation-bait house complex at Frank and Wava Borgert's property, commonly known as Steinke's Resort.

There is no established religion at the church services. Instead, meetings are non-denominational and "any old-time hymns someone wants to hear are sung," according to Earl Mack of Miamisburg, Ohio, who heads the church's five-person steering committee.

The minister is Pastor Larry Morrison of La Otto, Ind. He's retired, but no matter; he has a flock. An average of 45 persons, of all ages, attends the one-hour service on Sunday. In addition, he ministers at a Saturday afternoon Bible study session.

Attire at the services isn't questioned. You come as you are. A fellow can go fishing in the early hours, catch his limit and get back in time to find a seat in the complex before the first strains of the hymns begin.

Speaking of music, Mack said "in the beginning we kinda struck up duets and quartets for special music." But then the Borgerts got caught up in the doings and purchased a used organ.

"You ought to hear the music now," Mack said with a grin. "It's sure beautiful, rolling out over Long Lake on a Sunday morning."

The Borgerts refuse rent for the building use. The pastor also is not salaried. However, the committee and the parishioners felt a token payment should be made to the minister for his services and mimeographing bulletins distributed at the services. So a "love" offering, as the pastor calls it, is collected.

For the Macks, who have vacationed each summer at Steinke's Resort for 12 years, and since the 1930s in Michigan, the church service is special. "It makes the day right," the outgoing Mack said. "We missed our regular church and it was rather involved going into town for services each Sunday."

Mack said he's surprised at the turnout each week. "And the young people attending are such a delight – and surprise. So many of them are coming to the services."

The services are expected to slow down after Labor Day, when many of the families return to their own communities. A special holiday service is planned tomorrow, but that won't end the meetings. "I guess they'll hold services in a smaller structure, possibly one of the trailers," Mack said.

Mack said the gatherings are so successful that they'll start church the first Sunday in May next year, instead of July. "We realize we've got a winner in this church and we have to plan ahead."

The folks at the lake have become fast friends. They've scheduled a Fun Day and craft fairs. Several carry-in dinners have been held after church services.

Mack said the Borgerts refuse to accept money for anything they've provided for the fledging church. But there's a surprise in store for them, a secret that Mack said he might as well tell. "We're going to take our collections plate funds and give another 'love offering.' We're going to erect a sign on the building where the church services are held, announcing the events held here. It probably will include a bulletin board."

"It's our small way of saying thanks to the Borgert family, who have been so helpful in this endeavor. They stay in the background and let us do our thing. We're grateful to them."

Mack said he hopes the idea of lake churches springs up around the area. "There are many people who spend weekends or the summer in St. Joseph and Branch County. We here at the Long Lake Christian Fellowship know what it means to gather in the house of the Lord. We'd like for them to know that feeling, too."

If you want to worship somewhere different some Sunday morning, before the frost of fall sends the vacationers home, drive down Middle Colon Road and turn off at Steinke's Road. Travel a short way through the rural countryside and join the parishioners at their unique church in the wildwood.

Grandbabies – The Spice to Life

September 10, 1983

I have these half dozen grandchildren. And no, I'm sure they aren't cheaper by the dozen. A bit more fun.

They're a blend of Irish, English, Spanish, Mexican, German and a lot of other things thrown in. As my father once said, in exasperation when my sisters and I asked about family history and nationality, "you're half French and half frog." That statement went to class at school as I recall. The teacher wasn't amused.

There's not one of the grandchildren who closely resembles the other, not even brothers and sisters. And that makes it interesting.

They range from a boy of three to a boy of eleven. In between are nine-year-old and seven-year-old girls and two boys, ages four and five.

And are each of them his and her own person? You betcha. What they don't pick up from the others, they seem blessed with themselves. Sometimes it's confusing, but never boring. Not by a long shot.

There's the young fella who helped us pick up sacks of corn in a field to feed our squirrels. A cold, bone-chilling day, he insisted on hanging in there. And wryly commented: "Boy, you and Grandpa sure like corn."

And the little squirt, the youngest, happened to go potty on the car tire the other day. I admonished him a bit and he retorted with: "The dog did!"

Then there's the girl with the high IQ, the smartie of the group. When she was three, she outplayed everyone in card games. That's sure hard to admit, that a kid can outsmart you. Her Grandpa tried to cheat a bit in a card game. She tossed the cards down and refused to kiss him goodbye for weeks. Pointed out to her much later that she loved Grandpa and should kiss him. She haughtingly replied: "That jack of clubs wasn't in play." Settled that issue.

We've got black-eyed grandbabies, green-eyed, blue and brown-eyed. Hair that ranges from blond to black. And temperaments to match.

Each, of course, thinks he or she owns us. Though they like each other, there's always rivalry around the grandparents. The younger ones all want to sit on my lap. I'm a large lady. I don't have a lap left.

One kid dislikes school, another loves it. Our blond pixie delights in telling us her views about life in general, and another one won't give us the time of day in such matters. Takes too much time from his busy life. He's the one the others tag; drives him crazy.

Sometimes it's a bit dangerous to take them shopping, even though they are good and don't ask for anything. Their folks trained them well in that department. Point is, I was shopping for under-clothes for myself and one of the girls added her outspoken opinion: "Boy, them are big ones." That said it all, unfortunately.

The grandchildren love to visit – too much sometimes. But in fairness, I have to admit we love it. Each youngster has his own place he or she wants to sleep. Each has his own pillow and myriad of items to sleep with. Funny about that; not one of my four kids ever took a teddy bear or toy to bed.

Each grandchild also knows where certain goodies are tucked away. Some make sure treats are hidden away until they return. Rather funny to watch one of the others when something is taken from its hiding place. They're surprised another had the same idea.

These kids bring back popsicles, hair ribbons, dolls and miniature trucks. Our neat house is again beset with books scattered around the room, toys in every corner and always something they forgot to take home. The oldest boy summed it up: "If I leave it, I'll have to come back." Didn't raise any slow kids in this family.

So, for Grandpa and Grandma there are trips to the river, kites to fly, report cards to view, cookies to bake. Time must be taken to examine ant hills and explain how the moon and sun got up there (one child insists Grandpa threw them), why fireflies can't be found in the daytime, why brown sugar is brown and white sugar white. That was bluntly explained by one of the kids as being because brown sugar makes brown cookies.

Once again we are involved in frogs and angleworms in jean pockets, sand in sneakers, pocketbooks that include everything a little girl treasures.

Most of all, we are included again with the splendor of childhood, with looking at the world from a child's eye – and marveling in the wonderful honesty and good sense children have. And wonder how we lost it ourselves.

One thing more; I should be honest. I smile when I see them coming – and smile when they go.

No, these grandchildren aren't cheaper by the dozen, or half-dozen. And tomorrow, on the day they set aside for grandparents, I know these babies are worth a mint when it comes to realizing they belong to us. All those lucky people who have a grandchild hug them and whisper fervently "I love you best," know exactly what I mean.

Oh, to be Kuralt's Writing Clone

September 17, 1983

I envy Charles Kuralt. I envy him a lot. In my opinion, that guy has the best of all worlds.

Kuralt, that genial fellow who hosted the *On The Road* television show during the summer, gets to travel all over the country. That alone is something to appreciate. But what I envy Kuralt the most is that he gets to meet people – and interview them. That's the sin of my life: I covet that job. How I covet it.

Some reporters hate to write feature stories. They simply can't stand them. Hard news is their bag. So be it.

I love features. You learn more about people, their hobbies, disappointments, loves, history and just about everything else when you write features.

And meeting the people behind those stories is one of the most rewarding things of my life.

But then, when I start wishing I had Kuralt's job, I remember all the interesting folks I've met since working for the Journal. And they are many.

There was the violin maker over by Leonidas, the Sturgis railroad gandy, the beekeeper, the maple syrup makers, the lady from Fawn River who reopened the old mill, the local sheep herdsman, the man who is a master woodcarver.

And there's the lady who makes quilts. There are my good friends from the Amish sect. I remember the enjoyment interviewing the radish, gladiola and mint farmers.

And many, many more themes of articles. The story ideas abound in this area. Some are difficult to write: The fellow who was crippled from a swimming accident, the child suffering from cystic fibrosis, the man who committed suicide. But no matter how hard the stories are to relay to the public, they are part of life. You can't show the immense joy of living if you can't detail the difficulty in losing a loved one to death.

Each story brought me new experiences, new friends. I also learned that with all the so-called hard news, people want to read items about their next door neighbor. They want to read about things from the past. Those people already know what I learned through trial: you are what you have been. Maybe that doesn't explain it well, but it's what a crusty old codger told me once. He's right. I just wish I had listened closer years ago. That knowledge came to me years later. I learned hard.

I'm continually surprised at what people do with their lives. I thought one only found interesting interviews by traveling, like Kuralt. Wrong. They are here in my backyard, waiting to be discovered.

I've had a ball writing features. People still remain the most interesting thing in my life. Oh, I realize what they are doing may make the story, but why those people are doing it provides the depth to the tale.

So, I suppose I will continue to envy Kuralt for his poetry in expressing his tales, his freedom to go where stories beckon, his in-depth coverage of the American scene. But I think I've got the same privilege here, on a smaller scale.

You see, I just heard about this guy who . . .

The Elks: Giving a Kid a New Life

September 24, 1983

Craig Rowe, 12, goes to camp in the summer. That experience may not be new to most kids. It is to Craig. He's a diabetic. Until three years ago, Craig hesitated becoming involved in many things because his affliction overwhelmed him at times, especially among his peers.

The camp has made a world of difference for Craig, an 8th grader at Sturgis Middle School. And that difference came about through the Sturgis Elks Club, which paid the fees for Craig to spend two weeks on Camp Midichi near Marquette in the Upper Peninsula.

Midichi's name derives from the Michigan Diabetic Children's Association.

Al Weaver, chairman of the Elks program for handicapped children, said Craig is only one of many handicapped youngsters the Elks have assisted through the years.

"We've got 800 members in the Elks Club," Weaver said. "We do many service projects in the community, but our heart is in our young people. We especially try and help youngsters who have problems, whatever their handicaps."

Much of the money to handle youth projects is raised through community fund-raisers, such as dinner dances. A portion of the money is sent to the state, to be used in the Michigan Elks Major Project.

"But that doesn't mean the state Elks has the final say on who we help. And children don't have to be from Elk families. We just want to give youngsters an extra push; perhaps something their parents would like to do but are prevented from handling because of economic or other factors."

Craig, the son of Lonnie and Carolyn Rowe of Sturgis, has had juvenile diabetes since the age of five. He learned early on how to give himself the two injections necessary each day to keep him alive.

But Craig, by his mother's admission, "was fearful of many other things. He knew there were limitations concerning sports, such as when his blood sugar was high. He was called a sissy and taunted. He withdrew from many activities."

Craig's mother explained that even though Craig's disease can be controlled, "it is difficult for him. Especially at the age he is now, when kids are in so many sports."

Camp Midichi's staff knows this well. All staff members are diabetics. "The camp helped Craig so much," his mother said. "The Elks support allowed Craig to go the past three years. Craig learned assertiveness, how to handle teasing about his problem, how to deal with his feelings when he comes up with some things he can't do.

"We can't tell you the difference the camp has made in Craig's life – and through him, ours," Carolyn said.

The Rowe family has two other children, both girls, and the

chance the Elks provided for Craig to attend the two-week camp has been a "boost," Carolyn said.

"Kids ages four to 15 can go to Camp Midichi," Carolyn added. "What they learn there is more than adjusting; they learn to cope. That's a godsend."

"And the Elks Club did it. We're very thankful," she said.

But, as Al Weaver said, if "one little boost can make so much difference, you can see why the Elks Club is so involved in youth projects and why we try and find youngsters who need something special. Something that we can give."

While Weaver admits it "takes a lot of time and a lot of work by many Elks; seeing the look on a kid like Craig's face, and the new spirit and maturity in his voice – that makes it worthwhile."

A Run for the Railroad Again

October 1, 1983

Someday, if time doesn't run out for me, I will attempt some major projects. Actually, they are longtime dreams that have no connection to each other, no reasons, except mine. They are hold-ons from my younger days. I was a dreamer of sorts. Still am. It's something that never left me when I supposedly grew up.

I've completed some of those wild schemes and dreams, but there are a few remaining. Like going back in time and tracing the path of the school teacher lady who figured in the Butch Cassidy and Sundance Kid story. I'd like to know what happened in her lifetime after that remarkable tale. Don't ask me why. I just have this compulsion.

But mostly I want to walk down my childhood path again and locate three fellows who played a part of my younger life. One is Steve Marcino, a rascal of a pilot who flew in once a month to give airplane rides to CCCs at the camp in Sidnaw, my hometown in the Upper Pennisula.

But there are two more fellows who I know will be difficult to trace. I knew them only as Bill and Joe. They rode the rails in the late 1930s. They did the regular work, unhooking the trains, signaling, the usual stuff.

To explain, I should say I've had a major love affair in my life, one my husband understands. I've been in love with the railroad since my first remembrance. As a kid I lived close to the railroad in that old logging town. I spent the better part of my days keeping track of the trains.

There were two lines running into Sidnaw, but for some reason, I picked out one. And loved its trainmen. I don't know why those railroad fellows adopted me, but they did. I was allowed to ride the engine from the coal tower to the water tower. I could pull the throttle.

Bill and Joe were special. They took time to sit with me during stopovers. We'd sit on the high bank near the track. We discussed everything in life. Those guys and the trains were my ticket to the outside world. I had never been more than 40 miles from Sidnaw, my birthplace. The stories the trainmen told me spelled adventure.

I don't know much about the fellows to this day, except they were young, clean-cut guys who looked the other way when hobos climbed aboard boxcars. Looking back, I suppose Bill and Joe realized they were fortunate to have jobs. They understood the hoboes' plight. I re-member the train even slowed down near the hobo camp just outside of town – and there wasn't any other reason other than to allow the guys to hitch a ride.

Bill and Joe learned early on that I loved to read. There was no library in my small town. I had read everything at the school and stole looks at my dad's Detective Story magazines when he wasn't looking. I read everything, including the Sears and Roebuck catalog from cover to cover. Words were my escape. They were my world.

Joe and Bill caught on fast. They took to bringing me library books from up the line. They'd check them out and when I was done reading them, they'd return the books during another of their runs. I wonder what the librarians thought of two grown men in trainmen's overalls continually checking out children's books.

They bought me three Little Big Books my last year in Sidnaw. It was Christmas and they knew I was leaving to live in the Lower Peninsula. We never said goodby. The truth is, I didn't have the courage.

So, when I remember those days and how I learned to tell each engine by its whistle, I recall the days of those huge black locomotives. I also remember two fellows I'd like to find again and reconcile old memories. And talk about something else I recall about Sidnaw.

One day the railroad line replaced that black engine with a shiny new orange and yellow streamliner called the Chippewa. I was furious. How dare they name such a monster the Chippewa? I'm sure the Indians hated that idea. As for me, I despised that new engine. For months I prayed it would derail and they'd take if off the line.

It was more than I could bear. I remember standing in the shade of that weather-worn depot and seething with rage. That darned engine had no class, no decent whistle, no clouds of steam rolling out.

The railroad officials never brought my beloved locomotive back. But I got even; I never forgave them.

I'll bet Joe and Bill would appreciate that.

He Scrounged to Help Others

October 15, 1983

Merrill Friddle of Sturgis is a collector – and a giver-away. A collector who recently scrounged around in every nook and corner in Sturgis, in just about every store and business he could find.

Friddle admits to being a scrounger, but for good reason. He amassed some 60,000 Pepsi-Cola bottle caps. That's right: 60,000 of them turkeys. But turkeys they didn't turn out to be. Friddle turned the bottle caps into the Pepsi-Cola Company for points. Points that earned him four, 19-inch color television sets and an audio system.

And Friddle gave the items away. Gave them to the Mount Pleasant Regional Center for Development Disabilities, where Duane E. Chapman, director of community relations said "wow!" And quickly accepted the gift, given by a stranger who cared.

Friddle modestly says "I didn't do much." He said he heard about the bottle cap drive Pepsi offered. Friddle, who is divorced, has children living in the Lansing area. A son told him about the bottle cap drive and the need for equipment at the Mount Pleasant Center. Friddle's son was so enthused that Friddle decided to see what he could do in Sturgis.

He began at his place of employment, Sturgis Tool and Die, collecting used caps from the pop machines. That branched out to stops at party stores, The Chicken Coop, restaurants, gas stations, "anywhere they had machines." I've got this much to say for the businesses in Sturgis; they sure are cooperative. Sure helped me after I told them what I was doing," Friddle said.

Now, if you're wondering what 60,000 bottle caps amounts to, consider 300 pounds. That's the closest Chapman and Friddle came in tallying up the collection, which was turned in at a Pepsi plant in August when the drive ended.

Originally, Friddle had hoped to collect 100,000 caps to "exchange for an organ for the center," but when he found he only had 60,000, he told the Center to choose whatever it needed.

"And, we sure needed TV sets and the audio system," Chapman added.

The Center serves developmentally disabled persons from 11 counties in the Lansing area, Chapman said. It is part of the Eastern Region of the Department of Mental Health, and the facility has a certified bed capacity of 448.

Chapman explained that the Center handles persons with mental retardation, cerebral palsy, epilepsy, or neurological impairments. Charges are based on ability to pay and no one is denied services because of economic problems, Chapman said.

The Center was operated as an industrial school from 1880 through 1934 for students of American Indian parentage. It then was handled by the Michigan Legislature as a branch of the Michigan Home and Training School, Lapeer, until it was established as a separate facility in 1949. Since 1945, it has operated under the governship of the Michigan Department of Mental Health. Its name changed several times, eventually receiving its present title in 1978.

Friddle said he doesn't expect praise for what he's done. "I like to help others," the 41-year-old citizen of Sturgis the past five years, said.

And there's the 15,000 Coca-Cola bottle caps Friddle collected. "Well, I'm waiting to hear what Coca-Cola will do. They promised to match any program Pepsi had . . ."

Missives from a friend

October 22, 1983

He came into my life late, at a time, perhaps, when I needed him most. And he was needed. I hope he knew that.

I never met him. Strange how one can become so attached to an individual through phone calls or letters. But attached I became.

The first letter was very proper, but held a hint of warmness. He loved my columns, he said. Of course, you know that made my day. I'm not so humble as not to accept a good thing when it's offered.

The greeting on the first letter was most proper. "Dear Mrs. Carol Ankney of the Sturgis Journal," it began.

I loved him from the start.

His name was Lou Moon, Sr., he added, and he was an elder citizen in his 80s. He said he used to live in Sturgis.

I remember the Moon name. I knew the family owned and operated a funeral parlor here. But I had never met the elder Lou Moon.

The next letter was a bit warmer. "My Dear Mrs. Carol Ankney," it started, and went on to remark about something in a column that brought back memories of his early life.

The letters came unexpectedly. I never knew when they would arrive, but each time they were placed on my desk a good feeling came. He saw only light in the world and had only good things to say. How I wish there were more of his nature – especially in the backwash of handling a newspaper job.

The folks in the news room soon realized that I recognized Lou's writing on the envelope. That letter was opened first. It was important to hear what that important man said. Sometimes he'd include an article I had written, or an announcement from our paper about an award. One time, he scribbled "Right On!" at the top of the clipping.

As the letters became more numerous, the greeting changed. It evolved to "My Dear Mrs. Carol." Feeling more secure in our relationship, he wrote, "My Dear Carol." And then, he gave me the supreme compliment: he wrote "My Dear Lady."

I loved it.

I shared a lot with that lovable man, just from the knowledge that he understood me. It was that kind of relationship.

He was careful, though, from the beginning, to ensure that I didn't think he was out of line.

"I must tell you, my dear, that I'm not a masher. Do you mind me writing to you? I do feel I know you so well through your writing."

A lot of misery of the world disappeared while reading Lou Moon's letters. I never failed to feel good – and honored – that he cared enough to drop me a line.

I remember his first letter came on a day that I felt particularly bad about everything, including my job. I don't usually get that far down, but it was one of those times. Lou Moon's words that day gave me the lift and the courage to continue this job. I know that – and I owe him.

The other day I picked up the phone and the fellow on the

other end told me he had an item to dictate. The call was from the Kalamazoo area, where Lou resided.

It was an obituary notice concerning Lou's death. That was how I learned about Lou dying. I took the information down, like the reporter I'm supposed to be, but it was like a death in the family.

I wish I could have met him in person and told him what great joy he brought to my life.

Sleep well, dear Lou, my gentleman friend.

C.W. Kirsch: His Credo Continues

October 29, 1983

He had a personal credo: "It is always possible to evolve a plan whereby everybody wins and no one loses ... profit to all and loss to none."

The man who lived and worked by these words, Charles Wendell Kirsch, is long gone from the Sturgis scene. But only in person; his memory and deeds remain.

And because of his dedication to the workforce and its thousands of employees, Kirsch will receive a long overdue honor.

The auditorium in Western Michigan's University's new John E. Fetzer Business Development Center will be named in Kirsch's memory.

If Kirsch was alive and heard about that move, he would probably be a bit embarrassed. Those who remember him know he was not a man of personal gain. We believe, however, that Mr. Kirsch would be honored to have that facility carry his name.

Kirsch, as we all know, was founder of Kirsch Co. in Sturgis, a company known as the world's largest manufacturer of drapery hardware. Kirsch Co. is now owned by Cooper Industries. Kirsch is celebrating its 75th year in Sturgis and 76th year of its founding. It began in Three Rivers in 1907, and Mr. Kirsch moved the fledging business to this city the next year.

Several members of the Kirsch family made a major gift to WMU's Partners in Progress capital campaign to honor Charles Wendell Kirsch.

The $4.6 million Fetzer Center will be dedicated Nov. 2 and the 250-seat C.W. Kirsch Auditorium "will provide a staging point for interaction between international business and governmental leaders and the business community," Dr. Darrell G. Jones of Western's College of Business said.

Kirsch was born in 1867 and died in 1933. His deeds are still remembered. He provided well for his workers, installing an inside swimming pool, bowling alley and rooftop café at the company, among other items to ease the stress of a day's work.

His flat curtain rod revolutionized the drapery business world. The success of his company was attributed to his integrity, vision and hard work.

He cared about his employees and gave generously to community endeavors.

Charles Wendell Kirsch's personal commitment to his business, hometown and family bore rich fruit through the years.

It is only right that Charles Wendell Kirsch's ideas will continue in a magnificent new auditorium.

The Rise – and Fall – of Egos

November 5, 1983

I've got this promotion at the Journal and the congratulations starting coming in. Bound to make you feel like a swellhead.

Until the complaints come – and that's when I wish some of the nice cards I received had been letters of condolences.

I guess it's like anything else; folks think an individual can settle many of their issues, publish everything they want in the paper, keep everything they don't want in, out.

Not so. That's not the newspaper business.

Now, I wouldn't begin to tell someone else how to run their business, but I've got to admit that if their product doesn't suit me, I'll offer some suggestions.

I need – and want – constructive criticism on this job. What's a bit hard to take is the criticism whereby someone calls up and bluntly informs that "your paper stinks." I never said it was perfect, but neither was the caller who wouldn't give a name and slammed the phone down in my ear.

And there was the individual who called and said we had an item wrong; claimed the dates were mixed up. Well, in looking at the article while talking to the person, I pointed out that the dates were right: the caller quickly hung up the phone. It was a simple mistake, getting the dates wrong. I understand how that can happen while reading articles. And besides, we at the paper make mistakes.

What bothers me is that the person could chew me out and then hasten to hang up because the distress of making a mistake was too hard to admit.

That's the life of reporters, editors – or whatever title we happen to wear. And I would hasten to add that I don't appreciate the little titles they give the paper. Fun's fun – and sometimes it's not.

But, back to the promotion. I thought I'd worked pretty hard, paid my dues to get this editor post. So, some little spot in my ego corner expected a bit of puff about it from the family.

Well, I can tell you, they can deflate a swelled head faster than anyone out there in newspaper critic's circle.

"That's real nice," the husband said. (He knew, of course, that uncooked meals, lonesome hours, and chores he'd have to assume were ahead). That'll teach him for not changing the babies' britches so long ago.

I then turned to the four kids for a big boost. They didn't seem to think it made much difference, either. Titles don't mean much to them. I've always been just plain old Mom.

So, I wistfully searched for someone in the family who might think this new position would be a big deal. I latched on to every last grandchild I have (and I've got quite a few) and tried my luck with them.

"What's a managing editor?" one bright one asked. "Do you manage to do something?" Oh, great.

Another said, "Won't you be able to bake cookies anymore?"

That was followed by another who gravely questioned "Can't I come and stay overnight anymore – and wear your big nightgown?" I didn't need that. Talk about kids' honesty and fair appraisal.

And then there was the grandchild who knew a good thing when he saw it: "Oh boy, I'll take the story about Grandma's promotion to school – and I'll bet my English teacher will have to give me an 'A' for the next six weeks." Little does he know, poor lad.

I guess I'll have to suffer out the loss of accolades. I do know that one of the grandbabies made my promotion announcement a bit worthwhile – I think.

Brushing off the inference of what the newspaper article said, he glowingly looked at the picture and hollered loudly: "It's Grandma Babe!"

He's only three, of course.

Ode to Those Running Boards

November 12, 1983

Saw one of those cars the other day, one with a running board. That old car rolled down the road, like the queen she is, drawing homage from passersby.

I expect if I told the grandbabies about running boards they'd think I was crazy to talk of boards that run. I'm sure they'd go sorting through Grandpa's lumber pile to locate one.

They've missed a lot, these kids. Mercy, have they missed a lot.

Now, some things about the good old days weren't all that good. But running boards on cars were. Good for memories, too.

Those were the days when a kid could be a kid for the allotted time God set aside for them to remain a child. Nobody pushed you into wearing dress-up shoes and bras before it was time to wear them. A girl could wear overalls with the cuffs rolled up mid-calf and she didn't worry about freckles and wind-blown hair.

In short, life was lived at the pace it was supposed to be lived.

And then, there were running boards. You could stand on a running board when you were too big to be lifted to see inside a car window or a foot short of standing on the ground on tiptoe.

Running boards solve a lot of things. They were handy to use when you were taking a drive down to the creek to swim and there were too many kids to fit inside the vehicle. They worked pretty good for delivering newspapers and darned handy to toss water-filled balloons. (Wait until the kids hear about that).

You could even drive the old jalopy down the lane to fetch the cows. If those critters tarried, it was easy to give them a quick nudge from your perch on the running board. One has to remember that cars didn't go fast in those days, vintage a year I'm not going to be foolish enough to reveal.

Along with those running boards were rumble seats. Now, youths today think of rumbles as being gang wars or hustles of some sort. Come to think of it, you could hustle a bit in those rumble seats.

Anyway, if you were relegated to the rumble seat in the back of a car, you inherited many things. Like fresh air, the chance to see nature as it passed by, among others. And you also were heir to dust covering your body from head to toe, grit that lined your teeth and the ever present odors of nearby farm acreage. And heaven forbid if someone spit out the car window.

Those were the days when folks in the Northern Michigan town I lived in held watermelon parties. Events like summer picnics at a nearby lake. You tossed the watermelon in the lake or creek and sneaked frosting from cupcakes lining long tables.

I still remember those days as if they were yesterday. I recall listening during the long evenings to the sounds of the world around me as the crimson sun faded to shadows. We sat around campfires long into the night and joined in singing favorite tunes and hymns. I recall so quickly the sounds of those voices carrying out across the lake, sounds that filed away into a special place in my memory.

And then, when the festivities were over, the kids rode home on the running board in the cool night air, shivering as the rushing air stung our eyes – and the grit collected on our teeth and hair.

How very much I miss it.

Kennedy: The Light Glows

November 19, 1983

John Kennedy died 20 years ago. Although we sometimes attempt to show a different stance to the world, in some ways much of our youth and spirit died with him.

We knew John Kennedy wasn't perfect. Even in our youngness we were realistic enough to understand that truth.

But JFK made us feel good, proud of who we were, what we were and what we could be.

Maybe it is best that we deeply absorbed the charisma of those Camelot days of the Kennedy Administration. We would learn soon after his death that Kennedy was not that faithful, model husband and hardly the man we had naively put on a pedestal.

But incidents warned us. We knew he could be wrong. There was the Bay of Pigs disaster. Kennedy demonstrated he could also fail.

But there was more to the Kennedy man. Though he climbed late on the Civil Rights bandwagon, at least he joined it in high gear in the short time he had left.

And there is the Peace Corps he cared so much about and which survived him. That was a lasting, shining example of his dream for the world.

We will never know what Kennedy could have been or how far he might climb as president of this great nation. The answer to that was lost when an assassin's bullet shattered his skull in Dallas 20 years ago.

There is something in many of us that mourns for the young John Kennedy, because some of his dreams remain with us.

He gave us the courage to try, to hope, to have faith in what we could do. He showed us how to reach for a dream.

John Kennedy's promise will remain a mystery. But, if we mourned so deep that other November day when he died, why is it the hurt remains so sharp this November day?

Perhaps it is a simple thing. The good and bad that was in John Kennedy, the triumph and the error, is a mirror of ourselves.

But Kennedy dared. He at least dared. And he gave us a pride in America at a time when we desperately needed it.

When Kennedy fancied around the White House, splendid in hosting world heads of state, we acknowledged his leadership and the aura only the White House can bring. When he rejoiced in the birth of his child, we rejoiced. When he lost a child, we mourned.

John Kennedy was a cross section of America. We loved him because he saw the misery of America and instinctively knew that sometimes, a nation so chilled by war, so downcast by Recessions and Depressions, needs something more.

We needed lightness, the magic arena of splendor and the sheer enjoyment and brilliance of events that touches us. And, if we are truthful, many of us will admit that we have not felt quite the same since he died.

We still mourn the man cut down in his prime. And we mourn

because we admired his attempt to enjoy life to its fullest.

And if that is a weakness, then why is it we felt so powerful and so magnificent in the shining 1,000 days we had with him?

In a way, John Kennedy lived the dream so many Americans were afraid to attempt. Many of us will always thank him for allowing us in some small way to identify with his life in the short time he filled the presidency of this country.

Thanksgiving: Good Memories

November 26, 1983

Having just recovered – I think – from Thanksgiving dinner, it's always the time of the year when I swear I won't gorge again until the first of the year. Unfortunately, I just say that. Never do follow good instincts, it seems.

Thanksgiving to me always ushers in a special time of year. Special because of the holidays that begin at this time of the year – and special because of the food. Everyone knows I'm a good eater. They only have to look at me to know it.

But Thanksgiving reminds me of other days, and Barbara Miller of Mendon dropped off the menu of a restaurant in Chicago to joggle my recollections. What food. What buys in that restaurant.

The menu was from the year 1933. You could go to that restaurant and buy the following on Thanksgiving Day: Consommé with noodles, pickled beets, olives, green onions and celery; rose radishes, pickled peaches and fruit supreme; roast turkey with oyster stuffing; mashed potatoes; buttered green beans; cranberry sauce; molded vegetable salad with whipped cream dressing; Parker House rolls and Melba toast; ginger pudding with wine flavored sauce; salted nuts, coffee and milk.

That meal cost $10 – for six people!

180

That leads me into admitting I was three years old in 1933. And I know, just from memories of later years, what the menu usually was in my parents' house. It wasn't fancy food of the Chicago menu, but it was good, wholesome and lovingly prepared by a mother who many times rose from her sickbed to cook and bake for her husband and small children.

I recall from those days that we usually had chicken. Mother raised chickens and canned them so they'd last us through the winter.

Now we only had chicken after we moved to the Lower Peninsula. On the farm there it was my chore one year to whack off the heads of those unfortunate chickens. After about 40-odd chicken head decapitations, the mess got to me. I couldn't look any longer at the poor chickens. I turned my head away and just aimed. Now and then I'd hit the chopping block, and sometimes I hit the chicken.

For months afterwards, the family had an ongoing contest at the dinner table guessing how long a chicken neck in one of those canning jars measured.

I was the only one who didn't appreciate the humor.

We also had parsnips on our menu (I still love them, even if everyone in the family hates them). My dad left the parsnips in the ground and dug them up from under the snow.

Also on the dinner table in those days would be garden-grown and home-canned canned vegetables. We also had wild cranberries we had picked and current jelly from the bushes in a neighbor's yard.

There were potatoes and carrots we had harvested, fetched to the kitchen from a barrel buried in the yard and covered with straw.

Always, there were dinner rolls Mother had baked and the kids fought for the center roll which was considered the tastiest.

And then we were treated to blueberries or raspberries, also picked from the woods and fields in the Upper Peninsula.

Pumpkin and mincemeat pie topped off the meal, with cream whipped after we separated it from the milk.

The mincemeat was homemade. I remember coming home from school on a bitter-cold days and smelling the wonderful aroma as I entered the kitchen door. The copper boiler was always on the cook-stove, filled to the top with the slow-cooking mincemeat.

That mincemeat was made from wild cranberries and venison. And it was delicious, the best I've ever had.

We ate well in those days of the Depression for a simple reason: The garden harvest sustained us through the winter. I don't know what we would have done without a garden. There was little money to purchase groceries. I do know that while many of our friends swam in the creek, rode bicycles and played, the kids in my family worked much of the summer in the garden.

I can't say I liked it much, especially picking those darned potato bugs off, but at least the work in the potato rows put starch in my diet – and my backbone. Can't say as I regret it one bit.

And, though remembering those other times and wishing my parents were alive to spend this holiday with me, I am still thankful. Whatever adversity is ahead, Thanksgiving reminds me of things I know made – and continue to make – my life richer.

Mystery Solved; River Trip Set

December 3, 1983

A month or so ago I wrote a column about a fellow who had written to me concerning a diary he had purchased from a lady in Montague, Mich. It seems the woman had been in Sturgis and bought the diary "from a very nice lady" at a garage sale.

The letter writer, Brad Bogart, also of Montague, was fascinated by the diary, once owned by a man from Sturgis, G.E. (Frank) Lark.

What intrigued Bogart about the diary was that its pages were filled with items about a trip aboard the Steamship Saint Louis, to Mississippi, Ohio and Tennessee in June 1914.

The trip accounts and photographs were pasted on an old Crane Co. diary. The Crane Co., I have since learned, made valves for paddle wheelers.

What Bogart asked of me was how he could find out who sold the diary – and what had happened to Lark.

Shortly after the column was published, my phone rang. The caller was Mrs. John (Irene) Weaver of Sturgis. She said she was the one who had the garage sale and sold the diary to Sharon Briggs, the woman from Montague.

Mrs. Weaver told me she and her husband John rented a house on North Street in Sturgis many years ago. Frank and Bertha Lark owned a place on North Nottawa. The families were good friends.

Mrs. Weaver explained that Mr. Lark suffered a stroke while visiting in Florida, and he and his wife returned to Sturgis. Needing someone to look in on them now and then, they moved in with the Weavers.

Mrs. Weaver said Mr. Lark was unable to talk after his stroke, but was alert and in good spirits.

The couple had no children, so they remained with the Weavers 10 years.

After her husband's death, Mrs. Lark was admitted to Branch County nursing home.

Mrs. Weaver said the Larks are buried in Oak Lawn Cemetery.

With no one to claim the diary, it remained in the Weaver home. And that's how it came to be sold at the garage sale a while back.

The reason Bogart wants to learn more about the people in the diary is that he hopes to retrace the route taken down the Mississippi River by the passengers. He wants to stop at sites the passengers visited at the turn of the century. In short, Bogart, a lover of history and nostalgia, wants to retrace the steps of those from another era.

Bogart said he learned the Saint Louis had a short life. According to the National Archives, the steamship, a merchant vessel, was built in Jeffersonville, Ind., in 1912. Her gross weight was 374 tons; her length 210.0 feet and her breadth 37.0 feet. Her depth was 6.0 feet.

She was a passenger ship, had a crew of 35 and her home port was St. Louis, Mo.

According to the 1919 edition of "Merchant Vessels of the United States, Page 450, the Saint Louis foundered Sept. 2, 1918 at Sulphur Springs, Mo.

If anyone can trace history, Bogart appears to be the fellow to do it. He ran away from home at the age of 12, made his way by road and rail from Chicago to Los Angeles. He has been a hobo, dishwasher, motorcyclist, merchant seaman. He also is a drifter of sorts, which he readily admits, and apparently is a modern day Walt Whitman whose verse becomes visual through the medium of photography, a critic said.

A write-up I read about Bogart says he is "an ex-warrior who hates and fears war, a Jew who would like to sit down and talk with Christ, a man who thinks 'macho' is an adolescent reaching toward manhood that stems from ignorance, and an adult who trusts only children."

An artist of established talent and acclaim, Bogart has exhibited his work in several museums. But he mostly wants to travel the route of the Saint Louis and tie yesterday with today – and possibly, tomorrow.

Shades of Christmas Hoarding

December 10, 1983

I'm a saver, something that bugs my family to no end. I also have idiotic (they say) ways of doing things. It works, so why knock it?

For instance, I buy Christmas wrapping paper after Christmas. Makes sense to me; it's far cheaper and you can always find a bargain.

Buying the paper later makes sense to the family, but what they can't – or won't – accept is that I save Christmas wrapping paper. Used Christmas wrapping paper.

Now, if that seems silly, so be it. I don't think it's so crazy a trait.

I remember my parents saved cardboard. I never went to school in bad weather without three pieces of cardboard in my lunchpail. My shoes – and those of my sisters' – were used to their maximum. The soles of the shoes wore out and you just stuck it out until the shoes didn't fit anymore. There were few shoes thrown away. Families seldom purchased new shoes for as simple a thing as a hole in the bottom. There were more important things to consider, like survival, in those Depression days.

So, when the soles got big holes, one took a piece of cardboard, cut it in a circle and put it inside the shoe, over the hole. When the cardboard got soggy from the lousy weather, one replaced it. And so on.

My mom was a conscientious mother. Those three pieces of cardboard were always neatly stacked in my lunchpail – and much appreciated, I might add.

Moving on to something more delicate, I'd have to add another paper product to my saving list, even if I don't use the paper for the same reason today. But, old habits stick around awhile in the life of a person who's known some hard times.

Remember the outside shanties, or outhouses, better known as toilets? Those are the printable words for them. The good old Montgomery Ward and Sears Roebuck catalogues in those days came in mighty handy, the handiest thing in those buildings, I might add. And those catalogues had different types of paper: Regular, slick and soft pages. Suffice to say that the index, the soft pages, worked the best.

If some of you have never experienced the use of those catalogue pages, don't expect me to say much more in this column about it. Ask someone older to explain. I'm not about to describe those times any clearer.

I also save Christmas boxes. Never know when you might need one of them. I recall a few years ago when I pawed through a stack of them and discovered a shirt still in one. Now, the gift wasn't wrapped and apparently had never made it to the recipient. Trouble was when I found the shirt, I realized it was a kid's size 8. Now, my boys have been grown for years, so you understand that box had been kept for a long time. Wonder which kid got shortchanged that Christmas so long ago?

Back to the wrapping paper. Come Christmas morning, I'll do what I always do. Sit there and grab every available piece of paper the kids and grandchildren don't tear up. The kids have grown smarter. They crumple the paper before I can reach it. Their theory is they won't have to see "the same darned paper we've seen every year."

Now, if there is anyone out there who needs a piece of Christmas paper to wrap a thimble in, I've got it – secondhand, of course. Or, I can wrap a small buffalo if the need arises. You'd be surprised how many manufacturers sell the same paper design several years. One just has to be sharp and save enough of it to match.

I go another step. I make Christmas package nametags from old Christmas cards. Just use the front part of the card, cut around a particular design with pinking shears. Then, use a paper punch to make a hole and use colored string for the tie. Simple, and costs pennies.

Now, that's something the kids don't laugh at, even if they do make sure they throw out the old tags.

Now, did you know there's another thing you can do to save money? Remember that old turkey bird? Well, carefully take the meat off the bird's breastbone (I'm assuming the poor bird is deceased) and boil it. Invert it and you have an old-fashioned sleigh. Paint it, color it, or whatever.

Please, folks, don't save me any. Those I have plenty of for the next 10 years.

By this time, you've probably come to the conclusion that I'm a Christmas fan. Why not – it's my birthday. I figure if I got robbed a regular birthday and everyone overlooks mine because of the big holiday, I might just as well go whole hog.

I figure I've got a genuine right to hoard used Christmas wrapping paper.

Memories Make Rich Christmas

December 24, 1983

I have told part of this story before. Much of it remains good memories. But a portion of the story was too personal to tell. It hurt too much.

Christmas tugs memories from most people, memories sometimes buried too deep to easily disclose. Memories held in silence or in selfishness.

A lady called me the other day and pleaded "tell us again about the boots."

I thought a while about that request. Why bore captive readers with such trivia? But I've decided to tell the story again – all of it.

Our lives were entwined, the three of us, for years. There was my dad, Neil Hogmire; his best friend, Miles Burnside, and me, the upstart they referred to as the "kid."

A Miles trademark was a well-worn, red and black checked hunting shirt. Seldom saw him without it. I wore one like it, the sleeves rolled up and the shirttail hanging to the back of my knees.

We trapped together, fished together, hunted. We sought out the bee tree and collected the honey. They taught me how to use snowshoes.

And I was the one who kept their secrets – and they had plenty of them. They were rousers of sorts. Sometimes the trappings and binds of my dad's confining illness and family responsibilities were forgotten in his search to break loose. Why he and Miles allowed me on their adventures I'll never know.

They forever played jokes on each other. I recall my Dad made breakfast for Miles one morning and criss-crossed white thread through two layers of pancake batter.

I was there when Miles and dad wandered down to Watton, the town near my birthplace, Sidnaw, in the Upper Peninsula. Watton was overcrowded with Finnish descent folks. Miles got smacked in the jaw for insulting one. He and Dad were a bit under the weather, but sober enough to hightail it out of town – fast.

Well, not quite so fast when it came to Miles. He was knocked out. When he came to – with his jaw broken – he had no memory of what happened. I told his wife Miles had run into something. He had – someone's fist. When Miles asked me months later, when his jaw was functioning decently, how his accident happened, I just looked at him and howled with laughter.

"Blamed kid," he snorted. "I ain't going to ask any more about it. That laugh of yours told me enough."

I knew other secrets about Miles. I knew he bought groceries when my family needed them. I learned he paid for coal to be delivered to our house one winter. Miles was that kind of fellow.

Miles' referred to his missus as "her." And "her" was Goldie. She was a good woman, a hard worker, but the keeper of a biting tongue. Miles was usually the focus of it. Didn't bother him much, although he once told me "she better shut up, that woman. I might just go find me an Indian woman, marry up with her and have a passel of papooses." (Miles had a healthy, genuine respect for Indians, something that didn't escape my attention.)

Miles and Goldie were childless and Miles loved kids. I knew he also loved Goldie, despite his rancor. The Indian lady was an idle threat.

I remember one day we returned to the Burnside house from an outing. Goldie blocked the door and leveled a scathing look at Miles. "Hand over that bottle," she ordered Miles. He turned to Dad. "Give her the whiskey, Neil."

While Goldie was intent on watching Dad, Miles reached inside his shirt and slipped the bottle into Goldie's pail of mop water, retrieving it when she hurried to the kitchen to check the cookstove. I can still see that devil grin on his face.

One Christmas, as the story I've told before goes, I asked my parents for a pair of hip boots. I needed those boots to wade the streams while helping Dad trap. There wasn't money for boots. And, where would you find a kid's size?

When I asked my Dad, he just shook his head as he carefully polished his most treasured possession – a harmonica.

But Christmas morning, there those boots were, unwrapped, under the tree. I looked at Dad, the unspoken question of where he had found the money. He turned away. I ran to the dresser and looked. The harmonica was gone.

I never asked Dad where it went. I only knew he had sold it. He treasured that harmonica – but treasured me more. The harmonica's loss to Dad was enough. I didn't insult him by asking.

Years later I visited Goldie at the house in town where she moved after Miles' death. My Dad had been dead for years.

Goldie had just held a yard sale. It was a warm day and she was tired.

"I don't know where we collected all that junk," she said. "Miles was a scavenger. Never threw anything away."

She sighed. "I sure miss that dreamer, though. Beats me about that man. Do you know some stranger who stopped at the sale today bought something Miles kept for years – an old harmonica? Wasn't worth anything, you know."

"Miles never played that harmonica. Didn't know how. Why in the world would he keep it? He told me once it was none of my business. He was going to give it back some day to a kid. He mumbled something about the kid would know what to do with it.

"Miles nursed a lot of secrets, but I'll bet he didn't remember where he got that harmonica."

Miles knew. In that moment I also knew his secret. I remembered a Christmas from my childhood and two men who loved me enough to make a wish come true.

The Colonel, a Plane Ride and Life

December 31, 1983

He was a quiet, articulate man, with an air of grace. He came walking up the aisle of the plane, on my Washington to Dayton hop on my flight home just before Christmas.

I had talked to several servicemen at National Airport in Washington, D.C. Some had missed flights home to loved ones. They were impatient; some were distraught as they sat in the crowded terminal. A couple had served overseas and one wouldn't talk about his experiences. I had sense enough after I asked where he had served not to question further. It was Lebanon. His eyes mirrored the unspoken answer to any more of my questions.

But the colonel on the plane intrigued me. As luck would have it, he was assigned the seat beside me.

In his hand, the officer carried a copy of USA TODAY, Gannett's national newspaper. "I like this paper," he commented. "I can pretty well find out quickly what's happening in the nation and the world by reading it."

I thought about that a while. I knew a bit about USA TODAY. Seeing as how Gannett also owns the Sturgis Journal and I had just toured the USA TODAY complex in Virginia, I figured maybe the colonel and I could trade information.

We discussed the newspaper and that seemed an opportune time for me to lead the talk into the military issue (I'm known for my dogged persistence when I want to gain answers).

I learned a lot about where America is going during that conversation. I also gained healthy respect for the fellows who serve and guide our armed forces.

The colonel was soft-spoken, but firm. He was assigned to the Pentagon, he said, but was on his way home for the holiday. Two of his college kids would be home and he was eager to see them. It was clear he was a family man, and proud of it. He had that special sound in his voice when he spoke opinions of America's purpose.

The obvious question from me was a loaded one: What was the colonel's opinion of Lebanon and our mission there?

He thought a moment. He was not a man of quick answers. He looked beyond me out the window as our plane climbed. We could see the land that was Washington and Virginia. "Look at that sight," he said, nodding at the millions of lights that gave the appearance of a world of sparkling gems. For an instant, the Washington Monument and the Jefferson Memorial floated past our view.

"That sight never fails to stir me," he said, as if to himself.

"Washington – a city of decision," he said quietly, "a city that holds our future."

I wondered if I was unfair in asking an Air Force man, a career officer of 22 years, what he thought of the Lebanon affair. But then, he spoke.

"We are committed to our mission in Lebanon," he said firmly. "I admit I question at times whether we should re-evaluate our sense of purpose and mission in some of our overseas agreements. I would like to believe that I do not follow blindly in my career, that I am a free thinker and observer. But, I would have to say we must attempt to carry out our mission there, to help keep the peace."

He was silent a long while and then spoke again. "But I don't think it's fair that we put our Marines in the coastal plain position. And though I know that firing back can sometimes escalate into a war, I wouldn't want my sons or anyone's sons to have to sit there and not be able to defend themselves."

I liked the colonel. Here was a man who had spent all his adult life in the Air Force, but kept a strong perspective of what is right and wrong with world. And he wasn't a braggart, a know-it-all, a gung-ho officer. He was a man who valued humanity – and cared.

We didn't talk about the colonel's military career or where he had served during his long tenure. He didn't seem the kind of man who wanted to waste conversation by talking about himself.

Before he left the airport at Dayton, he accompanied me to a seat where I would wait to catch my next flight home. "I hope your Christmas is a good one and that peace is a major part of your life," he said before walking off into the dark, snowstorm night.

His name is Col. James Hobb. I only know that much about him and that his hometown is Dayton.

Oh yes, I know one other thing. This world is a lot safer – and wiser – with warriors such as Col. Hobb around. I hope he knows he made my Christmas – and my New Year's – richer for having met him.

I'm Going Aloft – Again

January 7, 1984

If you see a lady a' flying above your head someday, it'll be me. I'm going aloft again.

And no, I don't intend to climb aboard an airplane. I love flying, have since the day I hitched a free ride with a daredevil pilot in the 1930s and rode through two loops. I've been addicted ever since.

Through the years there wasn't money for airplanes, but some trips were memorable, like the time my seatmate upchucked his lunch. I didn't have time to feel sorry for the fellow: some of his secondhand lunch hit me. Talk about captive audiences.

I've been known to take airplane rides to interesting places. I even flew to the National Guard's training grounds in Grayling with Ron Riley, and had a marvelous time with our local Guard unit. Made some interesting reporting.

So, imagine my delight when I opened my Christmas gifts this year. I found a balloon, tied to a wicker basket. In the basket was a greenback – my ticket to a ride aloft – in a hot air balloon.

I've only been up once for a balloon ride. I tell you, it's some way to fly. You may not have horizontal control, but vertically you can do about anything.

My pilot was congenial Ron Centers, Kalamazoo, a guy

well-known in Sturgis. Ron married pretty Nancy, the daughter of Paul and Phyllis Stewart. The Stewarts own and operate Paul's TV Service.

Now, I'd never been up in a balloon before, but willing to try it. Ron, two others and myself lifted skyward a while back. Talk about fun. First of all, Ron and his ground crew fanned cold air into the 70-foot high, 55-foot wide balloon. Then, the propane heater took over, blasting warm air into the sphere. And that, simply, is what makes a balloon containing 77,500 cubic feet air fly. Once you're skyward, when the air cools, the balloon lowers; add warm air and it rises.

Ron's an experience balloon pilot and has a commercial pilot's license. He also is a licensed instructor.

Ron started in the business while he and Nancy were performing in a street theatre at Jones, Mich. The owner of Jones, Ed Lowe, asked Ron if he would like to fly the balloon Lowe used in the summer festivities. That was 1976 – and Ron being hooked on balloons since that first flight.

Ron flew and raced balloons in Albuquerque, N.M., four years for the World Balloon Corp., before coming to Michigan. He now flies balloons for First Federal Savings and Loan of Kalamazoo, and First of America, also of Kalamazoo. First Federal jobs take him throughout Michigan, and he also flies his own balloon, the second one he's owned.

Ron goes aloft day and night, weather permitting. And, he doesn't have to advertise for customers. Word of mouth keeps his business thriving, so much that he recently purchased a truck to handle his equipment and serve as chase vehicle.

In the summer, when the air is warmer, Ron can take two

passengers aloft. Cooler air allows three.

Our journey started at Wall School in Sturgis and were airborne a little over one hour, landing in the field beside E&K Restaurant in Centreville. You never know where you'll end up on a balloon flight. You go where the wind takes you. There is little sensation of height, no feeling of traveling through the air, because you are the wind.

We took off at dawn and drifted northwest over farmhouses and fields. We hedge-hopped, which means we came down close to the ground and 'jumped' over fences and trees, close enough to pick leaves off trees. We followed deer in the woods, surprised rabbits in fields. We dropped down to the waters of Lake Templene, close enough to see the fish. We hollered good morning to folks on the ground who streamed from homes to watch us drift by.

Ballooning is a strange experience to describe. I can only say it gives you a feeling of being part of the world, of nature. There is no urgency of time. It is a peaceful atmosphere that completely hypnotizes.

I had never viewed the earth from that altitude. Either I was high in an airplane or walking. One sees a different view of from a balloon. In short, it's a great experience.

So, if you see this large lady attempting to climb into the basket of an air balloon, don't worry. I manage to get inside, whether it's a dignified entrance or not. Besides, that balloon is tolerant of size. It is a vehicle to another world, regardless of its passengers. Nice.

A Resolution that Makes Sense

January 14, 1984

I don't make New Year's resolutions. They're too easy to make – and break. Maybe I should make them. Can't say as it would hurt me. But I find too much hypocrisy in some resolutions. The human beast seems to find the easy answer for the easy way out. I'm more than a bit guilty, too.

I try to find the good in others – and I've been fortunate. I've found a lot of it.

Perhaps the best resolution I can make is to continue to find interesting people to write about, to highlight their triumphs and good deeds, to give them a momentary place to shine.

There are sad things to report, too, and maybe by telling them we can resolve to make life a better place and to have a little more understanding of others. We could start with appreciation.

The year 1983 was a good one for me, for many reasons. I remember it was a year of reasonably good health, that I am fortunate to have a large, loving family. And among the good things a business promotion came along to give a morale boost.

And there were other things. I am forever surprised at the outpouring of letters I get from people. Personal letters that warm my heart and make the tough job of being in the newspaper business easier.

I remember one experience in particular. You will remember Lou Moon, the fellow I wrote about in a column last year. Lou was in his 80s. although I never met him, Lou decided to write to me. How much those letters meant in my life. And how much I valued his thoughts and suggestions.

Lou died. It is hard to express how you can miss someone so much when you never met him. But I do. I wonder if I ever conveyed the message to him of how much I enjoyed his letters.

His daughters came into the Journal one day and emotionally handed me a package. In it was an item found among Lou's effects after his death. It was a book. On the pages of that book were pasted columns and stories – with my byline. Lou Moon had kept every story I had written. And alongside of many of those stories he had jotted down personal reflections.

The note I liked best from Lou's book was the one that said "I love this lady."

Sometimes, if you are blessed, a reward comes your way in life. Lou's last gift to me is a treasured one.

And just this week, another of my old friends dropped me a line. Actually it was from his owner, although it was written in his words. You might recall Homer, the duck I wrote about in a story last year. Homer has no feet. He lost them in a mowing accident and was found by Lucille Stoll's family. Lucille, of Sherwood, decided that any duckling that spunky and full of grit should be allowed the chance to live. Although everyone said it couldn't be done, Homer is alive today, testimony to the care and love Mrs. Stoll has for animals and wildlife.

Homer is still wobbling around the Stoll farmyard on the stubs of his legs. And there is neither man nor beast who invades the Stoll domain. Homer rules the yard – and rightly so.

Homer had a mighty fine Christmas. Got wrapped up in a Christmas bow and was allowed to parade a bit inside the house, where he immediately pulled decorations from the tree, Lucille said.

So, I'm going to allow myself one resolution I know I will keep: This column will reflect what it always has: people, animals and everyday happenings. Life.

Honey Lake – and Friend George

January 28, 1984

Well, George, you finally made it. You were afraid of it and hoped I'd bypass you. Sorry, George. Eventually, ALL good friends make it here, WHETHER they like it or not.

George, so all my other friends will know, is George Mayer of old Honey Lake days in Branch County.

And no, don't ask me why they named it Honey Lake. I just lived in the area as a kid and didn't have the passion for history I now possess.

There's a lot of folks, however, who know about Honey Lake and the grocery store that used to be there. A lot of folks I love.

And then there was Trayer School, down the road from the lake.

I could cry when I drive by the old Trayer School site. The building burned down some years back, but the memories burn elsewhere – in the hearts and minds of the people who loved that structure and the days when they learned their early schooling.

Trayer was one of those country schools with eight grades and one teacher. That teacher did everything from shoveling snow, to hauling wood and coal.

There was no kindergarten. We had the largest county pupil population one year, around 38 kids. And let me tell you it was some education. When you went forward in the front of the room to study with the teacher, you listened. Had to, because when you went back to your row, you listened in on the other grades.

I'm incensed to this day that students in those days were required to take an examination in order to go on to town high school after completing eighth grade. Can you imagine? What did they think we were, country idiots or something?

I remember when I graduated from eighth grade (I still have my diploma) and went to Burr Oak High School. I learned something I smirked about for months: the schooling learned at that little country place put me half a year ahead of most of my classmates as far as book studies went.

Country schools are part of the past for most kids today, but they live in many folks' memories as fresh as the days we trudged a mile one way to classes. We didn't ride, we used those now-ignored transportation items – feet. And it didn't matter whether it was sleet, rain, snow, heat. We walked. Did we walk.

Well, not always. My Dad always said I never walked. I ran. You bet. There were too many adventures to experience on the way to school.

Like watching the mink and muskrats play in the river. Chasing blue racer snakes (which sometimes chased you), picking mushrooms, gathering hickory nuts, cattails and pussy willows.

I knew where the biggest and brightest cowslips first poked their heads to catch the early spring sun. my next-door neighbor, Bob Fennell, use to coax me to run a quarter mile just to get a drink from the spring alongside the curve in the road – and roll down the hillside into the cool water. I'd hate to say how many scoldings we got for going swimming with our shoes on.

School at Trayer was rigid, but recess was fun. I got drafted for the softball team and darned if I didn't turn out to be a pretty good shortstop. Well, didn't have a choice. One of those Cary kids had his big brother Scott line me up in front of the barn. Scott hefted balls at me until I learned it was better to catch them than catch one in the belly. Scott later went to the major leagues, so you know I learned pretty fast.

We had the basics at school and were required to learn what we had done wrong in our studies before going on to the next chapter. God forbid if we took home anything below a "C." Good grades were expected by parents and we knew enough to come through.

And on that report card was a place to mark your height and weight. Well, we marched down to Angelo Botzner's farm once a month and got weighed on the farm scales in his grainery. Things were flexible in those days.

We had some excellent teachers at Trayer. My favorite was Avis Smith, now Avis Brothers. If kids had teachers like her every day, they'd learn. She made you WANT to learn.

One teacher, however, was a bit strange. She loved to play the piano and we were smart enough to realize that if we kept her playing – and us singing – we could skip fractions. I never have been good at fractions.

And then, there was the swimming hole. You climbed over the fence, walked along a field back to the creek. From the bluff overlooking the water, you had a nice diving platform.

Things changed. The darned neighborhood boys got a bit older and learned they could keep the girls away from the swimming hole if they went skinny dipping. That worked for a while.

But I had a fondness for that swimming place. The water was clear and deep and wound around a long bend. So – with the faint hope my eyesight was weaker than my courage – I summoned a few of the girls. We invaded the place.

You never saw such carrying on and such hasty departures in all your life. There were a few well-spoken words and some scathing looks. But they left – and never bothered our swimming place again.

So, George, as I said, old friends eventually make it to this column, in all their finery – or without.

I still recall your hasty retreat – and marvel that you still call me friend. But you do – and now, with me telling everyone the truth, you can't deny even that.

Thanks, dear friend – for being a lifetime friend.

A Town, a Gym, and a Dream

February 4, 1984

I have tried to stay away from writing on this theme, mostly because I am blessed. I love this town. It is as simple as that.

Burr Oak is one of those villages small in population but big on heart. Well, more like huge when it comes to friendship and caring.

Citizens down there have had this dream a long time, a dream that came with a need for a school gym. The old gym, built in the 1930's, simply isn't large enough to handle league games. It's small for most school events.

Dreams, like everything else, are built on questionable foundations. Sometimes they are called air castles, these dreams one feels may never come true.

But the dream for a community gym persisted. It drove the passions of fruition into the school superintendent James Lindsey. Although new to the area when he was hired by the school board, he saw the immediate need for a gym.

His vision was shared by others who had tried, unsuccessfully, to get bond issues passed for a complex. Their dreams had not died; they were just on hold.

And that is how it started, with a simple dream. But the idea swept past the doubters, the scoffers, the know-it-alls who sat back and cast scornful words about the reality of raising funds in the community. It would take a lot of money to build a structure of that nature.

There would be no bond issues. That fact was clear. With less than 400 students in grades kindergarten through 12, the school had its hands full just attempting to make ends meet.

But there was the Athletic Booster Club. Its members were doers. They did not dream dreams; they made dreams come true. Boosters have funneled thousands of dollars into the school coffers for everything from band and athletic squad uniforms, to computers and supplies. They joined the bandwagon, earmarking funds from regular bingo games.

The urge to help did not exactly sweep the community. As in any other small-town endeavor, there is controversy, argument, doubters. But a few determined people kept the idea alive. They cajoled, enticed, ran fund-raisers, even took to downright begging. Begging is sometimes necessary when a cause is right.

And, with help from many many individuals and organizations, the funds started rolling in. Money for the foundation and shell were raised.

The community is a long way from having the fancy gym so many communities possess. But this gym will be constructed with money citizens gave from family budgets, kids who washed cars, mothers who baked pies, personalities who lent their names and resources to help.

And the age of those helping does not matter. The ranks were filled by young and old. Assistance has come through donations, anonymous gifts, memorials. Time and material have been donated.

Only $1,000 dollars of tax money has gone into the effort. That came from the Burr Oak School Board of Education, which noted taxpayers had turned thumbs down on a long-term bond issue. The board felt obligated not to bond the school district.

But that did not mean the board did not endorse the project. Not by a long shot.

And so, Burr Oak is cautiously and eagerly awaiting spring and more fund-raisers. Then, a gym floor and other needed materials can be purchased through more donations and events.

Oh, there are still those who resist the structure's completion. And they should be allowed their say. Opinions can differ, but friendship prevails.

What makes the special gym drive so important is not one group raised the money; not one individual paid the total cost; not one taxpayer will be forced to spend his and her remaining years paying for a structure the district had to borrow money to build.

This building comes from a simple source: Love. The unabashed love of a community that is spunky, independent and proud of its own—and willing to work to show it.

I am proud of that community.

Memories of Frank Abound

February 11, 1984

He is a man of singular mold. A man of strong principles. He is not shy, either, in advising you of his thoughts – on just about any subject.

I remember the first time I saw him. It was at the Journal and I was new.

"Wait'll you meet Frank," the staff told me, smiling. Smiling a bit too much, as I recall.

I was worried. Who was this institution called Frank Tennent? And what was in store for me when I met him.

Well, in he strode, hat centered on top of his head, coat unbuttoned, coattails flapping behind him as he nodded in all directions.

"And, who are you?" he boomed. And, before I could open my mouth to answer, he shook my hand, patted me on the shoulder and launched into a dialogue of what was good and what could be improved at the Journal.

I loved him at first sight. Well, Frank, there were times when we have tested each other's temper and patience. But, Lordy, how we have loved it all.

Frank has had a long association with the Journal. He is the fellow who faithfully called in the stock listings each day. On time, because he knows deadlines. Possibly he was on time because he did not enjoy getting return calls disturbing him at noon.

He began calling a few minutes late a few years back, and I learned what made Frank's calendar tick and how to get his time clock on the same schedule as the Journal's. I carefully waited until about five minutes before Frank left for one of his many service club lunches – and then called him. It cured the tardiness – I think.

Frank is Sturgis. He may deny it, but that is the way it is. He was born here in 1900 and his family was well-known in civic and business circles.

Frank forged his way in a new business. When securities are mentioned, the name Tennent crops up.

Frank entered the world of stocks and bonds in 1925, shortly after graduating from college. He stayed in the business until a couple of years after the market crash of 1929. He had a family to take care of and, with "Americans having no confidence" in the market, he realized he had to make his mark elsewhere.

He founded the Tennent Equipment and Supply Co., and operated it for 20 years. But his love of the stock market world lured him back in 1950 even if things were "pretty tough." He was allied with a Chicago securities firm 10 years and joined the William C. Roney office in 1960.

He laughs when he tells folks he runs his business out of a "horse barn." That is just what it used to be, but now serves as the Tennent garage and Frank's office.

He is a busy man, this fellow named Tennent. Belongs to the Shrine, Rotary and Klinger Lake County Club, plus several other endeavors, including being a charter member of the American Legion.

He admits he is sold on Sturgis and "this is a great town. You make it what it is."

There is a story the younger generation does not know about Frank. He recognized the need and single-handedly raised funds to build a Montgomery Ward complex on Chicago Road. Sold the bonds, raised the cash. He admits it is one of the proud accomplishments of his life.

And there is one more thing about the whirlwind fellow named Tennent. He retired yesterday from the securities business. And that means we at the Journal will not hear his quicksilver tongue each day. I know what not having Frank Tennent around means. Boring, boring, boring.

Frank said he is going to slow down in retirement and devote more time to his family, which includes his beloved wife, the former Doris Dewey. He also has three sons and grandchildren, and he is quick to boast about them.

And by the way, for all those interested, Frank is celebrating his 84th birthday tomorrow.

I have never known a man as young in spirit as Frank Tennent. Happy, anniversary, Frank. I wish you would tell me your secret for all that energy, but I will settle for having you call me friend.

Let us Bring Back the Cellar

March 3, 1984

Cellars, the old kind at least, belong to my childhood. My long-ago childhood.

The cellar monicker, I guess, evolves from early days, because the underhangings of new houses usually are called basements.

How terrible.

Cellar is a more impressive word, better for digesting all the memories from growing up times.

Cellars, at least the kind I remember, were actually Michigan basements. There is the ugly word again.

We just called our place the cellar.

Now, if you are the vintage age I am, or at least circa the 1930s, you will know what I am talking about.

Usually, one whitewashed the floors and walls of those cellars. That meant once a year the kids had the task of painting the cellar. My mother believed in clean floors. Clean cellar floors, too.

The problem was, when we were done with the painting, a goodly share was on us. Did you ever have paint brush fights? They are fun, I tell you.

We had the kind of cellar where the cement sides of the room were molded into shelf's. On those shelf's, displayed according to the contents and colors, were many jars containing my mother's canning talents. She set a goal each year—1,000 quarts—and reached it.

I guess the goal was not the important thing. It took that much food to tide the family over the long winter until garden harvest time.

Cellars always had a room for a coal bin, if you used coal. If not there was the old woodshed, good for warming the household or the backsides of errant kids. I visited there a few times and it was not always to carry wood.

You could find a lot of things in cellars. Spiders, flighty mice that kept their distance, and if you had a crawl space, a salamander could be located in the sand.

We made pickles in that old cellar. Used a big crock and filled it with cucumbers and brine. Always had a dinner plate with a rock on the top to hold everything down.

I was the kind of kid who tried anything. Ever munch on a half-seasoned pickle? I did. Ate several of them. Spent the next two days in the outhouse, bemoaning my stupidity.

The cellar at night was a place of mystery, where shadows cast eerie designs to make your heart climb into your throat. I always looked over my shoulder and into the dark corners. In the daytime, the cellar contents of baskets, family belongings and other articles made a fairy tale.

I wandered constantly from the attic to the cellar, each of them offering their own treasures.

In the winter the cellar was a cold tomb. Literally. My Dad skinned out minks and muskrats there. My mother would not step foot down there until the mess was gone. But I did. I helped stretch the furs over the boards Dad made and usually was rewarded at the end of the trapping season by receiving the money from a mink. That was pretty good pay for a youngster in those days. I remember one year a good mink skin brought $30 dollars. It lasted me until the next winter.

But cellars mostly contained pungent odors I cannot find anymore. There is too much opening cans from stores now. The old time cellars had dill hanging from the ceiling, apples in barrels, potatoes, parsnips, carrots, all kinds of seedpods. And baskets. I love baskets: round ones, oval ones, big ones, small ones. I have the darned things all over the house and still add to the collection.

I wish we had more cellars. I still call my basement a cellar. I suppose I always will. It rather resembles the old one, and certainly is not one of those remodeled, paneled, moved-in family rooms.

I suppose if I sorted everything out I would find the kids' old boots, roller skates, toys and everything we do not need—unless you collect memories.

I figure if I wait long enough, the items in the cellar will fit the grandkids. Come to think about it, I will have to let them explore down there.

If they belong in my family, they will have to like cellars.

Ode to the old Pitcher Pump

March 17, 1984

I got to comparing memories with some people the other day after my recent "cellar" column. Recollections went back to pitcher pumps. Remember them? I do, even if it's been years since I labored over one.

Up North, we had town pumps. That's right – town pumps at each end of town. Took our choice, whichever was the closest.

I had a close buddy, Tom Dentel. We usually managed to haul the daily water supply home together. Families didn't have inside pumps in those days, so all the water used for washing clothes, taking baths, cooking and drinking came from those pumps.

In winter a kid hauled the water in large milk cans on sleds. In the summer, a youngster's wagon was always handy.

Tom and I were the kind of rowdies who found trouble, or it found us. We usually sallied forth to fetch water and wet down every-thing along the way, be it passersby or ourselves. Pity the dog or cat that came by. We got 'em.

Tom's mother was a saint, but she became pretty upset once when we tarried along the way. Hours, if I remember correctly. Anyway, she came after us, picked up a pail of water and threw it at Tom. Trouble was, she let go of the pail, too. Tom learned wisely that day about the old adage, "haste makes waste."

Water from those pumps filled the big tubs for family baths. Usually a copper boiler sat on the cookstove and Mother would pour some of it into the tub to warm the water a bit. We didn't fool around taking baths. That water never got warm.

After moving to the Lower Peninsula, the water situation didn't improve, except the well out by the barn.

That meant I got the job of pumping the water tank full for the stock to drink. Did you ever go out on a cold morning, carrying a hatchet, chop the ice in the tank and stand there freezing to death while you pumped away?

And, worse of all, sometimes you had to prime the pump. I hated the job.

There were some rewards, though. Like having some town kid visit who never had to pump water and was innocent of how cold weather, wet tongues and pump handles go together. God forgive me, but I managed to entice a couple of kids to try that maneuver.

I didn't sit down very well for a couple of days after my folks realized – quickly, I might add – what had happened to my poor friend's tongues.

I'm surprised I ended up with any friends. But then, I remember getting baited to eating choke cherries up North. Alum has nothing on choke cherries, let me tell you. Nothing.

People who have fancy electric pumps will never realize how tough it was – and sometimes fun – working away at those old pumps. You developed arm muscles, colorful language and a lot of fringe benefits while pumping water.

One of those benefits was you could immerse your body in the horse tank in the summer. (I don't think I'd ever fit into one now.) But I still eye them when passing farmyards.

I wonder about the sterile, shiny glasses and cups we all use now. People wouldn't think of drinking out of the same glass. In my childhood there was the dipper. Everyone used the dipper. You had one cardinal rule: Never spit in the pail.

Thinking about those times, I can't remember having half as much illness as the kids of today. We had some tough diseases, such as polio, whooping cough, mumps and diphtheria, but few colds.

Maybe the reason was because we weren't inside the house, glued to a television set. We sure weren't. We were out in fresh air – pumping water.

Cemetery Witness to History

March 24, 1984

History is always being discovered, even in St. Joseph County. Witness the small cemetery in Section 34 of Leonidas Township. The tiny acreage, called McAuley Cemetery, was visited several months ago by Tom Weinberg, Helen Wickman and Virginia Hoekzema, all of St. Joseph County.

The cemetery chronology goes back to 1836, when John Patrick McAuley of Ireland bought 175 acres in Leonidas Township.

The purchase was made at the land office in Bronson. That town of Bronson wasn't in Branch County. This Bronson was the area later named Kalamazoo.

The certificate for the land, No. 3781, was signed by President Andrew Jackson's secretary, A.J. Donilson.

The cemetery is located on the north bank of the St. Joseph River near a small creek in a woodland area. Members of the St. Joseph County Historical Society say the tombstones are intact, but a fence built around the burying ground has fallen into disrepair.

Ownership of the cemetery plot is being investigated, Wickman said. Research indicates McAuley and Schellhous families were related. Both families were early settlers in the Colon-Leonidas area.

The McAuley land was inherited by Cyrus Schellhous' children after the death of their mother, Ann McAuley Schellhous.

Though research has not proved the case, it appears a fraction of land on which the cemetery is located was kept by the Schellhous family and never sold to Phineas Farrand, as Farrand believed. This leads to the assumption the Schellhous family wanted to insure the family plot would be preserved, leaving the present ownership in question.

The earliest legible inscription on a tombstone is that of John McAuley, who died Dec. 19, 1835. His epitaph reads simply: "Rest In Peace."

He was 40 years old.

The county historical unit has asked the Leonidas Township Board to allow the Colon Historical Society to clean up the interior of the cemetery, as the Colon society has volunteered to do.

The township board also has been asked by the county historical group to erect a fence around the cemetery.

Whatever happens, the cemetery is now in the public eye and so noted by Leonidas Township and the historical groups.

Perhaps John McAuley can rest in peace.

Friendship to Last a Lifetime

March 31, 1984

The folks will get a bit weepy today. Even the men will shed a few tears. And why not? It isn't every day two couples, good friends for long past a half century, will observe their 50th wedding anniversaries. Together.

Seems like the right thing to do. After all, Tracy and Ruth Lasco and Howard and Avis Hackenburg all of Three Rivers have been best friends since childhood. "And that was a mighty long time ago," mused Tracy.

According to Tracy, who afforded he is a "bit embarrassed to talk about it all," the couples' lives have been blessed.

Seems the couples married a month apart, Tracy and Ruth April 7 and Howard and Avis March 31. That was in 1934.

No, they didn't stand up for each other at the ceremonies. "We were lucky just to raise the $2 for the marriage certificates," Tracy said. "There weren't any frills in those days."

The couples got along so well they continued their friendship after their marriages. The couples even moved into a duplex to cement their friendship, Tracy added.

They weathered the years together, those four, helping each other in times of sorrow, sharing the happy times. They took pride in each other's kids and boasted about the dozen grandbabies the Lascos' two children and the Hackenburgs' three presented the couples.

Harry and Tracy worked for Eddy Paper Co. for years, with Harry retiring from employment there.

The girls had one difference. Avis liked being a homemaker but Ruth was a beautician for years.

And then, like most couples, they drifted apart – but only in a physical sense. The Lascos went to Las Vegas, where Tracy was employed several years.

"But Three Rivers drew us back," Tracy said. "We missed our old friends, even though the Hackenburgs visited us in Las Vegas."

The four missed each other so much the Hackenburgs recently moved into the apartment complex which the Lascos manage. "Yeah, we're about 20 steps apart," Tracy said.

They have many memories to share today, including a trip taken years ago to Kentucky and Tennessee. Seems Tracy wanted to locate his ancestors' homes in Kentucky.

"We pooled our money, $50 for each couple and set out in a Model A Ford," Tracy recalls. "We stopped at Gatlinburg, Tenn., stayed at motels and had a ball. Even had $5 left when we got back – and divided it."

"Some fun that trip was," Tracy remembered, as he described how they had to wade through a creek and push the car in the back hills of Kentucky. "What memories!"

And that's what Tracy terms the four's intertwined lives: "Experiences."

So who planned the big celebration today at the Three Rivers JOCO Center? "Well, our kids got together and set it up," Tracy said.

"We didn't argue. We think sharing a 50ᵗʰ anniversary – just like we share our lives – makes sense. After all, we're as close as brothers and sisters."

"It sure is going to be a fun time at that anniversary party."

And so today, the Hackenburgs and the Lascos will wade through the multitude of kids of all ages, people from all walks of life, old-time and new-time friends and acquaintances. The punch will flow, the cake will be cut.

And in the midst of this special day in their lives, Howard and Avis Hackenburg and Tracy and Ruth Lasco will make a special toast. That toast is sure to mean something to the four people who will hold their glasses high. In the warmth of this special day in the winter of their lives, they will give thanks for the meaning of friendship.

Milestone for Salvation Army

April 7, 1984

They'll have reason to celebrate at the Sturgis Salvation Army's annual civic dinner Thursday. They will have the usual speeches and a special speaker.

But what the Army is excited about is the enthusiasm and motivation that sparked fund-raising to pay off two mortgages.

The Army desperately needed additional space a couple of years ago. A campaign was started to pay the mortgage on a new building at 105 N. Fourth St. The fund drive began Jan. 1, 1983 and ended last September. The goal of $15,011.24 was reached.

There is a bonus to that fund-raiser. The Army headquarters in Grand Rapids said if the Sturgis unit raised the money to pay off the Army's new office complex mortgage, headquarters would provide funds to pay the $19,000 mortgage remaining on the Army officers' quarters. Lts. Paul and Barbara Logan reside at the home.

That leaves the Army debt-free as far as mortgages are concerned.

Lt. Paul said the campaign "was rewarding" and praised the devotion and dedication "so many persons gave to accomplish the goal."

The Salvation Army was organized in 1965. The Sturgis Post will observe its 50th anniversary in 1985.

Funds to operate the Army unit in Sturgis come through

donations from the public, the United Fund and church members.

Lt. Paul said the membership stands at 55 in the senior division and 25 in the junior.

The Army is an organization that quietly goes its way, helping the needy, offering spiritual assistance and boosting community activities. Their work doesn't usually gain spotlight, nor does the Army's workers seek it. Their foremost goal is to help others.

Among the contributors to the office fund drive were Cooper Industries, Northern Cashway Lumber, Sturgis Foundation, Gannett Foundation and many private donors. Lt. Logan said the list is extensive.

As always, there are many persons behind the Salvation Army scenes. Paramount are the advisory board members who give their time and effort: George Abel, John Browne, Max Harker, William Snyder, Robert Addison, Pat Heydlauff, Judy Reid, Clair Ickes, Jack Bell, Howard Bush, Virgil Weekly, John Mancini, John Fair, Fay Hart and Martin Bostetter.

The dinner will feature Carl Ehry, United Way director of Elkhart County, Ind. A good turnout is expected, and the public may attend. A $7.50 donation is asked.

Those who attend the dinner will be offered a chance to participate in a proud milestone in the Sturgis Salvation Army's history.

Dorothy: She Spiced Up Life

April 14, 1984

We knew her simply as Dorothy. A vocal lady whose opinions came often to us – in criticism and in praise. She didn't always like the Journal, but she loved us. And that's what matters.

Something else matters: The memory of the woman who was Dorothy Knox of Sturgis. She died recently. Sturgis is much dimmer without her vitality.

Dorothy was a native of Pennsylvania, where she first made her presence known in the halls of learning. Learn she did. She said once she never stopped learning. "That's the joy of life," she said with that particular piercing look one came to know so well.

Her degrees included an AB from Hood College in Maryland with a major in zoology and a minor in English Literature and composition. She was granted a teaching fellowship in the Zoology Department at Michigan State University and earned her way through a master of science degree, and one year toward a doctorate before giving up the fellowship. It was a simple thing, she always said: "I wanted to get my doctorate in a field not available at MSU. My major there was genetics." She eventually returned to Hood, teaching genetics, anatomy, physiology and embryology.

She married her Richard, the fellow she met when he was an

undergraduate at MSU. Richard transferred to George Washington University to be with his parents. Dorothy moved back to Frederick, Md., to teach. As she always said, "Richard and I resumed our friendship. It was love at second sight."

Dick worked for the War Department and Dorothy continued teaching. She also worked for Army Intelligence and then was offered a job with Upjohn Co., in Kalamazoo. From there, the couple came to Sturgis and Kirsch Co.

But there was more to Dorothy Knox. She had a favorite hobby: gardening. She grew her first flower garden at the age of six. It was a love that never waned. She became a naturalist, although she seldom admitted to being one.

Dorothy was one of the founders of the Sturgis Garden Club, which was organized in 1955. She served in every capacity on the board, garnering 24 years of tenure.

She was proud of the Sturgis Garden Club. And well she should be.

Among its accomplishments are winning the Purple Ribbon from the National Council for best flower show in Michigan. She helped institute the landscaping project for the Sturgis Post Office, which took two years. The project won the Sears Civic Improvement Contest. She also helped update the club's by-laws and constitution; celebrated the 10th anniversary of the club as a state affiliate; and helped with the first Glamor Tea at the Sturgis Woman's Club.

Dorothy was most proud of the educational/conservation exhibits staged at flower shows. She handled much of the photography work for the exhibits and enjoyed the landscaping projects for the hospital, swimming pool, Augspurger Tennis Courts and others.

She once said in a handwritten brief about her life she also "wrote articles for the Sturgis Journal – back in the days when they would publish anything about the club!"

Dorothy didn't mince her feelings. When there was a platform or a crusade, she spoke out. And didn't hold grudges, even if her words sometimes hinted her patience was a bit frayed.

We will miss her comments about the Journal. The Garden Club will miss her. Sturgis already misses her wit, warmth and great love for this city.

Charlotte intends to fill GAP

April 21, 1984

Charlotte Kaley is the king of gal who knows a good thing when she sees it. She doesn't profess to have a wealth of material things in life, but she knows when material things are needed.

Charlotte Kaley also has a big heart – and knows how to get a job done.

Charlotte, 65, 414 North St., Sturgis, is a booster of the Sturgis senior citizen mealsite. A vocal booster. A working booster.

Charlotte heard a lot about the Generation Activity Program and how Sturgis citizens are attempting to raise $75,000 to buy, renovate and equip a building to house senior citizen activities and a nutrition center. Total cost of the project is $125,000.

Charlotte is busy.

She has two passions in life, fishing and garage sales. "Well, fishing won't raise much money, so I figured I'd turn to my other love, garage sales," the spunky Charlotte said.

She hustled up her daughter, Patricia Salisbury, and sister, Abigail Augerbright, also of Sturgis, and they sorted, labeled and arranged items for the garage sale.

Successful they were. Charlotte turned in a $125 check for GAP at the Citizens State Bank, which oversees the account for the GAP

Council.

Charlotte retained only the amount necessary to pay for the newspaper ad.

Charlotte is a walking, talking advertisement for the proposed GAP center. "Mealsites and senior citizen events are absolutely wonderful," she gushed. "I never met so many people before, made so many friends. Why, I've met folks there I'd never know otherwise. And, I have a better outlook on life."

Charlotte had known a share of heartache. Her first husband died. Her 15-month-old twins, a boy and girl, died of pneumonia. Another daughter died in 1975. Her oldest daughter "went off years ago. I don't know if she's dead or alive," Charlotte said.

But Charlotte found happiness in her remaining four children and her second husband, James.

And she looks ahead to making her life interesting. Charlotte is planning a second garage sale in June – also to raise funds for the center. "I'd have more sales if I had enough items," she said.

Charlotte could sit back and let the world come to her. After all, she worked 25 years at a factory in Three Rivers before retiring. But she's not a chair sitter. Not Charlotte.

She knows the GAP Council needs funds, even though Gannett Foundation awarded $50,000 for the project. The Foundation, which authorized the funds under its Communities Priorities Program, on a matching basis. That means two Foundation dollars for every $3 raised locally to reach the $125,000 goal.

Donations, large and small, began to trickle in. the Veterans of Foreign Wars and its Auxiliary recently gave $1,200, raised from its bingo proceeds and breakfast funds. Citizens have pledged funds.

Roanne Fry is treasurer of the GAP Council. She said $30,000 in cash and pledges has been raised. But much more is needed if the goal is to be reached.

For those who don't know about the GAP building, it will be the site of all senior citizen activities. It is vitally-needed in Sturgis. And it will be a blend of young and old. Youths will learn how to prepare meals at the complex as part of Sturgis High School's food service program. Students will serve the meals to Commission on Aging participants.

It will be a unique generation tie.

And, while some pledges are large, GAP members know it is the small donations, the $10, the $25, the $100 gifts that will make the difference. And that's how it should be, donations from all walks of life. The more people who donate, the more realistic it is that the building's purchase will be gained through citizen's generosity.

And Charlotte? "I'd hold a garage sale every day if I could. That center is going to be a reality.

A Monitor to Child's Life

April 28, 1984

Most parents at one time or another face a terrifying moment when their baby or young child is seriously ill or experiences a dangerous moment.

One group of parents lives with that terror every day.

And because of their common concern, the Apnea Support Group of Southwestern Michigan was organized in May 1982. The unit is a non-profit group.

Apnea, in simple terms, means cessation of breathing. There are many reasons why babies stop breathing, but one known cause is when a baby has not developed close enough to term date. Their lungs are underdeveloped and they simply forget to breathe.

If they do not begin breathing on their own, or are stimulated to do so, death results. Many so-called crib deaths are caused by undetected apnea.

Most youngsters can be given medication to help overcome this problem, but in some cases, the youngsters must be connected to monitors to detect the cessation of breathing. An alarm goes off and the parents can stimulate the child or provide the necessary treatment to make the babies breathe.

Having a youngster connected to a monitor can be a strain on families. Some monitors go off as many as 60 times a night. Parents get little sleep. While parents learn after awhile the babies will be fine after being attended to, the fear remains the monitor might malfunction.

The alarm still draws concern for most parents, including Conni and Bob Wells, Burr Oak, whose children experience apnea problems.

Conni is active in the Apnea Support Group. She feels the more parents learn about apnea, the more children can be saved. According to Conni, one baby in the United States dies each half hour because it stops breathing. As Conni says, "what would the government be if one 30-year-old man died each hour in the USA of completely unexplainable causes? There would be hysteria all across the country."

And yet, no government money goes towards extensive apnea research.

But that hasn't stopped the area apnea group. They have many medical experts as advisers and support persons who speak at meetings. There are counseling sessions to help parents and families adjust to living in such an environment.

Newsletters go out every other month to keep families in touch and explain new testing procedures. Conni said group membership is growing as more parents become aware their children react in ways similar to known apnic tots.

Statistics, Conni says, show one of every 400 babies born will succumb to SID, Sudden Infant Death.

Most of these babies can be helped, if parents are aware their babies are breathing normally. Conni urges any parent who notices a child breathing differently to immediately check with a doctor. A youngster may manage to live many months without severe problems, but face emergency situations or be found dead.

Living with an apnea child is not, as Conni says, the easiest way to live. "But you can save that child by simply using medication in some cases or hooking the child up to a bradycardia monitor while it is sleeping. While the monitor doesn't correct the condition, it measures the heartbeat. If the beat falls below the normal rate, the monitor alarm sounds," Conni added.

Nearly all families take special training to handle apnea babies. Friends and relatives usually participate so they can babysit with the youngster and give the parents a night out. Many nursery schools now recognize the seriousness of this and undergo the training.

"When we learned one of our children had apnea problems, we were frightened," Conni said. "We still worry, having a couple of them on the monitors, but we know their lives can be saved with extra precautions."

That's why Conni and all the other parents of apnea babies want more people to learn about the apnea danger.

"Our kids are pretty special to us. We want to make sure other parents can keep their children alive, too," Conni said.

Sturgis Claims Witty Artist

May 5, 1984

Sturgis people remember the Clemmons brothers, Larry and Ralph. Larry, as most people know, achieved fame as one of Walt Disney's talented artists "from nearly Day 1," his sibling, Ralph says.

Brother Ralph says "I'm not as famous as brother Larry, but I'm just as smart." Ralph didn't end up in the slow lane, that's for sure.

Ralph is a witty gentleman. I've never met him, but I've heard about him through Henrietta (Sturgis) Richards, his former class-mate. She said Ralph is "one talented, lovely fellow." She's right.

Ralph graduated from Sturgis High School in 1923. He also remembers attending kindergarten in the old three-story school. He lays claim to being Sturgis' "proverbial barefoot boy." In summer, that is. He recalls raising the dust on Chicago Road when it was an "unpaved dirt road with plenty of horse watering troughs."

He remembers going through school with a girl named Mary, whose "dad was superintendent of schools many years. I was always secretly in love with her," he said. (Ralph has a wife, I should point out.)

Those early days meant smaller enrollments. Boys played all sports. Trouble was, Ralph says, the basketball court was in the as-sembly room and the baskets were on the walls. So were the steam radiators. "Those radiators were hard – and hot," Ralph remembers.

The girls basketball team "was better than ours. They seldom lost. We didn't win all that much," the honest Ralph adds.

Ralph says he learned he was "pretty much of a hick when I went away to Highland Park Junior College, a prep school." He also studied four years at Notre Dame, majoring in architecture.

And then it was on to Chicago, to join Corn Products. Yes, the makers of Argo Starch and Karo Corn Syrup. Yes, he worked in the architectural department.

Ralph wasn't content to put down roots. He journeyed to Portland, Ore. Hitchhiked out. He was employed in architectural offices a couple years and "got wiped out by the Depression."

He landed a job with Walt Disney Studios, but "didn't make connections even though brother Larry was working there." On to the Bank of California in the real estate department.

But Sturgis beckoned. He returned in 1937 to work at Scovill Manufacturing Co. and worked at Sturgis Products Co. during World War II, traveling the U.S. as a production engineer. He also worked at the State of Michigan Architectural Department.

Ralph transplanted roots again. Traveled to Montana for "browner pastures." Eventually, Ralph ended up in the state of Washington. He retired in 1971 at the age of 68 and he and wife, Ila, have "been living the good life."

That's the basics of Ralph's life. He's also an artist. A talented, sensitive artist. The talent was always there and now there is time to devote to his watercolors. His workshops did well; the sales "pretty good." But he will not admit to being a "known painter." Not Ralph.

"I've leaned one important aspect of art. Being an architect is to do renderings of buildings, generally for publication or to be displayed in public to show how the building will look upon completion. That is not a painting, being too literal and exact."

Ralph, by his own admission, says he is fighting to get away from that "cocoon and to paint with interpretation. A clever brush won't do it for you."

Ralph is right. An artist must have feelings, of experiences and growth. Joy and sadness. Life.

Ralph tends to look at himself and his work – even though he is very successful with his watercolors – with a clear eye. "If you fall in love with your own work, you stop growing."

One can't imagine the versatile, witty Ralph Clemmons as ever stop growing.

One more thing. Ralph Clemmons, Sturgis-boy-makes-good, may have left Sturgis, but he never left Sturgis behind.

A Rock in the Time of Need

May 12, 1984

He was six. And special. Their only son. Steven and Alice
Easterday knew something else: his life would be short. But still, like
most parents, each day they kept him was a triumph. And something
tugged at their subconscious. Maybe, just maybe. . .

But after each hospital stay, weary and drained, harsh reality
returned. Matthew, the Easterdays' first-born, would not live to
adulthood.

So Matthew's parents faced each day as it came, touching and
loving the boy, wrapping him in as much devotion as possible until
that inevitable day they knew was coming.

It came recently at Sturgis Hospital, two days after Matthew's
sixth birthday. Death took from the Easterdays what doctors, medicine, years of care, concern and closeness, could not deter. Not even
love.

Alice Easterday remembers those hospital days and nights, but
does not despair. "Matthew was born with several handicaps. He was
deaf. He had poly cystic kidney disease. He had diabetes, was subject
to seizures. I guess we always knew we would lose him young. But
yet, we hoped. . ."

What finally took small Matthew's life was heart failure. That gallant heart had beat on long after the measure of time doctors gave him.

In a soft, controlled voice, Alice Easterday talks about Matthew's life. And though she does not realize it, there is a bit of wonder, a sense of triumph that creeps into her words when she describes that long battle Matthew and his family fought.

The Easterdays were told after one of Matthew's operations in 1978 he had six months left. "But we were lucky. We got the kind of care that Matthew needed. We wrapped up as much love in our son as possible in the time he had. I believe that love sustained Matthew that extra time," Alice said.

The battle was not easy. The Easterdays have two daughters, Abbie, four, and Suzanne, one-and-a-half. Taking care of Matthew meant time away from the girls. But Alice believes what most parents who face problems such as Matthew had believed: Those who are well will adjust as long as there is sharing and love. Matthew's short time on earth demanded something extra.

Extra Matthew had. And it came from many individuals. Alice is especially grateful to Dr. John Robertson, Matthew's pediatrician. "You need someone who recognizes what you are going through. Someone who does not question, but offers understanding. That was Dr. Robertson."

And always, Alice's mind returns to those hours in Sturgis Hospital. Hours when Matthew was restless, when only his parents' hands could comfort him. "Those people at Sturgis Hospital. . . I can't begin to tell you what they did for us," Alice said. "They knew Matthew needed to be touched. They would round up the most comfortable chair to ease our tiredness."

Alice said the hospital staff went beyond their normal duties. "Matthew became their family. I guess it boils down to the fact that with Matthew hospitalized so often, they helped us raise him."

"And when Matthew died, they cried with us."

Mostly from that agony, Alice's mind focuses on those hospital hours and the time spent rocking Matthew. Rocking was all that seemed to soothe him at times. "I spent hours there, holding him, comforting him, trying to ease his pain and fright," she said.

But even Matthew's parents determination could not fight death. The rocking ceased.

Those hours of cramped weariness were paramount in Steven and Alice's mind in the days immediately after Matthew's death.

Alice recalls during that terrible time she came to realize bits of comfort helped to bear the long waiting hours of someone's death.

She knew how much the little things extended to her family meant while they waited at the hospital. Time and again her mind returned to the pediatrics ward at Sturgis Hospital.

And that is why the pediatrics ward has a new, upholstered rocking chair, a gift from the Easterdays.

Alice knows it will be appreciated. She knows many people will use it. "We're giving back part of what was given us."

She also reasons some small boy may be rocked by this parents through an illness that frightens him. The rocking will soothe him. His parents will draw a measure of physical comfort from the chair.

And maybe, when the rocking is over, the little boy will go home with his parents. Alice Easterday hopes for that more than anything.

She Keeps the Flame Burning

May 19, 1984

Dorothy Cossairt is no dreamer. She believes dreams become reality only if you work at them.

She's working.

If you see a strange-looking figure on county streets or in schools, granges or club meetings, rest assured it isn't foolishness or early Halloween.

Far from it. That's just Dorothy in her Statute of Liberty costume, on her way to drum up funding to restore the proud Liberty statute in New York Harbor.

Dorothy, 49, is wife to Therman "Stub" Cossairt and mother of four sons, ages 10 to 31. While some women would be content to sit back and take things easy in the midstream of life, Dorothy says she's just beginning life.

A native of Florida, but longtime Burr Oak-Colon resident, Dorothy is a patriot. A pure, undiluted patriot, who isn't ashamed to say so. She's the kind of gal who sheds tears when the colors pass, when the band strikes up the National Anthem.

Dorothy and Stub are active in the American Legion and Auxiliary, being longtime members of Post 354 in Colon. Both have served in important offices. Dorothy, for instance, is president of the

Auxiliary now and is past president of the district unit. She is now district treasurer.

At one the Auxiliary meetings, Dorothy learned of the fund drive to raise monies to restore the Statue of Liberty.

As a volunteer aide at Colon Community Schools two mornings a week, Dorothy realized she had not heard anything at school about the fund raiser.

"I believe kids, especially, should be aware of this important fund drive," the vibrant, outspoken Dorothy said. "I figured I had the time and inclination to do something."

Do something she did – and is. She fashioned a costume in copper hues. With head and purpose firmly established and her "light" held high, Dorothy marches into classrooms, grange halls and clubrooms to emphasize the need for American citizens to join her parade.

Dorothy figures if the original drive in France to raise funds for the statue came from donations of less than a dollar, then surely Americans can do no less than to give a bit of themselves for a symbol of what Americans stands for.

"Everyone should become involved," she said. "The Statue of Liberty is a national treasure, our heritage, our beacon of hope and light to the world. We cannot let that proud statue erode further. We must work to preserve its quality and meaning."

And so, that copper-colored costume will be seen in many places in the next months. And don't laugh. Dorothy is serious in her quest and determination.

For those of you who would like to join that quest, feel free to call Dorothy and set up a club meeting date with her. She'll go anywhere to spread the words of the Statue of Liberty.

Come to think of it, for a rather short gal, Dorothy Cossairt stands pretty tall – just like the Statue of Liberty lady. Very tall in patriotism.

Her Light Still Burns Brightly

May 26, 1984

She died quickly, like a bright flame extinguished before the candle burned long enough to shed light.

But she shed light in her short lifetime. And its thoughts about her accomplishments during those years that light the dark moments for Cindy Briggs' parents, Larry and Judy.

Larry agonizes about his young daughter's death at the age of 20, but realizes that without remembering the good times, the laughter, the successes, life would be unbearable without his sunshine girl.

Those successes were many before the car crash that took his oldest daughter's life.

"I guess it tears at me that she might be forgotten," he said softly, still finding it difficult to speak of death and endings.

She was a golden girl, in most everything she did. Her family takes solace in that she tasted life with a flavor unquenched up to her last moments.

Cindy was a champion athlete. A three-time swimming champion, she excelled in competition, winning many medals, her coach, Ray Martin, said. "Very few swimming stars – very few – are named to the All-State Team three times in high school," Martin said. "Cindy came into my program at the age of 12 and I coached her through high school. She had drive, she worked hard at goals she set up for herself. Sometimes those goals seemed pretty strong to me, but Cindy insisted."

Martin remembers Cindy was well-liked, was named varsity swimming team co-captain three years. "And Cindy gave up much for sports. She gave up a lot of social events in order to compete."

Martin was hurt deeply by Cindy's death. "We were very close. She was a sweet kid. She worked as assistant coach to help others. She was great in supporting her younger sister, Laura, in her swimming career. She was a warm, personality-loaded girl."

Carol Griffith, softball coach, also remembers bubbly, out-going Cindy. "She was always enthusiastic. Always here at practice time. Swimming came easier for Cindy than softball, but she made up her mind that she could make the team, coming out in her sophomore year. She was named most improved player in her senior year. That's unusual when you join a sport that late. She ended up as a starter."

Martin and Griffith said it was difficult when students learned of Cindy's death. "She was still so close to school," Griffith said. "On the bus ride to a game, the kids were sober. They said they were going to win the game for Cindy. They did. There was no rejoicing after the game. The kids were all crying."

And because of that kind of attachment to Sturgis High School, because their daughter held athletic programs so dear, the Briggs family established a scholarship in Cindy's name. Handled through the athletic department, the fund will support swimming programs.

Martin said he hopes enough money will be added to the fund to allow use of the interest. "It would make a lot of sense," he said quietly, "to send some kids to summer swimming camp. To help them develop into the kind of athlete Cindy was. Besides our good memories, a tangible part of Cindy would remain at Sturgis High School."

That same thought eases the dark moments for the Briggs family. As Martin said, "Cindy was special." The Briggs take comfort in that.

Hairbrushes Lead
You to Trouble

June 2, 1984

A lady called me a while back and mentioned she liked a story about cellars that appeared in this column space. Seems we had some of the same ideas about old times and use of places and things.

We recalled many items: pitcher pumps, loud screen doors, radios with crystals, milk cans.

And then, the conversation got more personal. We exchanged several laughs and reminiscences about our childhood and growing up days.

One thing in particular we discussed was brushes. Hair brushes.

Now, I always thought hair brushes were most useful. To begin with, being a tomboy, hairbrushes for me didn't mean brushing my hair, but they worked pretty good on cleaning sand burrs from the dog's fur.

Which brought me a paddling with the same brush, as I recall.

That hair brush disappeared, by chance. I know who found it: my Dad, when he spaded the garden the next spring. I also know how it got buried in the garden. I knew the guilty person pretty well.

Brushes also were good for scratching one's back. They were good

246

for making designs in sandpiles. They also were great for dipping in paint pails and flipping paint at someone.

More spankings. With paint designs on you know where.

Brushes were good for whacking wasps that strayed into my bedroom from the attic. They worked pretty well to anger the wasp if you missed on the first try. They were questionable when you missed the wasp and batted out an upstairs window.

They were also great for tossing out the window of the top barn floor to see if they would land handle first in the mud hole in the pig pen, or seeing how many bulls-eyes you could score in cow piles.

Life, as you may have guessed, was rather colorful and aroma filled on a farm.

I was sometimes forced to tackle the real use of those brushes. My youngest sister, Donna, had long hair. She usually wore it in braids, which my mother carefully wove each day. Now, if you have ever worn braids (which I never did, thank heavens), you know how tangled, how snarled, hair becomes. When mother was ill, I got the challenge – and chore – of untangling that hair. I learned early on how to get out of the job. Hair bristles can be murderous to the scalp if you press hard enough. Amid determination from me and resulting wails from Donna, I was relieved from the job.

More spankings.

Well, I never said I was a perfect kid. I never aimed to be one. I still wonder how many prayers my folks must have made to change my errant ways.

I hear the new owners of the farm found a couple of hair brushes in the old garden plot after we moved away.

John Schworm left his Mark

June 16, 1984

John Schworm says he's retired. Nobody's betting on it, including his wife, Opal.

Schworm, who lives on South Lakeview, Sturgis, is the kind of fellow who finds work interesting. "Good for you," he drawls.

Schworm was born in Howe, Ind., and began adult life as a school teacher. That lasted three years. Turns out he taught country school near Orland, Ind., a couple of years and then taught at the orphans home near LaGrange, Ind. one year.

When it appeared Schworm was going to be moved back to a one-room country school, he decided it was a bit too much.

"Looked elsewhere for work," he said. That search took him to the Harold E. Beadle Store in Sturgis. Beadle had purchased the Burdick business. The store was on the site where Bisel's Store later was located, on Chicago Road in downtown Sturgis.

When the Hagerman-Freeland Block on Chicago Road was built, Beadle moved into the building.

Schworm went to work for Beadle in 1928. In those days the trade was mostly floor coverings, carpets and window shades.

"I guess those first 20 years I was on my knees in about every other home in the city, laying linoleum," Schworm said.

In 1945 Milton Seger bought the Beadle business and kept Schworm on. In 1954 Seger moved to the E.C. Wright building, where Seger's is now located, on the corner of Chicago Road and Clay Street. Wright was Seger's father-in-law.

The store was modernized. Sundries, jewelry, glassware, gifts and draperies were added to the growing business' line of goods. Seger's became a popular spot in Sturgis.

Schworm had his own "corner" at Seger's. "I pretty well took care of the draperies, notions," he said. "I sure put up a lot of draperies in this county."

When Robert Myers bought the store in 1973, John was past retirement age. He had retired once before, but stayed on at Milt Seger's request, working part-time.

Believing Myers probably had his own crew to handle store duties, John went to the basement to "pick up my tools. I stopped by to wish Mr. Myers well. He looked surprised. Asked me where was I going."

Myers told Schworm he hadn't considered replacing him. "You're too valuable to me." And so, Schworm's "retirement" continued, although he worked only half days until his official retirement last January.

Schworm admits he'd still be working if "my legs would hold up," but figures it's time he and Opal did some more traveling. They used to travel a lot.

For now, the couple spend much of their time working in their immaculate flower and vegetable gardens.

Schworm said he will continue to make furniture. That's another of his talents. He grins a bit when he speaks of an old cherry tree he "grew up with down in Indiana." Seems Schworm cut it down when he and Opal were married back in 1932, and he used the wood to make furniture for their living room.

His woodworking talent is obvious. Items in the Schworm home and furniture he made for friends shows fine detail and craftsmanship.

And what does the 83-year-old Schworm intend to do next? "Never know," he said. "I always look ahead. Have all my life. Each day is a new one. New opportunities to excel, to share experiences."

But his trademark is left in one place, the Seger store, where John Schworm spent the major part of his life.

One can't turn his back on something that's being shared for 56 years. Schworm is proud of the 56-year record with the Beadle-Seger-Myers folks. Mighty proud.

Making a Case for Being Stern

June 23, 1984

I must have been a cruel mother. I never let my kids run free in laundromats. And they weren't allowed to open sealed boxes at department stores and run toys up and down aisles.

There's a bit of the wicked in me that says I wish I had let them loose a bit.

Especially when I get run down from behind by a four-year-old wielding a fast-moving laundry cart.

Now my girls were big enough to help sort laundry, but the younger kids, the boys, were required to sit on the chairs when they accompanied me to public places.

Not that they wouldn't have run a few carts if I had let them. Not that they were perfect angels. Hardly. They knew every trick in the book – and they travel when they got a foot away from me.

They tried it a couple of times, I'll admit. But those were times when they didn't sit down – they hurt too much. They stood against the wall, glaring at me as I recall.

It amazes me how some kids, and mind you I said some kids, are turned loose so often. How they keep from being picked up or hurt is beyond me.

But, getting back to my laundromat days, I should add I've

experienced sucker sticks thrown into my washer, had my clothes baskets disappear.

And, speaking of baskets, I remember standing speechless while a youngster calmly walked up to the basket and went potty in it.

When I admonished him, the frank young man cut loose with some of the most colorful language I've heard.

And then, to rub it in, his mom (I assume it was his mom – who knows when no one had been near the kid for more than an hour) lambasted me for "picking on my little kid."

I wish I had picked on him. Ever try to clean up potty remains in a basket? No fun, I can tell you.

Maybe I won't be spoken to again, at least in friendship, after this column comes out. But it sure would be nice to be able to sit down in a public place and not have some youngster toddle up and plant two chocolate-covered patties on my freshly dry-cleaned slacks. It sure would be nice not to have a kid toss a pop bottle and have it clang down on my foot.

You might think I don't like kids. Sorry, you're wrong. I love them. And I have grandchildren who know I'm a soft touch. I truly like kids. I also like kids whose parents teach them a few manners.

Come to think of it, the kids aren't to blame. They don't know any different. And, to be charitable, I realize mothers are tired and laundromats can be a busy time.

But I sure don't want to have that potty routine repeated.

Shriners Help Boy Step Ahead

June 30, 1984

Mike Carper is off and running, thanks to a plucky spirit. And he runs on two feet, with an artificial leg supplied through efforts by the Sturgis Shrine Club.

Mike has known more misfortune than most fellow his age. He developed osteogenic sarcoma – cancer – two years ago.

The cancer was discovered in June 1982. Mike underwent four sessions of chemotherapy. He experienced the devastating embarrassment of losing his hair. And pain. Lots of pain. He underwent a skin graft on his arm because of a reaction from chemotherapy.

Mike lives with his mother, Marsha, his sister and grandmother on Jefferson Street in Sturgis. His parents were divorced eight years ago. Mike learned early to deal with that trauma.

Dealing with cancer at the age of 12 was harder. Mike admits it. While most kids his age were thinking of bicycles, fishing, ballgames, Mike's concentration focused on a simple course: living.

Overwhelmed at the possibility of his future – if he had a future – Mike underwent surgery in September 1982. Doctors removed one of his legs four inches above the knee to guard against the cancer spreading. That danger still lurked, because Mike's type of cancer has a history of spreading to the heart and lungs.

Though those months, the Sturgis Shrine Club played an important role in Mike's medical progress. Not one cent was charged to his family for transportation, and later hospitalization and medical treatment at Riley's Children's Hospital in Indianapolis.

Ken Johnson, who chairs the Sturgis Shrine committee to help people in Mike's predicament, said that's what the Shrine Club means. "Helping those who need help. Especially kids," Johnson said.

In December 1982, Mike traveled to Illinois to be fitted for an artificial leg. Again, the Shriners picked up the tab. In February 1983, Mike tried out his new leg. He had a wheelchair and walker, and his mother thought it would be some time before he mastered the new leg.

On the second day, Mike walked by himself. "He had his life ahead of him and he didn't want to waste it," his mother said.

Mike received lengthy physical therapy at Sturgis Hospital and other medical facilities to learn how to walk properly. The Shriners were "always there. We never had to worry. A phone call and there was the Sturgis group, willing to help," Marsha said.

Mike has broken the new leg several times. "Well, he's an active boy," his mother said. "Each time, the Shriners stepped in and had the leg repaired."

Mike, an eighth grader at Holy Angel School, plays kickball, swims (without the leg) and rides his bike. He has adjusted to the new leg and doesn't consider it a handicap, his mother said.

He's even taken to visiting wards at children's hospitals, showing other kids they can triumph over losses such as his, life goes on, there is meaning in their world.

Mike will return in September for a new leg. Like all kids, he's growing by "leaps and bounds and the leg is becoming too short," his mother said.

If someone asks the Carper family about the Shriners, prepare to hear a long tale. Marsha can't say enough to express her thanks for the moral and financial support the Shriners gave in her family's time of need.

But others know. For instance, in Michigan last year, the state Shriners sponsored medical care for 610 children, 258 of them new cases. There were 312 cases closed, meaning medical care is no longer needed. Six clinics are sponsored by Michigan Shriners. At least 324 youngsters found medical help at the Chicago Shriner-sponsored hospital as surgical or outpatients.

Nationwide, the Shriners have four hospitals to treat burned patients – at no cost to patients or families. At least $32,580 was spent by Shrine Clubs to provide transportation to hospitals. The 1984 Saladin Foundation had a budget of $250,000. And work continues to support a total of 22 Shrine Hospitals. A new hospital is being built in Tampa, Fla. It costs $110 million a year to operate all Shriners hospitals. It can run $1,000 a day to treat a severely burned patient, Shriners say. One child's treatment came to $840,000, Shriners said. All free. All paid through nationwide Shrine fundraisers.

Those statistics astound people who hear them the first time
Not Mike Carper. He knows firsthand.

The spunky youth was too busy to take time out to be photographed by the Journal staff. "He's busy. Life is too challenging for him to stand still," his grateful mother said.

One kid. One life. Heading toward the future on two legs—one of his own and one contributed by a caring Shriners Club.

A Little Good
Sometimes Helps

July 14, 1984

Sometimes, if one is fortunate, good things will come into your life. Like Lou Moon, my elderly gentleman friend, whose death I still mourn.

Lou came into my life when I needed him most. Our friendship continued only through letters. We never met.

When Lou died, something special went out of my life. I missed his notes and letters.

Shortly after Lou died, another fellow came into my life, as if Lou had willed it so.

Ralph Clemmons, a former Sturgis fellow, started writing to me. So now, to take some of the edge off from missing Lou, Ralph's paintings, wry humor and notes keep me watching for the mail.

Ralph has a way with words. Even the newsroom staff takes an interest in his witty letters. Some of his watercolors I will frame. They are gems.

Having this kind of job, I get somewhat accustomed to being phoned and berated about mistakes the Journal makes. I feel journalists should take responsibility. But sometimes, the verbal abuse is pretty bad. I've been shouted at, sworn at, threatened.

My colleagues and I don't want to make mistakes. We feel the embarrassment, the shame, quicker than most. Our errors are in print forever.

Coupled with that is the knowledge mistakes can hurt the public, ruin a story about them they wanted to keep.

I understand their anger. I respect their right to tell me about it. But I can't understand how verbal abuse comes so easy.

I've received unsigned letters about editorial stands. I happen to recognize the handwriting. I wouldn't say a word to the people who wrote them because I respect and like those folks. They were angered at my position and said so. They even went so far as to say I shouldn't berate Gov. James Blanchard for not showing up at our Michigan Week kickoff parade because he was receiving a personal award out of state.

The writer pointedly said I probably never turned down the chance to receive a journalism award. Oh yes, I have. The latest time was the same week I got that letter. Duty kept me here at the Journal. That's part of life.

I guess what I'm saying is everyone has feelings, including the so-called tough press.

And that's why notes from Lou Moon were appreciated. And why notes from Ralph Clemmons are special.

I should add Lou Moon didn't always agree with me. Lou said it like it was, but always with grace. I knew his point was made. I was toned down – but gently and left with some measure of dignity.

Part of getting along in life, I believe, is understanding the faults of others. I don't expect to find a perfect individual out in the public

– and surely there isn't one here.

Lou and Ralph were right. A little good goes a long ways farther than the bad.

Just Call Me Confused, Please

July 21, 1984

Why is it directions always confuse me? Or is it because I don't follow them?

For instance, the Mister at my house claims I haven't learned to put the plastic tag back on the bread wrapper after I'm done with it. Then, why is it I can never find the blamed tag? He claims it's because he finds them all over the place, such as in the refrigerator, on the window ledge. That's hard to believe, of course.

And tell me, please, why directions on the big boxes of laundry soap say "Push Here To Open" and all that gives is my fingernails?

And why is it when I go shopping the things I want to sort through are always on the lowest or highest shelves? Everyone knows I'm a big girl and I can't bend down that far, and my tummy won't allow me to stretch close or high enough to reach that elusive shelf.

And why is it the car always needs gas when the Mister happens to leave his billfold at home? Is that why he allows me to drive?

And those television programs. The producers must spend weeks gloating about how they will run the good programs at the same time. I will never believe ABC, CBS and NBC feud. Not by a long shot. They must sit in their ivory towers and think of how they can pool their so-called wisdom and frustrate us common folks.

How come its always me – who ought to know how to choose ripe muskmelons – who manages to either buy a green or a mushy one?

And then there are the labels on canned goods. Someone will rip off the label to get some free coupon offer – before the can is open. Oh well, it's always interesting to see what vegetable we end up with at mealtime.

I think I have the only family whose members buy shoes and only try one on – and months later learns they are different sizes. What fun. Now I know why the kids walk so strangely.

I swear I'm the only woman on our block who had the clothesline break just when all the white clothes were hung. The other women's always managed to break when overalls were hanging.

And if I remember correctly, I believe I'm the gal whose kid always told me it was his time to have a cake raffled off during the athletic game intermission. Told me about an hour before the game.

Maybe that's why I hid the bugger's jock strap once in a while. I believe in being fair, even if some folks call it getting even.

And how come my kids had a knack for catching chicken pox, measles and mumps in one winter – all three of the older ones. The youngest kid never caught a communicable disease in his life. He's 25 and I still check him over when he comes home. And while I'm at it, let me tell you I know why they call them communicable diseases. Because no one wants to communicate when those nasty kids catch 'em.

I'm also the person who can wait in line patiently to purchase a bargain – and the commodity runs out just when I reach the head of the line.

There's another thing I seem to be rather good at: I can bust those little caps off from canned pop easy – before the can opens, of course.

I guess if there is a mud puddle to step in, I find it. I even weeded my flowers one year and thought rain was dripping softly on my hair. Hardly. Just the tar from the roof where the Mister had patched a hole. Never, never, never weed close to a house that has a tarred roof, especially in hot weather.

And there is something else. Dozens of people can sit under our huge maple tree – and out of that mass, I'm the only one the darned robin baptizes.

I guess I ought to know by now that I'm a hard luck gal. I should have realized it when I was a kid and we used to go swimming in the creek out in Trayer School territory. Most of the kids picked up one bloodsucker – if they were lucky. Talented me usually could climb out of the creek with a couple of dozen.

So I suppose I shouldn't expect order in my disorderly life. But when I go to all the trouble of folding my washcloths into a matching towel and then find some member of the household picks another washcloth . . . well I can lose my temper.

A guy called me here at the newspaper some months ago and complained that one of our stories on one page was supposed to be continued on another. He was nice enough; just wanted to know which page the rest of the story was on because he wanted to read it.

I didn't have the heart to tell him it wasn't on another page. Why should he be privileged to have the same bad luck as me?

I have a monopoly on that area.

Warm Memories of the CCC

July 28, 1984

They were young, poor and without motivation. For some youths, caught up in the hopelessness, the turmoil of the Depression, there would be no future.

But a new vista beckoned. Those who tried it found a new path, a measure of success.

They earned about $30 a month. Twenty-five of that was sent home to keep the family fed. In some cases, it was the only family income.

And serving their time, earning their keep, some men found a mission in life, a haven. A reason for pride.

They were the CCC.

Most were young, few were married. Their officers were members of the regular Army. Rules were rigid. Work was hard, living difficult.

But at least they had a place to sleep and eat. And the feeling they were men, not vagabonds. Previously they were called bums, but that monicker drew few derogatory remarks because most of America was bumming in those days.

I knew many of those 1930's fellows. The Upper Peninsula town I was raised in, Sidnaw, had a CCC camp at the edge of town. There were more than 300 men stationed there before World War II.

During the war, the camp was used to house German war prisoners.

My memories of those CCC days remain strong. My mother hired on to wash officers' clothes. And many of the men were guests at our table.

One, Capt. Arthur Wermuth, later gained worldwide fame as the "One-Man Army of Bataan." His face and deeds were spread over *Life* magazine pages. I recall him only as a young, lonely man, far from his birthplace.

My mother's food drew some of the boys to our home. Most of the young guys missed their homes and mothers.

The CCC units were organized 51 years ago. The first camp was named Camp Roosevelt in honor of President Franklin D. Roosevelt, who championed the corps development.

The projects the men completed those earlier days are evident today: Parks, roads, forest preservation, bridges, campgrounds. They worked well. They built well. It was a lasting endeavor.

And the men remember.

Thirty-one years ago, members of CCC Company 556 barracked at Pokagon Park, Angola, Ind.

On Sunday they will return to the campground. Young bucks who tossed shovels of dirt in the 1930s now cradle great-grandchildren. They may be far older in age, but their memories are as close as yesterday.

Ask Jim Sendo, Mendon. He came out of an orphanage in his teens, with no home, untrained for the Depression world, unskilled in earning a living. That is if a living was to be found.

The CCC was his answer, and he is proud of that service. And quick to boast about it. The CCC gave him direction, motivation.

After his CCC and war service, he worked his way through college and eventually joined the staff at Western Michigan University.

But of all his accomplishments, Sendo holds the CCC years closest. He will rekindle that spirit Sunday with his friends at Pokagon when they gather for a reunion.

The first project the CCCs completed at Pokagon was the park shelterhouse. A county bridge was the next job. Many of their projects remain in the park.

But Sendo and his friends have another goal. They intend to record their CCC experiences. Sendo explained "we have to put down historical notes. After we are gone, the memories, too, will go. We must have personal reminiscences and documentation of those important years."

And so the men will put down, not only in writing, but in voice, what the CCC was and what it meant to them.

And Sunday, Sendo will spend a day with important people. Men who are part of his youth, his dreams, his long-ago goal for a future.

Sendo admits he will shed a few tears.

He's not a bit ashamed.

Goodbye, Christopher Robin

August 4, 1984

He came to the Journal 11 ½ years ago, a young man with a mission. He wanted to become a top newspaper writer and photographer. He did that. And added something more to the Journal: Vitality and spirit.

And he became my friend.

I should be honest. Trace Christenson is like a third son to me.

And here I am, wondering how I allowed it to happen again. I know from experience how it feels to care about someone at the Journal.

The old-timers in the community will remember Bill Light, the personable fellow who worked several years on the sports beat. That young man became family to me and it hurt like the devil when he left. We are still close friends, but it is long distance. That makes it tough.

It comes full circle and here I am again, wallowing in self-pity, in sorrow that Trace transfers today to our sister paper at Battle Creek.

I call him Kris, a nickname his family tagged on him as a small boy. He has always been Kris to me, will always be Kris. I'm the only staff member who uses that monicker and he tolerates it. And sometimes, when the mood is right, I call him Christopher Robin.

When you become attached to someone, you tend to assume you have a right to interfere in their life. If I think Kris is out of line in his personal behavior, he hears about it. He suffers the indignity of listening to me – and holds his tongue.

When he hurts, I hurt. I try to hide it, but when you've raised four kids and have a bunch of grandbabies, the maternal side emerges. You want to help, to share, to laugh and to cry.

Kris and I have a wealth of memories of our years at the Journal. We've gone through some leadership crises. We suffered the insult when our old computer system tested our last ounce of strength. And in the midst of those miserable times, when I was at my lowest mood, Kris' wonderful cynicism from his corner desk never failed to dilute the problems. That cynicism always tinged with humor – and I need humor in my life. I will be forever grateful to Kris for that.

And there are memories of other times, when we staggered in the midst of abuse from the public, took deep breaths and forged ahead. We've been cursed and berated. And blessed. And we hold close the other side – thoughts of the public's warmth and understanding.

Kris should have left the Journal long ago, simply because he is more talented than most small newspaper writer/photographers. His talent with the camera is unforgettable. As unforgettable as the photos that graced the Journal's pages these many years. The awards he won, not only for himself, but the Journal, are proof his peers found his work exciting and superior.

We will not find his replacement easily. I already know that. Few journalists today can handle writing and photo duty with equal skills. Few even want to attempt the challenge.

There is always more to life than a byline, a picture credit. There are things like dedication, dependability, sensitivity and grace. Kris' pictures were not always received with warmth, especially the photos that intruded on the public's feelings. But Kris, knowing photos, as words, are the mirror of life, continued his path of honesty and truth.

That is hard for any individual, but rare to find in a man as young as Kris.

Kris can be serious when the need arises, a keeper of confidences and sources when a story is developing, and a man of his word. He was always candid with the public in handling an assignment – and when that assignment was finished, he had the sense to leave it behind him.

In one of my lighter moments, I told Kris he'd better straighten up or I'd adopt him. That seemed to be as bad as anything that could happen to him. (At least he smiled). Or maybe it was a smile of resignation.

If one shares good moments with another, there is always a feeling that maybe, just maybe, the friendship is mutual.

So, Kris, my own Christopher Robin, you are stuck with knowing in some small way, you belong to me. Because if you love someone you can never really cut the ties that strongly weave a bond.

I will miss his grin, the comments from his desk in the corner. That corner will always be a bit empty for me.

Somehow, writing this, it's like I am sending another kid into the world.

I miss him already.

On Track to the Railroad Days

August 11, 1984

I wish Amtrak would get back on track. For a lot of reasons. One being I'd like to take a trip and the possibility of running off the tracks somewhere doesn't sound like much of a vacation.

Another reason is more personal: I've been crazy about trains since I was a child. Some of my best childhood friends were train engineers, trackmen and gandy dancers. If trainmen had mascots, then that's what I was.

I remember when trains did it all. Moved the vegetables from California to the East and fruit from one coast to another. Trains were the pathway to the world beyond – and the dreams all kids held dear.

In the Depression years another commodity traveled the rails. They were the people out of work, the hoboes, who traveled the railroads and established camps alongside the tracks. Those camps, called hobo jungles, cropped up all over this nation, as a generation of men sought the way to a future.

We had a hobo jungle outside Sidnaw, the town I lived in up north. I was forbidden to go to the jungle, but being rambunctious, I went.

It was another world. And those men, who never acted anything but respectful to me, opened my eyes to what misery really was – and how the human spirit can prevail.

I remember sitting by a fire one afternoon (there was always a fire going in the jungle) and one young man with tattered clothing and pain-filled eyes spoke about another time.

"You remind me of my kid," he said finally, stoking the fire with a long stick. He was silent a long time, as he moved a tin can filled with turnips and carrots closer to the flames.

He never looked at me, but bent his head lower. "She's one fine little girl."

In bluntness and innocence, I asked "How come you left your kid?"

"Weren't enough food for all of us," he said, with a finality in his voice even in my youngness I knew was the truth.

The hoboes weren't tramps. Even if some people called them bums, they weren't bums in the sense the word is used today. They received that monicker from bumming around the country, looking for work, searching for some measure of stability. That stability was a long time coming. It was so long coming I didn't recognize it when it did arrive.

The hoboes came from the field, the farms, the factories, the cities of America. Not one region was immune to the Depression's relentless onslaught.

One fellow I talked to was from Nebraska. Now, Nebraska to me meant words and pictures from books, an ever-stretching land I thought had promise and a magic way of producing food.

The Nebraskan was sad. "Oh, yeah, in good times, Nebraska has everything. But now . . . well there's nothing there. Nothing to make a living on. I've got to keep looking. I'd be a burden back home."

I used to wonder why my mother always fed the hoboes that wandered from the railroad grounds to our house, which was just across the road. It wasn't just food. I know now it was something more. She was a mother, a housewife. There were kids in our family, parents, an established routine. We went to school, church. We gathered in the town for picnics and town meetings.

It was simple enough. They were homesick. My mother knew it – and did not question.

She treated them with dignity, as though they were guests. They used the outhouse, drank from the same dipper in the water pail, took baths in the Sidnaw Creek before they came to our supper table.

And they did something else. Those hoboes taught me to dream. They opened my eyes to other places, traditions and this nation's wealth of changing landscapes.

The only thing about the hoboes that distressed me, but which irresistibly drew me like a magnet – were the songs they sang. At night, I'd sneak out the door and go with my friends to their campfires. Their songs were haunting revelations of their broken dreams, the frailties of life, fate's dealing of the cards and hopes and loves lost forever.

Some of those songs, if I happen to hear them on some vintage program, never fail to draw from deep within me a sense of sadness. And a sense of determination.

I wonder about all of those men, so many of them young boys, and where they went on to and what became of them. They were good boys, from good homes, but turned loose in a bewildering, unbending world not of their making.

I hope they found a measure of their dreams and at least a token of what they deserved.

And mostly, I hope one Nebraskan hobo returned to a little girl he loved so much he left her so she would have enough to eat.

Down Memory Lane to School

August 18, 1984

I knew someday I would have to write again about Trayer School. But I am a bit selfish with my memories. Some I can write about; others I store like hidden treasures, available only to myself.

I went back to Trayer School last Sunday. Almost. Actually, it was a reunion of Trayer School alumni, and it turned out to be a reunion of memories.

Trayer School is no longer there in terms of the physical structure. But in the minds and hearts of those who attended that one-room school house, it remains. It is alive as the recollections of the children, teachers and parents who spent so much time within its walls.

Trayer School burned down several years ago. The loss devastated the Honey Lake community in Branch County.

The first Trayer School was established in Noble Township in 1840. Classes ceased in 1962. Three structures housed school children during that time. All were lost to fires.

In years past, rural schools were the backbone of the community. It was no different at Honey Lake. Trayer School was the focal point. There were church meetings there, picnics, community gatherings.

Just about every kind of session possible in a farm community was an event at the school.

Schools knit communities. They draw them together, cement friendships more solidly, enforce lifelong commitments.

Country schools were much different than town schools. I know. I attended both. I don't mean to take anything away from city schools, but there still was an aura of oneness, of togetherness about country schools.

When I arrived in the middle of fourth grade at Trayer, the nation was on the brink of World War II. But in the quiet community, there was a feeling of contentment. The outside world seemed far away to a young kid content with neighborhood life.

My first teacher at Trayer was Avis (Smith) Brothers, a lady I proudly say is one of the best teachers I ever had in my lifetime. I only had two teachers at Trayer and the other one, who will go unnamed, didn't teach much. We did sing a lot. And swim in the creek and play baseball. Apparently the teacher enjoyed music more than mathematics. I learned many songs – and regret not learning mathematics.

Life a Trayer School was a mixed experience. We walked more than a mile to school, regardless of weather. We carried our lunches and shared or traded food. On cold days we would gather around the floor register in the middle of the room to study. Avis used to have to start the fire early in the morning. Oh yes, in those days, one did that. A teacher was janitor, instructor, playground supervisor, ball team coach. And thought nothing of it. That was the way it was.

Sunday, when we gathered at the Harold Shufelt home on Round Lake Road for the reunion, people kept arriving in cars. We gawked.

There were questions of who was arriving and, my, hadn't they changed.

One must realize for some people at the reunion it was the first time they had seen classmates in years. I met friends I hadn't seen in 35 years. Saw some I hadn't run into since 1941. That has to be a shock both ways.

My good friend George Mayer, who knows all my younger day secrets, also has a passion for telling them. None was lost during the day, I might add.

Names kept cropping up during the picnic. Mayer, Cary, Beery, Shufelt, Nofsinger, Phillips, Jones, Botzner, Shultz, Pagels, Fennell, Arver, Burnside, Miller, Grove, Hackett, Royer, Monroe, Moffett, Eberhard, Bontrager, Garbine, Hurley, Bowdish, Gable, Russell.

And memories emerged of those already gone. Some far too young, like Marjorie (Cary) Cossairt, the lovely lady and fine mother, who lost her battle with cancer. And so many recollections came forth about others who graced this world during their years here.

But there were happy times recalled. Such as when we pulled jokes on teachers, the many Christmas programs and events when the school would be jammed with proud parents.

Sometime during that sunlit afternoon last Sunday, watching the grandchildren and children of Trayer School alumni, we spoke about other days and where the world is going.

Eventually it boiled down to wishing the world would slow down, people would return to the neighborly attitudes they had in those long ago years.

Mostly, there was a prayer gatherings such as one Sunday would continue. That friends would gather again, and places as beloved as Trayer School would be remembered.

A Cry that should be Heard

August 25, 1984

She was only a few days old. Her eyes, which had opened to the world a short while before, were large and luminous. She was the cuddly kind, who might fit just right in some caring person's lap.

Instead, the small kitten was thrown away with the garbage.

Worst yet, she was infested with fleas. Maggots had wormed their way inside her, eating her flesh.

Her faint cries were heard two weeks ago on a hot summer day. A young boy walking past a dumpster behind a Sturgis business place looked in and found her.

Investigation would determine the kitten had only been in the dumpster overnight. It had been emptied the day before.

The message was simple: The kitten meant nothing to someone and she was thrown away like yesterday's trash.

The youth's family tried to help the kitten, taking it home and tending to it. But the kitten needed experienced medical attention. The family called Pet Haven for assistance.

Officials at Pet Haven attempted to keep the kitten alive, and with help from a caring veterinarian the plucky kitten rallied. But the maggots had done their work. The kitten died.

Lois Rosenberg told the kitten's story. Shock and disbelief crept into her voice. "How can anyone do such a thing?" she asked angrily. She knew the answer – because she and Pet Haven officials have seen what mankind can do to God's creatures.

Lois, secretary-treasurer of the Pet Haven organization, spoke of inconsideration in handling animals.

Just the past weekend another small kitten was discovered in the middle of the road, and a kindly motorists stopped. The kitten was starving, dehydrated. She could not be saved either and her suffering was ended in a humane way.

Pet Haven is a non-profit organization, with no facility to house pets or cast-off cats and dogs. Operating through the assistance of veterinarians, who cut the cost of their fees, the unit has one means of support: Donations from individuals and organizations.

Donated food also has helped the program stay afloat financially.

Pet Haven, simply enough, exists only on paper – and in the hearts of people who care. Pet Haven will accept animals families cannot care for or don't want, but Pet Haven must rely on foster homes for the animals until a permanent home is located.

"We have several foster homes where pets can be kept for a short time," Lois said. "Our goal is to keep animals from being destroyed. We are an alternative to the dog pound and animals having to be put asleep."

Animals turned over to Pet Haven are checked by vets. In many cases the animals are neutered or spayed.

A co-op index of people who will temporarily care for a pet is kept at all times by Pet Haven. Numbers are available in case of emergency.

If someone wants to obtain a pet from Pet Haven they must be referred by a veterinarian. "We must know that a family or person not only wants a pet, but has a record on file of past history in taking care of an animal. We don't mean a one-time visit to a vet, but continued good care of animals."

If a pet is placed in a foster home, Pet Haven usually picks up the vet and food bills. Sometimes the foster homes are able to handle the food bill, but generous neighbors in some instances make the difference in what Pet Haven can do, Lois said.

The basic goal of Pet Haven is to provide homes for animals and control animals through neutering and spaying programs. Pet Haven officials promote good animal care.

"We will not buy an animal," Lois said, "nor do we sell one. We are looking for good homes for animals."

Since Pet Haven was established a little over three years ago, 360 dogs and 380 cats have been placed.

Lois cautions stray or unwanted animals should not be left at foster care homes. "We must have animals registered in our files, so we know where foster homes are available for what animals. Foster homes are not dumping off places. Each home is carefully selected. We work closely with foster home officials to ensure they are notified ahead and can handle animals."

"We are, simply said, an animal adoption agency," Lois said.

Anyone can join the Pet Haven crusade by sending donations to Pet Haven, P.O. Box 853, Sturgis, MI, 49091.

And maybe, if individuals will think first and care a little bit more, there will be no more calico and white kittens thrown out like yesterday's used trash.

September School
Blues Return

September 1, 1984

It is that time of year again. September. The month means many things. A new beginning of sorts for those who choose to plan it that way. Or the end of an unhurried summer.

For the past several years, it has meant something else to me. An ending.

I no longer send a child to school.

Oh, I may say it's nice not to worry about lunch tickets and class schedules, but it would be false to say I don't mind.

Hardly, I still miss so many things. Each year the edge comes off the pain, but it is still there. I don't have a child to worry about.

I will miss the arguments, the morning re-change of clothes until just the right dress is chosen for school. Oh yes, in my daughter's school years, they wore dresses. And I will wonder if kids attempt to dress like their best friends.

I miss the phone calls from a distraught kid who forgot lunch money or left the tickets at home. It would be fair to say I'm not too sorry about that being over.

But there is so much more. Like the boys who flocked to the yard after school when they were youngsters, and ate me out of all the homemade popsicles. In those days, you couldn't buy popsicle sticks, so we scoured the town for them, boiled them an hour and reused them. Talk about all the sugar I used to freeze those popsicles!

And I defy anyone to tell me you can raise healthy lawns and kids at the same time. Not if you really allow kids to use your yard. My yard never knew what it was like to sport anything green until three years after the last youngster left for college.

I will never again experience the pangs of walking a kindergartener to school and leaving him. Of my four kids, two were hesitant to let go of my hand and two were eager to begin the first day. One bluntly told me "go home." I could have swatted him.

And the stories some of them told during "Show and Tell." One discreet teacher advised me she was sorry to hear my husband and I were having problems. Turns out I had lost my temper and said I was going to leave forever. I said a lot. Not my husband's fault, just my exasperation of being tied in a house with four kids. Needless to say, it took a lot of explaining. I don't think the concerned teacher believed me.

And the broken bones in athletics. One son did it up right. Broke a wrist in a fall from a school swing. Did it again the day before football season opened. Same wrist.

Report cards. Who will miss them? Me. I sat on the porch in good weather, waiting. If a kid brought a bad mark home, I could always tell by watching the road. Eventually the errant kid would peek his head around the Johnson house next door, looking for a swift way around me. I was always waiting.

I sent those kids to school and they didn't just get a ho hum if their marks were low. They were disciplined. Disciplined hard. Never did bother one kid, though.

I wish again for the prom days, when hesitant boys came to the door and tried to get the courage to knock. And watched radiant daughters grasp the arm of their beaus as if their new world was wrapped up in them. And I grinned a bit when I saw the scowl on their father's face. He never thought any boy was good enough for his daughters.

And I will miss the washdays, when just about everything possible, from pencils, gum (used), nasty notes from classmates, and frogs (dead) were removed from school pockets. Did you know you can tell more about your kids from what they carry around than what they ever confide to you?

I realize I said many times I would be happy when I didn't have to keep meals warm each night for four kids because school schedules didn't overlap close enough, or ball practice was staggered. It isn't true. I enjoyed it. I miss those young men and women who overflowed the house, who slept in corners or four to a bed, who could find food where I hid it. Kids who filled the bathroom sink with hair strands of all colors, and tracked mud on brand new carpets.

I never knew how many kids would be at the supper table. I know there were few times when only four were there.

And I suppose I will never attend an athletic event, graduation, or Honor Society induction without feeling a bit lost. I will never feel the same when our school team runs out on a court or a ballfield with the colors and numbers brightly saying what school we are. And knowing special names will not be there again.

Oh, yes, school has started and for some parents it will be a relief they can pack the kids off and sit down for a minute. Well, let me tell all of you harried parents there will come a time when you will regret not spending more time with the kids. And feel despair you may not have listened close enough to a teacher when she said a kid needed more help.

I have found one avenue of repose these days. I have grandchildren. This week I complimented the grandbabies on their new school clothes and got a special charge when one granddaughter asked my opinion on her new gym clothes. I grasp every straw I can.

But it is still not the same as when my own kids were in school. September has come again – and I still mourn.

Tomorrow is Surely My Day

September 8, 1984

Tomorrow is National Grandparents Day. I love it. But selfishly, I hope my brood doesn't all decide to come say hello to the Mister and me on this special day. Have you ever been invaded by kids of all sizes and temperaments? Did you ever add up the number of arms and legs of several kids and try to find lap enough for all?

I used to think my own kids couldn't be topped by anyone else's. Well, that was before grandbabies came on the scene.

There was a time I believed it was nauseating for grandparents to carry scads of kids' photos in their billfolds. That was my biased opinion before I had a grandchild. Opinions change, let me tell you, when a grandbaby comes onto the scene.

When else can you spoil a kid rotten and not feel guilty about it (and secretly feel satisfaction at finally getting even with the kids' parent)? What fun it is to watch a grandchild throw a tantrum and realize nobody will blame me. After all, I didn't rear the rascal. Doesn't fall to me to take criticism, thank you.

And where else can you find such a generous person as the grandchild who lovingly offers you his most treasured gift – a toad? That's love, I tell you.

I've got nine of the little ones, ranging in age from four to 12.

They have blond, black and brown hair, and eyes that run from black to blue. And temperaments that would test the patience of a pope.

I think I added up all the nationalities of these grandchildren once and realized we have Irish (it gets the blame for the tempers, of course), German, English, Pennsylvania Dutch, French, Spanish-Mexican. Don't ever let anyone say I'm a bigot. With this family?

Those kids have names that are a cross section of America: Stephen, Charlie, Becky, Matt, Natalie, Nick, Jimmy, Blake and Hollee.

I wouldn't trade one of these youngsters, but I am more than ready to send them back to their parents after a few hours. I tell you, it's a good thing nature decreed women should have children at certain ages. I couldn't handle it at my age.

But there are times when being a grandmother pays off, such as when a parent reprimands one of the kids and they remark "I'm going to run away – to Grandma's house." I love it.

Seriously, grandparents are necessary in every kid's life. Grandparents are far enough removed from kids to value their innocence, their questions, their honesty. Grandparents, if they are smart, hold their tongue when a kid misbehaves, and know when to hug and when to pat – on the rear, that is.

A child needs the comfort and security of knowing there are grandparents who will love them, right or wrong, and who think they are the most fascinating things God put on earth.

I grin a bit when I listen to some the folks who recently were blessed with a new grandchild, or perhaps their first grandchild. Ran into Howard Kendricks the other day. They welcomed their first grandchild – and the first boy in the family. Now that child wonder was touted all over Sturgis. And Donald Easterday had a puffed-out chest for the new grandson named after him. And I know the happiness of the Sam Curriers, who received a welcome present in their first grandson after several girls.

I knew those grandparents' pride would be re-echoed whenever another child came to bridge the generation gap. Having been there, I know it well – and offer no excuses for biased pride.

And while I'm at it, perhaps I should mention that it's been more than four years since we've had a grandchild at our house . . . anyone listening?

Let's Share Their World Again

September 15, 1984

Two county women observed their 90th anniversary this month. Each has given more than her share of time, energy and dedication to this county. And love.

Love is perhaps the most important ingredient the women have in common.

One lady is Esther Hartman. The other is Nora Hagen. Both are longtime Sturgis-Centreville area residents, but now reside in nursing facilities. Esther lives at the Clark Memorial Home in Grand Rapids. Nora resides at Fairview Medical Care Facility in Centreville.

Heart is what makes people stand out. Heart is what makes people notice Nora and Esther.

Esther is remembered as Centreville's most extensive letter writer. Write she did, from World War I through the Vietnam war. She wrote as many as 50 letters a day to service personnel during World War II.

Esther got a lot of response from soldiers and civilians. From that following she initiated the "Ringing Bells for Peace" crusade in 1951. She got hundreds of churches and courthouses to ring bells for peace July 4.

She has many honors, including being named Centreville's Santa Claus for 30 years, visiting hospitals, homes, shut-ins.

And Esther still writes to service people and wears the American Flag pin.

Nora Hagen started life in a homestead on Sauger Lake Road. She loved the country, animals, flowers and nature. When her folks died, Nora continued living in the Centennial Home near Glen Oaks Community College.

Nora never married. But she had children. Hundreds of children. Nora taught school in Burr Oak, Bronson, Sturgis and St. Joseph. Language and literature were her courses, and many a student will remember she was a strict, but fair instructor.

Her life was dedicated to students. A child of Henry and Johannah Hagen, she encouraged education to anyone who would spend time of day with her. Her nieces and nephews remember she preached one should work hard to obtain the best education possible.

Born in the log cabin that preceded the large home she was reared in, Esther knew the meaning of family. And she knows the meaning of brotherhood.

In her later years, Esther decided to donate her land for a college site. She also donated the family homestead to Glen Oaks, retaining a life lease on the property.

Nora best liked the quiet life, reading, tending her garden and flowers. But she welcomed visits from folks who stopped at the spacious farm home.

Esther and Nora spend their time today in places away from their beloved homes.

Reaching their 90th birthday is no small endeavor in this busy world. Nora will observe hers Sept. 23. Esther's anniversary is Sept. 29.

For those of you who remember what these women gave this world, perhaps a card or call would be a small token of appreciation. It would certainly brighten their days. A visit would be better.

The County Fair is a Grand Place

September 22, 1984

Fair week. I don't know what it means to other folks, but it means many things to me. And if you haven't journeyed to Centreville for the Grange Fair, it's about time you did.

What you'll get from it is pride. Undiluted, immense pride.

First of all, Fair Manager Floyd Loudenslager has put together a county fair second to none in this state. Apparently he must have the right crew working for him, because communications and events have gone smoothly and on time.

For those of us who consider the fair part of our lives, this week in September is special.

I first started going to the fair as a young child, usually riding the school bus for an all-day outing.

We didn't need chaperones in those days. You were always safe at the fair. Enough of your family friends were around to keep you in line.

During high school, we rode rides, pitched in (literally), helping our 4-H friends who had animals to show. We slept overnight in the barns. We cooked sloppy joes over campfires and roasted potatoes and apples in the coals. Life was a bit more simple then.

Kids teamed up with students from other towns and formed lasting friendships. We hit every eating joint on the grounds and every booth on the midway. And mixed the heady aromas of the horse barns and the doughnut shop.

And all this on $4.

Through the years fair events attracted people of all ages. One of the most popular spots always has been the Grange building. For those who believe the Grange is for older folks, be advised to step inside their building today and notice how many young people tour it.

And who can resist wandering over to the merry-go-round and watching the small fry. Does this tell us no matter how many years have passed, how many generations, the merry-go-round is still popular?

Think of how many times we've visited the animal barns and marveled at what rural youths are doing today in this time of big farm takeovers. The small farmers still produce bright kids, who end up champions.

Those 4-H'ers. Their achievements continue to astound me. If there is a category to enter, you'll find an entry. And what prizes. Competition that guides them to being better human beings.

Think of all the 4-H leaders who provided leadership for those kids. Consider the time and effort involved.

And if you want to get a lump in your throat you should attend at least one fair sale in your lifetime. Watching proud kids as their prize entry is auctioned off is a bittersweet moment. I've seen more than one kid shed tears.

Maybe it's a mixture of things, this event called the county fair. A mixture of friendship, fun, and awe. A viewing of harness races and grandstand shows.

Whatever its drawing card, the county fair is a mainstay in September. A grand way to begin winding down the year. Try and get there today. It's your last chance this year.

Fall brings Golden Memories

September 29, 1984

I lost him in another season of the year, but it is always fall that brings him back to me. And though I have written about him before, the memories return unbidden.

When leaves start to spiral earthward, covering the ground with a patchwork blanket, the memories come back the strongest.

The man who shaped my young life the most was my mother's brother.

He was the last of the clan, born after seven sisters. It was as though the Powell genes had, in one last effort, put all their Irish markings on him. His face was the Ireland map. Curly red hair, freckles and a temper to match the mold.

Although he was my uncle, I always called him Don. That was his order, not my choice.

He went with me one fall, when I was a kid of seven, to hunt colored leaves to take to school. He followed my begging to fetch the reddest, brightest leaves at the top of the tree.

But then, in pensive tone, he told me I should gather some of the yellow and orange leaves, the softer shades.

"Kid," he said, in that soft drawl I loved so much, "you have to have some of the less pretty ones, the ones from the shade, to make a complete bouquet."

I guessed, as best a youngster can understand, he was explaining what he had said once before when I told him he was my golden boy.

"Naw, kid, I can't be your golden boy." But seeing the hurt on my face, he grinned. "But I'll be your silver boy."

He looked away. "Silver tarnishes you," he said.

I did not fully understand until many years later what he meant.

He lived hard and fast. He drank too much, always had a girl hanging on his arm. He was quick with his fists.

But I knew the gentleness in him, as only a young child can know. He could build a kite that flew high. He knew where the arbutus grew. He could mend the wing of a bird and then give it back its freedom. He loved the outdoors. He showed me where the beavers dammed the pond, where the wild geese flew undisturbed by man's intrusion.

And he taught me about life's harshness. He asked no quarter from any man and certainly gave little.

He learned to drink too young, my mother and her sisters would cluck. And then, when their mothering instinct for their sibling surfaced, they'd say Don still searched for the mother who died when he was seven.

I always knew where to find him when he erred. At his mother's grave. I knew better than to question why.

I realize now why he paid so much attention to me the year I was seven. My mother was hospitalized with an illness that threatened her life. Not one other family member understood why I sought the solitude of the woods.

Don did. He searched me out and said only "I know."

We lost track of him for years, of his choice. He was ashamed he had done so little to make a good mark on life.

We know some things about those years. During World War II he left behind in England a bride he would not bring home because he felt he had nothing to give her.

Later, in a relationship with another woman, a child was born. He named the baby after his mother.

And when his woman died, he signed papers so his cousin could adopt the child because, as he wrote me, "It was best for her."

That child came to his funeral, brought by her parents who understood his sacrifice in giving up the child he adored. She was told about her real father.

Each fall I remember so many things Don said to me in my early years. He scorched my feelings once when I felt betrayed by a childhood friend. There was no sympathy, only rage that I did not have the courage to overcome my hurt.

"There's no prizes for just living, kid," he said. "If you get down and have to fight alone, you'd better find the starch to hang in there."

Many years later, lying in a hospital when the knowledge life might be taken from me, it was his words that came back to me.

I know he was not a golden boy. He was a silver boy who tarnished his own life, without much help from anyone else.

He died in his thirties, much too young. And alone.

Well, not quite. He took part of me with him. That's how if felt when I heard he was gone.

Someday I will find the daughter he loved enough to give up, my red-haired cousin Athena, and tell her the good things about her father.

Love Always makes Difference

October 20, 1984

They call him "Skeeter," but his name is really Millard Harvey, Jr. He's 29 and lives in Colon. To say it up front, in medical terms, Skeeter is mentally handicapped.

But his sister, Vanessa Kurzowski, also of the Magic City, says his family and friends don't really categorize Skeeter. "If you knew Skeeter as I do, you don't think about that," Vanessa says. "Sure, he can't do what a lot of other people can, but Skeeter has brought more joy, more richness into our lives than you can imagine."

Skeeter was born in Germany, while his parents, Millard Sr., and Alberta, were in the armed services. Skeeter had a tough time coming into the world, but hasn't stopped going forward since.

Skeeter is a man with a mind of his own. And Vanessa knew Skeeter had promise. She was determined he would have his chance. She pushed, she supported Skeeter attending Pathfinder at Centreville, a training facility for people like Skeeter. That was back when it wasn't know as Pathfinder and sessions were in a church. Only three people attended. Skeeter was one of them.

Two years ago, Skeeter graduated from Pathfinder. His family was there, smiling through proud tears. Vanessa's smile, friends say, was the biggest.

And, not being one to sit on a subject very long, Vanessa encouraged Skeeter to work at ARCH, where he earns money to help provide his living. "And he's proud of it, too," Vanessa says.

Skeeter is a vocal person. According to his family, he is a happy, warm individual. He loves to hug folks, Vanessa says, and always is first to say hello and shake hands. "He knows no stranger," Vanessa says. "He radiates friendship. That's one of his strong points."

Skeeter holds his own in the family and takes an active part in activities. Vanessa invited him to participate in her wedding – and he did. "And had a grand time, I tell you," Vanessa says.

There's another side to Skeeter. He has loved country singer Glen Campbell for about 18 years. According to Vanessa, Skeeter plays Campbell's records over and over and carries them around.

"He has lived, breathed and worshipped Glen Campbell – and that has been his focal point in life," Vanessa says.

That got Vanessa thinking. Maybe, just maybe, there was a way Skeeter could meet Campbell. Her friend, Nancy Percival, knew about WESTOPS, the public service office at Western Michigan University. The office can do about anything, Nancy says. So Vanessa called and told them about Skeeter. They got in touch with Miller Auditorium Manager, Ken Farrance. The wheels turned. The next thing Vanessa knew, arrangements were made with Ron Newhouse, road manager for Campbell, so Skeeter could meet Campbell when he appeared in Kalamazoo.

Recently, Skeeter met his idol, backstage at Miller Auditorium. Vanessa said for once, Skeeter was speechless. "He was so happy."

Campbell asked Skeeter to sing with him in the dressing room. Skeeter did – a Campbell song.

Vanessa said it was one of her happiest days, because she knew what it meant to Skeeter.

It is evident there is a special closeness between Vanessa and her brother. She treats him with respect and nudges him to excel. "I guess I push him sometimes," Vanessa says, "but I know he can do better. And eventually, he does."

One reason Vanessa cares so much about Skeeter is because she's his sister. But the main reason is probably because Vanessa has the rare capacity to look at Skeeter as a human being, as a person who is special for being himself.

Vanessa has an important character trait that is most evident when she speaks of handicapped people.

"I guess I just consider them individuals," Vanessa says. The truth in that statement is borne out by another: "Sometimes I forget Skeeter is mentally handicapped."

How Come the Kid Out-Authored Me?

October 27, 1984

I remember him most as the kid next door who couldn't swing a bat worth a darn. He was an intense, wiry kid, but smart. He could talk on the same level as an adult when he was 11 years old.

He had that one problem, though. He confided to me one day he couldn't hit a baseball. Being an old softball player, I figured I could remedy that. I stood him up against the back of the house and pitched away. He learned to bat.

I never did tell my mister what caused all those paint chips and dents in the siding on the house. That kid missed a lot of balls before he finally got the swing of it.

And here he is now, an author. Who'd have thought it?

Certainly not me. Oh, I knew he taped some spots for radio broadcasts and wrote articles for several publications.

But now I hear Ted Stone, oldest son of my neighbors, Tracy and Shirley Stone, Burr Oak, has written a book.

Sure puts me to shame. I haven't done that. Probably never will.

Ted was a joy to have next door. He was energetic, warm – and outspoken. He had solid views on politics and didn't hesitate to say them.

His life has turned around completely from what I thought it would be. For instance, let's discuss animals. Ted loved animals. But he was the only kid on the block our hoot owl (we raised one from a baby) couldn't stand. Every time poor Ted tried to touch Hoot or talk to him, that owl would puff up like a basketball.

And here Ted is now, a rancher of sorts, and owns land near Eriksdale, Manitoba, Canada. He and his wife, Patti, have two small daughters they are teaching about life on their acreage, named "Wild Rose Farm."

Ted and Patti raise sheep. Patti takes the sheep wool and does all those intricate things you do before it becomes something to wear. She dyes the material with wild flowers and then weaves beautiful shawls, blankets and other items. Many of her creations are in stores in Canada and some available in Michigan.

Ted's book is called "Hailstones and Hoop Snakes, Tales From the General Store." And that's what the book is about. Ted might have been a talker in his early years, but he was – and still is – a better listener. From those memories and his travels he collected stories told around pot-bellied stoves, general stores, fencerows and park benches. His stories portray people who are close to the land, to their neighbors.

Point is, some of Ted's characters in the book have a tendency to stretch things a bit. But all the stories are pure and simple Americana.

Come to think of it, I recognized some of the characters, or think I did. My worst thought when I started reading the publication was I might find some vestige of myself.

Thank God he still respects age.

I've not visited Ted and his family, but some day I'd like to travel to Ted's place. I'd like to see how the world was when it moved at a slower pace. I can only remember what it was like around the Depression, which is as far back as I care to remember.

I've read Ted's book a couple of times. It still amazes me how well he puts his words together. I hope other folks feel the same. His writing certainly is good. Anyone who wants to get a copy can contact his parents in Burr Oak.

And to think the darned kid never asked me about words, or writing. I can't take one ounce of credit for him doing so well as an author.

Darned if I don't wish I had never taught him to bat that ball. Never pays.

Hospital Stay What You Make It

December 1, 1984

I'll be back at the Journal next week, finally. And for those of you who wondered where I've been, you might say I just finished paying for an exclusive medical room, by way of Borgess Hospital, Kalamazoo, and Sturgis Hospital.

Seriously, I learned something from this recent heart problem: I know I have limitations. That is the hardest fact to accept, but I learned it the hard way.

A card from a lovely lady named Eleanor Eckhardt said it all. Her words will be my motto. She said "It is easy to go from working to live, to living to work." How true.

I learned something else. I realize working for the public means there are many people who know me, but their faces and names are hard for me to sort out sometimes. But I've received calls, letters, visits and cards from folks out there in three counties. Some were people I had never heard from.

One indignant lady, however, called me up and angrily demanded "How dare you quit the Journal? I like your stories!"

Well, I never did get in enough words to explain I had been on sick leave, not an exodus. No matter; her call gave me a chuckle. You need a bit of laughter in the middle of an illness. At least I do.

And while I'm at it, I have a few reflections on hospitals. And please, all my good friends in the medical world, don't call me. You know how much I respect and love you, but there are some weird things that happen in hospitals.

Like at Borgess in the intensive care unit. There were three patients in the room, with one television set. The set was controlled only by the middle bed. The patient they put in the middle bed was deaf and blind. Nice lady, but that TV didn't help her, let alone the other two. No TV.

And for all of you who cringe at the sight of those big needles, let me inform you those little "butterfly" needles for blood can be as painful on the top on your foot as the needle to take a blood gas sample from an artery.

And no, heart cauterization isn't as bad as you might think, or maybe it's because I'm a nosy reporter and had to know what everything was all about.

Still, there is one problem during cauterization. They go through the femoral artery in the groin and feed a catheter up into the heart. Then they inject a dye. Now, that dye causes instant warmth – and you swear you've wet your pants. I wasn't satisfied until the technician checked and assured me I hadn't lost control.

And then there was the episode in Sturgis Hospital, when my old friend in radiology, Dr. Ormsbee, came in. Now, to set the scene, there I was, on my stomach, with the X-ray machine immediately over my back. My head was buried in a pillow. I couldn't move, my behind was uncovered. I was, quite frankly, exposed.

In comes Dr. Ormsbee, who can see only the obvious. He calls out merrily, "Hi, Carol."

How'd he recognize me?

And tell me, please, why bedpans don't fit. They really don't. But at least that beats something else that I haven't told anyone about before, because I didn't know who might recognize whom. Borgess has a new potty. A gentleman patient ambled into the sunroom, did his duty on a large potted plant and ambled out. Being a courteous person of sorts and not too surprised at what takes place, I didn't question.

Oh, I can tell you lots of things patients do, too, like dumping medicine out the window. Fools. Why do they think they are hospitalized? Maybe they are in the wrong kind of hospital.

Being a practical joker, I usually turn medical problems into a bit of fun. I was wired up to a portable heart monitor tape for 24 hours last week as an outpatient. Now, the thing is, you keep a diary of everything you do, sitting, walking, working, sleeping, medication. And sex.

How in the world one can engage in anything romantic with a four-pound package tied around you, and five electrodes taped across your chest is beyond me.

But I did have this little notion, mind you, to write sex in the diary and then let the experts in Kalamazoo try and figure out why nothing different showed on the tape during that time.

I didn't.

But to all of you, the hundreds it seems, who asked about me, who cared enough to stop by, my grateful appreciation. And to those of you I did not know, rest assured you will never be a stranger to me again.

One Needs the Right Xmas Tree

December 8, 1984

I went Christmas tree shopping this week. Let me tell you, I ran into some polite people. It's a good thing they are patient. I'm probably the pickiest person around when it comes to trees.

I usually have to have a tall, fat tree. Now, trying to find a tall, fat tree is difficult. There are tall and skinny, short and fat trees, but few tall and fat trees.

I'll bet I spend an hour looking at trees. And the people who sell Christmas trees have to be the most patient folks in the world. It must be a bit tiresome to tromp all over the lot and hold up about 50 trees for picky old me.

To explain why I chose such a big tree, you have to remember I'm from the Northern Peninsula and haven't forgotten the times when my family journeyed into the woods to select the right tree for the holidays. It was some event.

I suppose with my folks making such a big deal out of Christmas, the tradition continued on in the children. And that's strange, because we didn't have fancy wrapped, store-bought presents in those years. But we had love.

Some Christmases were sad. My folks were ill a lot and they were hospitalized three Christmases. Two years they were in different hospitals. I also spent a Christmas in Sturgis Hospital a few years ago after surgery, but the hospital staff and my family made sure things were as normal as possible.

Another reason I'm so particular about tree selection is I have about 600 tree decorations. That's right, about 600. Don't ask me why. I have boxes and boxes of them packed away. Upstairs and downstairs.

Most of the decorations are homemade. Years back, when the kids were small, we'd go to Belle and Vic Decker's home. Belle and I made ornaments and decorations the whole month of December. I still have most of them, even though they are getting tattered and worn.

My family also has had strange encounters with Christmas trees. One year the overladden tree fell in the middle of the night. The noise was shattering. The kids woke up and one remarked Santa Claus wasn't very nice to knock our tree down.

Another year we had just installed a new sub floor in the living room and the Christmas tree we chose was rather large. The Mister got mad after wrestling with the tree for an hour. He finally solved the problem. Nailed the tree to the floor.

So, this week, I will begin sorting out the many decorations, put a wreath on the front door and wait for the visitors.

And I will remember the early years when stringing popcorn and cranberries was a tradition in our northern home.

And recall how my father could never wait until morning to awaken the kids to see what Santa left us.

Maybe my dad knew he and my mother wouldn't be around many years to share the Christmas seasons with us. My folks even missed out on knowing most of the grandchildren. If we still had him, I know my dad would awaken the grandbabies shortly after midnight.

I don't know what other folks are doing for Christmas, but I hope their holiday will be as joyous and satisfying as mine.

That's what Christmas should mean.

UAW Local 797
Thanks Their Man

December 15, 1984

Kirsch Co's United Auto Workers Local 797 displayed their solidarity Friday to the man who taught them what the word means.

The union repaid Chuck Williams, in part, for his long service to Local 797.

By recommendation of the UAW executive board and a union membership vote, the building on South Centreville Road in Sturgis was officially named the Charles N. Williams Hall, Local 797 UAW.

It was supposed to be a retirement party for popular Chuck, known in union circles as "The Young Turk."

But the secret about the hall dedication was kept secret from Chuck.

Old-timers from Kirsch know what the honor means to Chuck. Building a union hall had been a long time dream. That wish was realized during Chuck's tenure as Local 797 president.

The idea for the building dedication surfaced in October when Gene Trine, union president, said something should be done to acknowledge Chuck's union efforts.

Gene, not the kind of fellow who would simply present a

certificate, took the proposal to the union membership.

Then it was secrecy time – and anyone who knows Chuck realizes keeping a secret from him is near impossible. He's been known to finagle all kinds of information concerning contract negotiations and union business.

Chuck has a long history with the UAW. His early career began as a fiery, outspoken union member. He'd be the first to admit he hasn't mellowed much when it comes to union work. He's fought for equal pay, benefits, increased management-union cooperation.

And drew grudging admiration from the other side of the table – management – on his ability at the contract table.

Chuck's tenure with Kirsch began at the age of 18 in 1946, making 93 ½ cents an hour on the second shift. He left the company in 1948, but hired back the next year.

In 1951 he was recalled to armed forces duty, serving in Korea. He returned to Kirsch in 1952, where he was elected union steward.

He was named Local 797 president in 1953 and in 1955 took a nine-month leave of absence to help the Furniture Workers Union organize plants in Michigan, Illinois, Indiana and Kentucky.

In 1956, Chuck served as union committeeman and was re-elected Local 797 president in 1961.

He moved up to UAW international representation in January of 1965.

A former Sturgis resident, Chuck and his wife Barbara Jean live in Vicksburg. But not for long. Their hearts have always been in St. Joseph County and they'll return here soon. They hope to locate along the St. Joseph River, a favorite spot for fisherman Chuck.

The couple also intend to travel and spent more time with their children.

And Friday night, surrounded by UAW friends he served so many years, Chuck accepted a plaque representing the union hall dedication. Joining Trine in the presentation were union past presidents Louis Green, Kenneth Culp and Charles Keefer.

A union move to the end.

The Heart Knows
the Difference

December 22, 1984

Mary Buono, wife of Mario and mother of four, has many reasons to celebrate Christmas this year. The main one is being alive.

Mary, formerly of Sturgis and now of Kankakee, Ill., is a fighter. But Sturgis, Burr Oak and Bronson residents who remember the young Mary they used to know, wouldn't recognize her now.

Mary is 100 pounds thinner and off the insulin she took for years because of diabetes.

And all because Mary is a fighter.

She had to be. Mary underwent three open heart surgeries in as many years. She has had 11 bypasses.

It wasn't accomplished easily. Mary, the shy girl of rural Trayer School days in Branch County, is a new woman. Husband Mario, who worked for years at Garden City Supermarket in Sturgis, testifies to that.

Mary was forced to make a complete change in her lifestyle. To live.

Mary's heart problem emerged in January 1981 when doctors found 95 percent of her heart arteries blocked. Four bypasses gave

Mary a chance for survival. But losing weight and overcoming her smoking habit were necessities in her health schedule.

Stopping her smoking habit was easy, Mary said. Losing weight wasn't. Mary had never "done anything athletic in my whole life." She found walking difficult, so she began private swimming lessons to make exercise easier.

"When I swam the length of the pool the first time, it was a milestone," Mary said. "It was the most athletic thing I had ever done."

But fate again intervened. Heart pain returned a little over two years after her first surgery. Tests revealed a new problem.

This time, however, Mary's specialist told her nothing could be done. Her condition would not allow surgery.

In that moment, Mary changed. She vowed she was going to live. She and Mario had weathered many crisis in their lives. She remembered difficult times as a youngster. The product of a broken home, Mary and her sister and brother were raised by their maternal grandparents. Her grandfather lost his life in a home fire.

But Mary prevailed. When her doctor walked into her room the next morning, Mary greeted him with a smile. He had told her the day before she would be bedridden and probably die within a year. Now, at the sight of her smile, he realized that Mary wasn't giving up.

Neither was the doctor at that point. Another surgery was scheduled June 22, 1983. Although Mary had only a 20 percent chance of survival, she came through the operation with two bypasses. Mary went home with a firm attitude to make her life better.

She struggled. She lost weight, improved her exercise program.

Again, tragedy struck. Mary was hospitalized last March and

underwent a third open heart surgery, with five bypasses. This time, a new technique was undertaken. Surgeons grafted fabric on the back side of her heart to make it easier if surgery was required again. Surgeons assured Mary that if more operations are necessary, they will be able to perform them.

So, what's Mary doing now? She has a busier schedule than most folks who have never been ill. She speaks to clubs about coronary disease. She visits patients in the cardiac units at hospitals, offering them living proof that one can survive serious heart problems.

But Mary recognizes it took more than physical strength to get her through her surgeries. She knows her faith brought her along the road to recovery. She also is aware she needs the help to handle stress which surfaces when she realizes surgery may be necessary again.

So Mary faces reality. She meets with a Christian counselor to help her handle the mental stress. Mary is up front with statement that you can't always handle problems alone.

It is a new Mary who prides herself on her accomplishments. There is a new assertiveness in her manner. She looks and acts years younger.

Her mental attitude is centered on "living today, while planning for tomorrow." She vows she will not die without reaching her full potential.

And this year Mary Buono will observe a special Christmas with her family and friends.

She has made up her mind that dying is relative. Mary believes it is more important not to let something die within oneself while one still lives. That something is one's spirit, a commodity Mary will not allow to be conquered.

And this joyous holiday season, those of you who want to re-member a spunky Mary Buono may find it rewarding to take the time to drop her a line at Rt. 4, Box 306, Kankakee, Ill., 60901. Or call 315-939-7480.

You'll be surprised – and happy – to hear what she has to say.

New Year brings Commitments

December 29, 1984

I didn't write the customary New Year's resolution column. My resolutions seem to come easy and disappear just as quickly.

But I do intend to take time this year to talk more to people, to drive quiet countrysides and reflect on God's splendors, to walk a little slower and enjoy the prattle of the grandbabies.

There are reasons for these promises to myself. Although I've said them all before, I mean them this time. And coming to a commitment to do all these things came hard, by way of a hospital stay.

Like meeting new friends. Oh, I had heard their names for years, read the happenings on our news pages, but I did not really know them well. I do now.

There is J.C. Perry, a wonderful gentleman who gave me some information for story, but took the time to come back into my office for a chat. A lovely man.

There is a fellow who had a comment on how we could do things better at the paper. We talked a long while and I hope we learned where each is coming from. I found him to be a likeable, informed fellow. I hope he stops by again.

There is my unmet, but close friend Ralph Clemmons of Seattle, Wash., who entered my life just after I lost my old friend, Lou Moon. Ralph's notes, letters and drawings spark my days. I love him. I wonder if somewhere in that place we mortals have not reached, that Lou did some arranging on my behalf.

There are special people in Leonidas – and they know who they are and what they mean for their kindness to me at a time when I really felt down.

There are the Labon Smiths, a delightful couple my husband and I have come to know quite well. Their friendship has enriched our lives.

And so many people who somehow crossed my life the past year and convinced me this world is not so bad after all. Compassion, empathy, the caring and reaching out of people is still there. How well I know.

I could write about a Sturgis businessman who provided a needy family with some necessary items at Christmastime. All it took was a call and the response was immediate. I did not dwell before on people behind counters, but a gut feeling told me to reach out and ask the businessman to help a family less fortunate than his and mine. And I learned another valuable lesson: Those people look beyond the everyday scramble for a buck.

I remember two doctors, Hugh McCullough and Vicente Cabansag, who went beyond the usual care for a patient during a trying time. They'll probably be a bit embarrassed when I blab this. Tough. I'm not too swift on some things, but I recognize when some-one goes the extra step. They don't know that I'm aware they made calls to Borgess Hospital before I even arrived there on an emergency transfer. I know they didn't sleep much that night and kept in close touch later to learn how I was doing. I don't forget such things.

And there is the young kid whose name was lost to me in the rush of a noon deadline, who called to say "I like you, lady." God bless such kids. (Now, if I could only find out why he likes me.)

And the boys at Queenie's, or the Golden Cone, or whatever the proper store name. Those fellows' witty comments keep me on my toes. Journalism toes, that is. They sure can lay it on. I love it.

I shouldn't forget the boys and girls at Gannett Corporate, for bearing up under my never ending tirade on where I want to see this newspaper go. Surprisingly, they agree more than the public realizes. So I'm telling the public.

But mostly, this new year will mean new responsibilities, new challenges, and old commitments that must be realized.

And one new commitment: No resolution, just a firm resolve. I'm going to listen a little better to people, learn a whole lot more, and appreciate the things that make my life meaningful.

Happy New Year to all of you.

The Happy Man Has a Story

January 19, 1985

He is a man with minimal education in the halls of learning, but matchless in his knowledge of how to live.

At 86, he is still active, a recent traveler to Hawaii. He also is a man who does not live in his yesterdays. Remembers them, yes. But he knows time does not wait for him so he travels with it and cherishes it as a gentle companion.

I call him Happy. So does everyone else. Few hail him with his proper name, Angelo, and still fewer people know his first name is Willman. So there, I have said it all: Willman Angelo Botzner of Honey Lake, Branch County.

Well, there is something to add. That monicker is his second legal name. The first was Baby Weaver. He lost his mother at the age of two and his father turned over his care to his sister and her husband, the Botzners, who adopted him.

Happy learned an important trait early in life: he knows how to be a neighbor and how to treat his friends. Ask anyone in the Honey Lake community. Happy is a man respected for his warmth and wit, his word and integrity.

There's more one can say about Happy Botzner. He was pretty much of a confirmed bachelor until pretty Erma Unterkircher came along. Now, everyone knew Erma was much younger than Happy. That didn't bother the wonderful lady named Erma. She knew the worth of the love of the man called Happy. She married him. When the first child came along, some questions arose on whether Happy would live long enough to see the child grown. No worry. The three Botzner kids, Caryl, Clyde, and Mary, are full grown and settled. And Happy, still going strong, is living it up, visiting one child after the other, taking heart in his grandchildren.

But doing it without his beloved Erma, who died a couple of years ago of a swift moving cancer.

There's another tale centered around Happy Botzner for years. Seems when his mother died, the family returned to Honey Lake by train from Grand Rapids, where they had been living. The body of Happy's mother was in the baggage car ahead of the coach.

Happy, at the age of two, was confused and a bit restless. When a woman traveling on the train heard him ask, "Where's Momma?" she heard the hushed reply "she's in the baggage car ahead."

The woman was so touched by the incident she wrote a song, "In The Baggage Car Ahead."

Happy has heard the song, but doesn't remember the name of its author. He recently visited the home of new neighbors and they sang several verses for him. And then another friend hosted visitors from Pennsylvania, one of whose mother had known the song's composer. The woman repeated several verses for Happy.

Happy said he didn't know about the circumstances of his birth until a half-brother told him. He now knows the Weavers buried in Fry Cemetery in Branch County are his natural parents.

Happy does not dwell on what might have been. The Botzners

raised him and loved him. He had a good life and does not regret one minute of it, except for losing Erma.

I am sure the lady of the "baggage car ahead" would be proud of the baby she bore, the fellow, Happy, who is the epitome of the word character.

This makes Swimming Success

February 2, 1985

Ever wonder what the Knights of Pythias and the Pythian Sisters do? You'd be surprised. The group is much more than a service or private club. Members also reach out to provide assistance to the community. Especially youths.

In one case, it is Sturgis High School's swimming program. And head Coach Ray Martin can tell you how they help.

For the past 10 years, the Knights of Pythias have sponsored an open swim meet in the Stingray division. The event usually attracts 200-300 swimmers from the surrounding area, and as far away as Grand Rapids and South Haven. Many parents stay overnight in Sturgis to make it a family event. The meet draws many public supporters.

According to Martin, nearly all of the Stingray swimmers go on to compete at varsity level.

Sponsorship of the open meet affords the Pythians "means to raise funds that are used for items the competitive swimming teams need." It's a round robin effect.

The next "B" meet is 9 a.m., Feb. 9, at the Sturgis Community Swimming Pool, 216 Vinewood. Martin expects a good turnout.

Martin praises the Knights of Pythias and the Pythian Sisters for their efforts. He knows schools find it difficult to meet the growing needs of athletic teams. He knows boosters and service clubs make the difference that puts programs ahead. And Martin says the pivot to the success of the program are the parents and individuals who give of their time to assist at meets.

And the long-term efforts of the programs pay off. Presently, there are 7 Sturgis graduates swimming at the college level. All went through the Sturgis Stingray program. They are Cheryl Lawrence, Hope College; Dan Schessel and Nick Petruska, Kalamazoo College; Phil Pattengale and Steve Scribner, Alma college; Blake Barkley, a diving competitor at Purdue University, and John Scholl, Arizona State University.

Sholl made All American in swimming, the first athlete from Sturgis to accomplish that feat in 20 years, Martin said.

Another promising athlete, Cindy Briggs, died in an automobile accident. She was enrolled in Western Michigan University's program.

Back to the Knights of Pythias. Besides sponsoring the swim meet all these years, at a cost of $500 to $800 yearly, the members gave funds to purchase the high school Record Board. Not to be left out, the Pythian Sisters contributed $1,200. The Knights of Pythias also helped raise funds for a diving board, bleachers and electronic timing system.

The swimming club has grown from 15 swimmers in 1974 to as high as 110. This year the number is 80.

And the enthusiasm for the swimming teams has grown, as evidenced by the need for swim coach Donna Bullock and diving coach Steve Belote to assist Martin.

The school's swimmers have proved their athletic prowess. The program has stimulated student and community response.

And for those interested in the Stingrays, it should be noted these are swimmers in 8th grade and lower.

Martin said school officials are very supportive of the program, but the Knights of Pythias and the Pythian Sisters are the spearheads. "They make the difference," he said. "They and the parents and interested people. And folks like Harold and Isabelle Abbs, who have given more to this project then the public know."

Why not go out to the community pool next Saturday and watch a bunch of wholesome kids, engaged in a wholesome sport. You're bound to enjoy it – and be proud of these students.

And there's no admission charge. Where else can you find so much good entertainment so cheap?

Words to Happy's Song Learned

February 9, 1985

If possible, I try to follow up stories and events. And the column written recently about Angelo "Happy" Botzner, 86, is a case in point. Happy, as you recall, is a longtime resident of the Honey Lake area in Branch County.

His mother died when Happy was a baby. Happy was taken by this father from Grand Rapids to live with his family, where Happy was adopted by an aunt.

On that trip home, the father and child were riding on a train, with the mother's body in the baggage coach ahead. The baby began to fuss and passengers complained. When the question arose of where the mother was, the father replied, "in the baggage coach ahead."

Passengers were stirred to tears. They helped the young father tend to the baby until they reached home.

But the interesting follow-up from that tragedy was a passenger wrote a song about the event, a song popular many years ago. Happy Botzner had heard some of the words, but always wanted to have a copy of the song.

I got calls, letters, notes from people who remembered some of the song's words or recalled their parents singing it. But no copies of the song.

Enter a gentleman named Jess Morrisson, Sturgis, who called to say he had the sheet music. He gave it to me in the hope Happy would finally learn the words. And Happy has.

And for those of you who wonder about the words of that poignant song and the sorrow of a young father, let me repeat the song's words and chorus, written by Gussie L. Davis:

"On a dark stormy night, as the train rattled on, all the passengers had gone to bed,

"Except one young man with a babe in his arms, who sat there with a bowed-down head.

"The innocent one began crying just then, as though its poor heart would break,

"One angry man said 'make that child stop its noise, for it's keeping all of us awake.

"Put it out,' said another. 'Don't keep it in here. We've paid for our berths and want rest.'

"But never a word said the man with the child, as he fondled it close to his breast.

"Where is its mother, go take it to her,' this a lady then softly said.

"I wish that I could,' was the man's sad reply. "But she's dead, in the coach ahead."

Every eye filled with tears, when his story he told, of a wife who was faithful and true.

"He told how he'd saved all his earnings for years, just to build up a home for two.

"*How, when Heaven had sent them this sweet little babe, their young lives were blessed,*

"*His heart seemed to break when he mentioned her name, and in tears tried to tell them the rest.*

"*Every woman arose to assist with the child, there were mothers and wives on that train.*

"*And soon was the little one sleeping in peace, with no tho't of sorrow or pain.*

"*Next morning at a station, he bade them goodbye. 'God bless you,' he softly said.*

"*Each one had a story to tell in their home, of the baggage coach ahead.*"

Chorus:

"*While the train rolled onward, a husband sat in tears, thinking of the happiness of just a few short years.*

"*For baby's face brings pictures of a cherished hope that's dead, but baby's cries can't awaken her, in the baggage coach ahead.*"

So, a fellow named Happy Botzner has finally received the complete text of the song written more than 80 years ago about him, his father and mother, the lady in the baggage coach ahead.

Happy appreciates the generosity of Morrisson, a man who also knows the meaning of family love.

Have the Heart to Reach Out

February 16, 1985

They are a young family attempting to find the good life. But that dream mocks them at every turn. Bob and Conni Wells, Burr Oak, know what adversity is. They know it strikes swiftly and unasked. They understand it can force a family from a dream into a nightmare.

Their nightmare is medical bills. Costs necessary to keep three of their four children alive.

The Wells children are Stacy, 10, Lindsay, 7, Janell, 4, and Bobby Jr., 2. Stacy, Janell and Bobby, or B.J. as he is called, all have chronic health problems. Life threatening problems.

Janell and B.J. are on monitors because they stop breathing. Sometimes once a night, sometimes many times. Janell also has a heart problems, super ventricular pathacardia, which means her heart rate becomes very rapid.

B.J. sometimes stops breathing, whether awake or asleep. He also has a valve in his heart that doesn't work properly and doctors recently discovered a mass in his neck. Doctors disagree on whether the mass is malignant, but he faces expensive surgery soon. If it is not malignant, the family's insurance carrier will not pay the bill, Bob says.

Stacy began having seizures at the age of 7. She was given drugs to control convulsions, but developed a reaction to one drug.

Removed from the drug, Stacy still has seizures about once a week.

Although Lindsay doesn't appear to have health problems, her parents worry that some may develop.

There is another worry. Medical bills have reached the limit on what the carrier will pay. The family owes $18,540. The Crippled Childrens organization will not pay further costs for diagnosis or treatment of seizures for Stacy, the family said. And B.J. must return to Mott Childrens Hospital in Ann Arbor.

Bob is employed. He knows if he quit working and went on welfare, Medicaid would pick up the health costs. But Bob and Conni want to support their family. They don't want to be dependent on taxpayers.

Inez Ultz, who lives near the Wells, has decided to do something about the Well's problems. She requested the help of her Aid Association for Lutherans Branch of Burr Oak, working through the AAL's co-op project. This means the AAL will match half the family's unpaid health care costs.

AAL units from Trinity Lutheran Church and St. Timothy Lutheran Church in Sturgis joined in, as did St. Paul's Lutheran Church in Centreville and St. Paul's Lutheran Church in Coldwater.

But members know their share won't be easy to raise, so fund raiser bus tours are scheduled to the Lutheran School for the Deaf, Henry Ford Museum, Frankenmuth and St. Lorenz Lutheran Church. Inez also is organizing a gospel concert at Sturgis-Young Auditorium in May. In addition, scrap paper drives have been scheduled.

The Wells haven't given up in their attempts to make life better for their children. And in the midst of their anguish, they remain active in 4-H work, serving as leaders.

Neighbors say the Wells are hard-working, caring parents, whose primary goal is to help their children reach maturity, healthy and happy.

It's My Turn to Speak my Piece

February 23, 1985

I should have known. You can't please everybody. But one has to keep trying. At least that's what I tell myself after a recent unsigned letter arrived at the Journal.

I don't usually respond to anonymous letters. But seeing as how it was directed at something I wrote, I'll answer it. And sign my name. And put it in print.

The author of the letter claimed I had "hurt" all the other Sturgis High School graduates who had found their own "niche" in the world. She (I presume it was a she, because she put Mrs. and initials) claimed I shouldn't have played up the accomplishments of only a few.

The letter referred to a column I wrote about four former Sturgis people. The copy for that column was a combination of news I had saved up about the people.

The letter writer was right in that there are many other young people to write about. The author made another point: good things about our young people should be highlighted. I wish I had the answer on how to do it all, but we simply don't have news space for everything. And there are other graduates out there, from communities besides Sturgis. Our readership area isn't just Sturgis. So, occasionally, I work something into my column.

Perhaps, in the letter writer's opinion, I didn't do something exactly as she believes I should. And she's entitled to say so.

A newspaper can't do everything. We work within budgets and time schedules, just like any business. It amazes me the public expects us to work evenings, weekends, give up family gatherings, holidays. We have a small staff and I am bewildered that we receive calls to cover events that will happen in a couple of hours – after reporters are assigned to other schedules.

And I am confused when we receive news items and reports (some we have trouble reading) and bear the tirade when we print information from those reports that we have to accept as correct. We could say in our corrected column whose fault it is each time, but what real purpose would there be in pointing fingers at someone else's mistake? So, we take the lumps. Those lumps include telephone calls, nasty unsigned letters, snide remarks and sarcasm.

I won't argue that there is room for improvement in the journalism world. There is. But there's also space for improvement in the public sector. I'm a bit tired of hearing about the "uncaring" media. Perhaps the public is unaware that we sometimes agonize about how to present a story. There are reporters who have covered tragedies – and came back to the office emotionally and physically sick.

And maybe the public needs to understand that our days are saturated with man's inhumanity, life's brutality and anguish, court cases, family disturbances, death, murder and child abuse. And we still care. We couldn't cope if we didn't feel something. And we do reach out to present the other side of life, the good things. And many of them are told – in this paper.

Our words are here forever. We can't change our mistakes. We work under many daily deadlines that cannot be altered. Most other people have occupations where their work mistakes can be rebuilt or remanufactured, without public scrutiny each day. We don't.

That letter struck a nerve. And while I understand the letter writer's need to complain, this column theme will not change. It will continue to feature a cross section of life. It's my opinion and so I sign it. Editorials are a consensus of four editorial board members at the Journal. A column is one person's opinion. That's why the former is unsigned, the latter signed.

I just hope the next anonymous individual remembers if it's important enough to write and give a personal opinion, it should befit character to stand behind it.

She's a Cut-up at the Age of 90

March 2, 1985

Florence Hagen can still cut it at the age of 90 – literally. She manages her own hairdresser shop on South Fourth Street, Sturgis.

Florence doesn't know how to retire. Doesn't want to learn. She's plenty satisfied to keep working. Keeps her young, she always tells folks.

Those who know the spry, witty Florence are constantly amazed she continues business as usual, just as she did when she entered the beautician field 56 years ago.

She established the shop in her home because her husband, Louis, was in a wheelchair 36 years. He died 27 years ago. But being near him all day made it a strong, loving marriage, Florence said.

Florence lived in Sturgis since 1924, coming from Constantine, her birthplace. She worked at Kirsch Co., in her earlier years and always liked to cut and style people's hair. So she began studying barbering, cutting men's hair. Later on, she decided to go into women's hairdressing.

She still gets up early – about 6:30 a.m. Her favorite answer why is a simple one: "Don't want to miss anything."

Nearly all her customers have standing appointments. Many of them, like Lucile VanDeventer, have had their hair needs handled by Florence for years. Some of her clients have been with her a half century. Florence usually says with a chuckle that "I ought to know their hair pretty well by now."

She used to have other hairdressers in her shop, but now prefers to work alone. That way she can "pack up and go anywhere I want, when I want."

The only sadness in Florence's business is that being at it so long, so many of her customers have died. She dreads cleaning out her files because each name is a memory of someone she cared about.

Florence's birthday is March 8 and for a 90-year-old gal, you wouldn't know it. She's articulate, bright and quick with the quips. She loves a good conversation and enjoys company.

She is a longtime member of the Philatheas and enjoys needle-craft. Many of her friends can testify to her needlework skills, because Florence is a generous lady. Gives most of her items away.

When she isn't working in her shop, Florence can be found in her large garden. Or spending time with her family. She delights in being around young people, too. Friends quote her on that, too. "Keeps you young, and I'm all for that."

At the time in life when most people her age look back on life, Florence looks ahead.

So, to a lady who manages to find the good things in life, who enjoys helping others and finds life a challenge, Happy 90th Birthday, Florence.

The Hunter's Likeness Returns

March 9, 1985

They hunted and fished together for years, the fellows named Paul Cowles and Paul Work. They shared the love of country fields, quiet rivers and north woods. It was a good life and a warm friendship. Then Paul Work died.

But those who knew him are sure he'd get a kick out of a recent happening. Although Work wasn't a braggart, he'd be mighty pleased to know his picture graces the license application guide for the 1985 Wild Turkey Gobbler Season.

A photo of Work and the large gobbler he nabbed in 1965, the first year the wild turkeys were available for open hunting, was selected for the guide by the Department of Natural Resources.

Cowles, Burr Oak, was surprised to see his friend's photo when he went to pick up his license application to hunt this year. "There was Paul, toting the 19 lb., 12 oz., gobbler he bagged the first day of the season in 1965," Cowles said. Work's turkey was the 21st killed out of 52 the first day of the 1965 season. The event was the first wild turkey shoot in the 20th Century. The turkey was bagged in the Allegan Game Area, a favorite hunting site of Cowles and Work.

Work was a Bronson resident, longtime city councilman and mayor. He also was a founder of Bronson Tool & Die. But aside from business, Work's favorite hobbies were hunting and fishing.

Cowles doesn't know why the DNR is using the old picture of Work and the gobbler, but he has another reason for recognizing the picture. He was standing a couple of feet from Work when the photo was taken in 1965 by DNR officials.

For those unfamiliar with wild turkey hunts and wanting to join the hunt this year, you need a 1985 Wild Turkey Hunting License and a 1985 Small Game Stamp (unless hunting on enclosed farmland on which you live). A Turkey Stamp will not be issued this year.

Last year, the DNR transferred 462 turkeys to habitats in mid-Michigan, of which 35 percent were gobblers. In addition, 143 square miles of hunting lands were added for the 1985 season.

Another reminder. Designated districts are set up, as well as separate turkey hunts. There are 14 areas available to hunt and 1 to 5 hunts scheduled in each area.

Hunters aren't guaranteed a license. If there are more applicants than the number of licenses allowed, a random drawing decides who will hunt.

Wild turkeys are popular. Turkeys recently were exchanged for moose from Canada. The Canada moose were released near Michigamme in the Upper Peninsula.

Cowles hopes to obtain a permit to hunt wild turkeys this year. And if he does, he'll carry the application guide along. With the picture of his old friend close to his heart.

Sheilia's Outlook Face-Saving

March 16, 1985

Sheilia Hendrick grew up fast. She had to. During her childhood years, at the age when most kids naturally fit in with their peers, Sheilia knew mostly pain, fear, taunts from her classmates and stares from adults.

Sheilia, 12, who lives with her parents Hank and Sue and sister Michelle, at 1411 Sunnyfield Rd., Sturgis, has Sclaraderma, a disease that struck when she was 4.

Her parents first noticed a dark spot near her left eye, similar to a bruise. Sue and Hank weren't alarmed because Sheilia's face didn't look damaged other than the dark spot.

But concern came when they noticed part of Sheilia's face – the left side – began to look different. Besides the dark spot near her eye, another discoloration appeared above the eye on the forehead.

Doctors said the spots were birthmarks.

But then, tissue underneath the spots began to sink in, to "disappear" as Sue puts it. Part of the contour of Sheilia's face receded at the jawline as more tissue below the skin deteriorated.

Referred to a Three Rivers doctor, Sheilia's parents soon found themselves on the way to Mott's Children's Hospital, Ann Arbor.

Doctors confirmed the facial tissue was shrinking, causing a distortion of Sheilia's face. Her left eyelid would not close and eyedrops were needed so the eye would not dry out. The vision in that eye became weakened as Sheilia's face changed.

After a barrage of specialists examined Sheilia, a steroid was prescribed, which apparently stopped the disease's progress after six month's treatment.

But the damage was done. Sheilia's face was disfigured.

And then people began to whisper that she had been beaten. Her classmates taunted her about her appearance. Life became nightmares for Sheilia as she entered her first year of school.
Life became more difficult when the family moved from Constantine, where Sheilia's friends had become used to her appearance. "I faced new taunting," Sheilia said with a matter-of-factness.

When she was 6, plastic surgeons began the first of a series of operations to reconstruct Sheilia's face. She has undergone five surgeries and more are needed. Her forehead has been repaired from skin taken from other parts of her face. While cartilage inserts did not work, plastic surgery on her jaw improved her looks. Her eyelid was repaired.

Sheilia, a blue-eyed blonde, maintains a sense of reality and acceptance of her problem. While she knows other children can be cruel in their teasing, something in Sheilia's character brought forth an outlook that makes others forget her facial problem.

"I figured I had to learn to accept what others thought of me and what they said," Sheilia said. "I guess I just knew that early. But what people said hurt more than the pain from my operations."

She has suffered a great deal of pain from surgery, including an operation on her jaw when surgeons worked from inside of her mouth to repair the damage.

Sue said some doctors believe silicon injections would work well on Sheilia's face, but the government won't allow them.

But Sheilia, waiting for her next operation, faces the world with truth and clarity. And most of all, understanding.

She is far more mature than most 12-year-olds. She has good insight. She knows what she wants to do in life. "I'd like to teach math," the honor roll student said.

And she has not withdrawn socially. She likes school, is a "sticker" collector and recently was baptized. She especially enjoys going to church with her grandmother.

One can learn a lot from Sheilia Hendrick. Things like suffering, pain and cruelty. But most of all what shines brightest in this young girl is something far more brilliant than the usual childhood character.

Sheilia, in simple terms, has grace. She learned it the hard way. She carries it well.

I've Lost Part of My Childhood

March 23, 1985

They closed the last grocery store in Sidnaw, in the Upper Peninsula. And they didn't even tell me.

I heard about the closing of the last tavern, but I didn't know about the grocery store. Not until friends told me they read it in another newspaper.

That's like rubbing salt into a wound.

How could they close part of my childhood? It's like every chapter of my memories are being edited. And I don't like it.

Sidnaw, as most of you know from my other tales about the town, is located about 60 miles southwest of Marquette, on M-28. It was a busy town in the late 1880's, when white pine was king. I grew up knowing lumberjacks who took hot pasties to work in their lunch-pails to get them through the bitter winters on the logging trails.

It is a town that educated kids from 1st though 12th grades when I was a youngster. Now the school has 4th through 8th grades.

And there were many kids. Now, the town has only 19.

Sidnaw used to have a depot, water and coal towers, two railroads, passenger trains that stopped twice a day and two freight trains. They had two taverns, two grocery stores, a dry goods store, two garages, a small hotel, several rooming houses, two water pumps (few people had running water), three churches, and a CCC camp that housed 300 men.

Sidnaw is an Indian name, meaning hill by the creek. And it was only a creek, but it gave kids a chance to learn to swim, to fish, to pick up bloodsuckers. You could even drive a car into the creek to wash it.

That dates me back to the end of the Depression days, when ice cream cones were a nickel. When Three Musketeers candy bars included three bars, each a different flavor. When Kool-Aid and candy suckers cost a penny. Those were the days of Airline radios, Gabriel Heater, Gangbusters and The Shadow.

Sidnaw will always be my hometown. I have never been able to forget it, to fully accept another locality. Sidnaw formed my character, as surely as it put a stamp on me. I am Sidnaw.

And now, with Dorothy Barrow closing her grocery store, it is as though part of me died. I knew that store when the Beck family ran it and the Barrows operated the tavern next door.

I loved Sidnaw when the post office was located in the old Keith Shingler grocery store. Marian Shingler was postmistress and her daughter, Karroll, was my best friend. Still is. Another childhood friend, Betty Tschury, is postmistress now.

I don't know what the population of Sidnaw is. I don't want to know. Too discouraging. I know it was about 1,000 in 1917, when the hamlet was thriving.

There are only 3 places open full time in the town: The school, post office and a gas station.

Railroad officials tore down my beloved depot, the water and coal towers (I will never forgive them).

There are only a few people left in Sidnaw that I remember. When I went back years ago, some confused me with my mother, who died many years ago.

When I was a kid, Sidnaw was a close-knit town. People got together for card games, picnics and visiting. Television changed some of that, I'm told.

But the town can't die. I can't reconcile myself to a ghost town.

Part of me is buried in that cemetery on the edge of town, where my grandparents and uncle sleep. The names on many of the tombstones are friends from my childhood.

Even though a sawmill was later located where the old CCC camp and later a German prisoner of war camp was, I still see faces of the CCC men of the 1930s.

I remember the school where I wrote my first poem, the creek where we caught trout, the rail cars loaded with logs.

I remember that my mother's parents homesteaded in the woods a few miles from town, that they carved land from the woods by hand. It was in Sidnaw that my father met my mother. It is my birthplace.

And I cherish the recollections of those days, the freedom a kid had when life moved slower, neighbors were important and lifetime friendships were forged.

I will never forget the northwoods, the pure, wholesome beauty it retains today.

So, I can't accept the demise of Sidnaw. It will always be vital and alive to me. Memories don't die that easily

Norris Earned Mason Award

April 6, 1985

They only give one award out in the state each year. This year a Sturgis man, Donald Norris, will receive the Grand Chapter of Royal Arch Masons of Michigan's Meritorious Service Award. And deservedly so, although he modestly says, "I was only doing what I was supposed to do. I figure if you belong to an organization you should be dedicated and involved."

And involved Don Norris has been for more than a half century.

Just as his great-grandfather was a Mason, so was his grandfather. His father was a Mason 67 years, so the Masonry spirit was handed down through the generations.

A native of Ohio, Don came to Sturgis as a 21-year-old in 1927 – to manage the first Kroger store. He stayed with the Kroger chain until accepting a position at Cavin Lumber Co., where he retired as president of the firm in 1945.

If the Masonic award is for dedication, Don paid his dues – in more ways than one. And when he walks up April 21 at the testimonial dinner at Sturges-Young Auditorium to accept his award, the people there know he earned it.

When the Masons choose a man for their coveted service award, that man is one of 20, 000 individuals in Michigan who can be nominated. The award is based on Masonic, civic and church work.

Don's history fills those qualifications.

For instance: He is a life member and past master of Meridian Sun Lodge No. 49, where he earned the Mason of the Year Award in 1984. He is past high priest and life member of Sturgis Chapter 26 Royal Arch Masons, a life member of Columbia Commandery No. 18. He received the grand commander's service award in 1975, as well as the Knights Templar meritorious service award in 1982.

Don also is a life member of Olive Branch Chapter No. 2, Order of Eastern Star.

And there is more. He is a member of Saladin Shrine Temple AAONMS Oasis of Grand Rapids, member and past president of the Sturgis Shrine Club, ambassador at the Sturgis Shrine Club from Saladin Temple, earned the Shriner of the Year award twice. His credits also include six diamond merit service awards, the highest awards given to a Shriner.

He is a member of the board of directors at the local Masonic Temple.

His church duties are numerous, including member of the First Presbyterian Church of Sturgis for nearly 50 years, where he is an elder serving on the Session for 17 years. He belonged to the church building committee when the church was constructed and serves on the Foundation Committee.

His civic history is just as distinguished. He served on the Sturgis City Commission for 16 years, with two years as vice mayor and two years as mayor. He is now a member of the Sturgis Housing Commission (Maple Towers), serves on the city election commission and the board of directors for the Jane A. Sturges Memorial Home.

He also is a member of the Sturgis Elks Lodge and a 50-year member and past president of the Sturgis Exchange Club.

Busy man? You bet. And still says he enjoys it.

There are other titles Don holds in the business world, but it takes a while to get that information from him. He's usually too busy to find.

Among the work he cherishes is helping youngsters the Shrine Club sponsors, many of them handicapped children or those the club helps with operations or other problems.

One of the reasons Don is so interested in children is because he is a family man. Married to Margaret, the couple have two daughters. Don said he'd still like to see his daughters become Eastern Star members.

But asked about his interest in so many organizations, Don has a simple answer. "Involvement is what it's all about. You have to put your heart in it."

He lives and breathes the Mason creed. "I strongly believe in the ethics and goals of Masonry," Don says. "It is one of the oldest organizations in the nation and its belief in furthering the goals of civic, Masonic and church is a good one."

And April 21, when the Sturgis Chapter of the Royal Arch Masons sponsors a testimonial dinner for Don, you can believe the reason why he will receive the meritorious service award, the only one in Michigan this year.

Don Norris, Sturgis citizen, earned it.

The Hints from Yesteryear

April 13, 1985

I like old things. Tools, pictures, cabinets, knickknacks, you name it, I like it. And I just received a copy of a fascinating book. Titled "Homestead Hints," the publication is edited by Donald J. Berg and is an interesting look at hints from yesteryears. Some have merit today. Don't say the old-fashioned way is outdated. Not by a long shot.

Articles in the book contain many ideas to improve the home, garden and household.

For instance, did you know that to set fence posts, the earth from the hole is placed directly under the line of the fence, thus forming a ridge which is a saving equal to 12 feet of boards in four lengths of fence?

Want to know how to remove rust from a stovepipe? Rub with linseed oil, and then build a slow fire until the pipe is dry. Oil in the spring to keep the pipe from rusting.

And if you should decide to cut wood for fuel, cut hardwood in August, September or October. Hoop-poles should be cut before frost. Otherwise, there's danger of worms.

And now I know how to get rid of tree stumps. Bore a two-inch hole 18 inches deep into the stump. Do it in the fall and fill with a concentrated solution of saltpeter. Plug the hole up and leave it. By spring the solution will have saturated the stump. Dump on kerosene and burn away. Even the roots will be consumed.

And if you'd like to cut a glass jar in two, fill a Mason jar with lard-oil to the point where you want to cut it. Heat an iron-rod or bar to red-hot, immerse in the oil and the unequal expansion will crack the jar all-around at the surface of the oil.

Everyone knows the pain of bee stings. To ease it, make a paste of saleratus (baking soda) and water.

Want to make plants grow? Boil potatoes, dilute the cooled water and pour it on the plants.

Another good hint. If mosquitoes or other bloodsuckers invade the home, uncork a bottle of pennyroyal or other mint extract. The publication says the thirsty creatures will depart in haste.

To keep freshly-cut flowers looking great, immediately put them into a vessel of soapsuds. Each morning rinse in clean water and replace with soapsuds. The author says the flowers will bloom as nice as when first gathered and stay fresh for a month.

And, for wallpapered rooms when they get dirty, here's the answer to the cleaning. Cut large loaves of two-day-old bread into eight pieces. Blow dust off the wall with bellows, rub down with the bread. Dry corn meal also can be used.

And finally, how to cure a cold. Bundle up overly warm in bed with a bottle of hot water at your feet. The object is to create a mild perspiration the entire night. Before dressing in the morning, take a sponge bath in cool water and apply friction to the skin until it is a glow. The cold will probably have disappeared. This will work only if the remedy is done promptly noting the first indications of a cold

– sneezing or running of the nose. Often toasting the feet the whole evening by the fire will work.

When Don Berg sent me a copy of his book, I laughed at some of the ideas. And then I read some more. It wouldn't hurt to try some of those hints.

If you're interested in Don's book (and I don't usually do this, so don't all you authors line up with your books), write to him at Antiquity Reprints, Box 370, Rockville Centre, N.Y. 11571, and ask about Homestead Hints.

Family with International Flavor

April 20, 1985

Michael and Joanne Gresh are in the middle of an international family life. And loving every minute of it. Joanne will be remembered in the Sturgis-Burr Oak area as one of the twin daughters of Herman and Thelma Highley.

The Gresh family recently moved to Djursholm, Sweden, where they will live at least three years. Michael heads the Scandinavian branch of Northwest Orient Airlines, where he has been employed since leaving his teaching job.

The Greshes are a couple who began marriage with a bright future. But tragedy struck when Michael was stricken with cancer. His life threatened, Michael bolstered courage rare to one so young. He conquered his illness and looked ahead.

The Greshes had planned to have a family, but then they learned they would not be able to have natural children. Devastated, but knowing they would make good parents and that they had love to give youngsters, the couple decided to adopt.

A new barrier emerged. U.S. authorities would not approve adoption because of Michael's cancer.

Undaunted, Joanne and Michael applied for a child from Korea. Five years ago, they flew to Korea to get Katie, a 5-month-old charmer. Katie captivated her parents. And four years ago, Michael and Joanne returned to Korea to adopt Jennifer, a pixie 3-month-old.

Michael and Joanne are 31. They face their future unafraid, willing to take on two children because they had love to spare. And according to Grandma Highley, the family is "doing wonderful, just wonderful."

While living in a hotel until their home in Sweden is ready, the Greshes are adjusting to life there. They have toured the city, enrolled the girls in a British school and are learning the customs of a land.

Joanne said the girls may not understand the language yet, but they enjoy Swedish television, which is only broadcast a few hours in the afternoon.

The Greshes compensated for the lack of TV by taping programs and movies here too use on their VCR.

Joanne reports the weather is a bit colder in Sweden, but warming up. She also found food is much different from what she was used to, but some of the same staples are in the stores as in the United States.

Restaurant dining costs about the same as American meals, but there is a larger variety of fish.

Converter adapters are necessary for electrical items bought in the U.S., and must be ordered ahead of time, so the family is experiencing some problems in that area, Joanne said.

Joanne finds Djursholm is a charming city and plans to continue her education while the family is overseas.

And Jennifer and Katie?

"Well, they are like most kids everywhere," Grandma Highley said. "They adjust to new environments."

Grandma Highley also said it will be interesting when the little girls return to the states. "Here they are, two babies from Korea, who have grown to little girls in America. Now, they are in another land and will pick up the customs and language of Sweden.

Thelma Highley says she can't wait to see what Jennifer and Katie are like after living in three countries.

Neither can the Greshes, who consider themselves the luckiest parents in the world, even considering Korea, America and Sweden.

The Shriner's Work Shines

April 27, 1985

Mike Carper walked up to speak to the Sturgis Shrine Club the other night on the leg the Shriners gave him.

Mike, 14, who lost a leg to cancer several years ago, didn't give a long speech. He didn't have to. His words, more than any other's, spoke the simple meaning of what the Shriners' gift meant to him.

"Thanks for making my leg," he said. And with emotion, said it all: "Thanks for helping me walk again."

Mike and his mother, Marsha, were at the meeting to tell the Shriners how Mike is doing. His mother said "he's on his second artificial leg. He broke the first one several times—he's so active!"

Mike was using the leg three days after he got it.

He will need new parts as he grows taller. The Shriners will be there to help. Mike knows that. He also knows the Shriners will pay for costs when he returns to the hospital in September for plastic surgery to repair an arm damaged from chemotherapy reaction.

The Shriners are accustomed to helping kids. It's one of their goals as a unit. The local Shriners have helped many youngsters overcome disabling problems.

But the Shriners never become accustomed to the words of the youngsters they help. You could hear a pin drop when Mike gave his short speech—and then the Shriners applauded.

Mike is a success story for the Shriners—and they pray each of their young clients will be able to reach the stage Mike has—and look forward to a fruitful life.

The Shriners are picking up the cost of health care for six youths in the area. The youngsters have various ailments or handicaps. It doesn't matter what the problem is, the Shriners help. The families don't pay a cent. And that's how the Shriners want it.

Ken Johnson has headed a committee to select and oversee the youngsters' health care. He'll be joined soon by Dale Bishop and his wife. Many other members assist in driving the kids to hospitals for treatment. It's a united effort.

How does the local club pay for all this? Simple enough: They work at it. For instance, their main fund raiser is a candy sale, planned for May 10-11 this year. Members will sell candy at various banks and businesses. All funds will be used for Sturgis Shrine projects.

Shriner Bob Myers said the Saladin Shrine area, which is the western half of Lower Michigan, paid hospital and clinic costs for 791 youths.

"We're here to help kids," Myers said. "We've had that goal for years and we aim to continue it."

And this year the Sturgis unit will join others on a trip to Chicago to visit the Shrine Orthopedic Unit.

As Shriner Ron Roth said: "If we don't know how far-reaching the total Shrine crippled children's program is, a visit to one of the Shrine hospitals convinces us. It makes you understand the plight of others—and want to help."

Monday evening, as Mike's mother told the Shriners "the people at the hospital have been wonderful. Anything we want—anything they can do for us is given freely and warmly. They treat us like family."

Every Shriner is a Mason. Freemasonry is the oldest, largest and most widely known fraternal organization in the world.

A recent Harris poll found 73 percent of the people surveyed in the United States knew about Shriners, but only 27 percent knew about their public service.

For those who don't know, Shriners have operated hospitals in North America since 1922, when the first facility was founded. Shriners pay the total cost of operating 19 orthopedic hospitals and three burn units. No taxes, no insurances. All services are free and no money is accepted from patients.

It's a gift of love. Ask Mike Carper. He knows about that.

History Can Be Restored

May 4, 1985

Harold Carr, White Pigeon, had a dream. He was a man who respected the present and looked forward to the future.

He also was a man who was dedicated to preserving the past, knowing that it is history that provides a link to understanding times, events and people.

Carr did not live to see his dream realized. But he worked for that dream and did something about it – he invested his own money in it.

And that dream wasn't for himself. It would benefit a community, a county and people who know that yesterday is as important as today and tomorrow.

Carr always had his eye on the old D&E Restaurant in White Pigeon.

He knew its history, that it was the only original land office remaining in Michigan.

Carr feared the building would go the way of many other historical sites – demolition.

The structure was built prior to 1830 when Michigan was a territory. The original slat sides and bark timbers supporting the roof and ceiling remain, but the building needs extensive restoration to make it the proud structure it once was.

The land office location was later moved, but the building continued in use as various business sites throughout its proud history.

Carr wanted to restore the building for use as a community museum. His untimely death prevented that.

But he made sure that after his death, the building would be given to the St. Joseph County Historical Society. His wife agreed.

But there is a problem. It takes people – and funds – to spark a restoration endeavor.

There are sparkplugs in the effort, including Mary Starmann and John Guyton. There are Helen Wickman and members of the Society, who worked long hours with the other committee members to research the building's history.

Their efforts drew approval for the structure to be placed on the State Register of Historic Sites. The Society is now seeking recognition on the national level.

Concerned citizens have joined in the campaign. There is a concerted effort that the building plans will be finalized.

At 7 p.m. Tuesday, a meeting is planned in the White Pigeon Township Hall.

Guest speakers will be Dr. Peter Schmidt, Western Michigan University's architectural historian, and Larry Massey, archives historian.

The county historical unit is sponsoring the event, which promises insight into historical preservation methods. Awareness of the need for more interest in preserving buildings must be emphasized.

Too many of the county's historical buildings are gone. There is no chance to redeem what foolishness and a lack of interest allowed.

This is a time citizens can do something about it. Attending the Tuesday session can be the beginning.

REA turned on Nation's Lights

May 11, 1985

It seemed so strange. Here I was, a kid born in a small logging town in the Upper Peninsula, bereft of many of the modern conveniences. We had an outhouse, our drinking and bath water was hauled from the village pump a block away and my mother washed clothes the hard way. We had an icebox to keep things cool.

But we had electric lights. I was always used to having that.

And now, when we drove into the yard of my grandparent's farm in Branch County near the Indiana border that December of 1940, I was shocked.

A fellow was installing lines, wiring the house for electricity.

I had heard about the Lower Peninsula, how everything was so streamlined and modern. And here I was, literally back in the Dark Ages.

Oh, we still had the outhouse, the water pump out by the barn and the icebox.

But no electricity.

I couldn't wait to have it again. The radio was my best friend. There wasn't a TV set in those days and I sure didn't want to miss my favorite radio programs.

Some farms and homes outside cities didn't hook up to electric lines until later, but for me it was a signal of where I'd been – and where I aimed to go.

And today, the Postal Department issued a first day stamp in commemoration of 50 years of rural electrification, to signify signing of the Rural Electrification Act a half century ago.

And a good thing, too, because President Reagan's proposed 1986 federal budget calls for cutting Rural Electrification Administration loans in half for next year. And, according to the publication "Michigan County Lines," the REA will be phased out in five years.

There are still many rural utilities whose birth offered farm and rural families their first chance to join the modern era. Many of those utilities will be threatened by Reagan's budget, some folks say, and their very existence may be in danger.

The REA portion of the budget calls for reducing the agency's programs from about $2.5 billion this year to less than $1.1 billion for the fiscal year that ends Oct.1. The interest rate also would be hiked from 5 percent to the market rate, currently 11.2 percent, plus 1.1 percent service charge.

In addition, there probably will be a reduction of insured loans, which probably will mean rate increases for customers.

I guess time changes a lot of things and there probably is a reason for all these new moves.

But one has to understand what life was like before the REA act in 1935. For instance, laundry was a physically punishing chore for women. It meant huge kettles of water heated on a wood burning stove. There was no machinery, just muscle power. The laundry was handled piece by piece, which meant hours of beating, rinsing and wringing – all by hands. Gallons and gallons of water were carried.

No electric pumps, you see. No electric stoves, no electric washers and wringers. Sheer labor. An all-day job.

And then the ironing – all with those old irons heated on the stove. And, of course, no air conditioning to help ease the misery.

With electric power on the scene, there came a means to run machinery of all kinds. That included toasters, irons, mixmasters, griddles, coffee makers and many other items that, for the first time, made homemakers' lives a bit easier.

And one should remember that rural electrification meant a success story for our nation. The program was funded by loans, not grants. Since 1935 the REA approved almost $60 billion in loans for electrical and telephone service for nearly 12 million electrical customers and 5.2 million telephone subscribers.

Look at it this way: In 1935 10.9 percent of our nation's farms had electricity. That number is now 99 percent.

And for folks who like to cast a dim view of President Franklin D. Roosevelt, remember his was the hand that signed – and supported – the Rural Electrification Act – and turned on the light for America's rural communities.

Arbutus – A Promise Kept

May 18, 1985

It was there, poking its fragrant head through the grass and leaves, just as it did 45 years ago.

I had vowed there would be no tears. This would be a celebration of sorts. One should not weep at triumphs.

I had returned to the northwoods in the spring – for the first time since I was nine years old. Many things had changed in that time, including me.

But one thing remained the same, and time and events could not alter it – my memory and love of arbutus.

You can find the wild, trailing arbutus in the Upper Peninsula, but I'm not sure you can find it everywhere up there. It's a lot like a small woods warbler that nests only in the pine trees of some Upper Michigan counties. It's native to that area.

Arbutus is a member of the heath family and frequents the areas where pine trees grow. It is usually found in acid soil, in cool, damp areas. It grows low to the ground, its clusters of pinkish-white flowers wafting a wonderful fragrance. It looks a bit like violets, but nothing compares with arbutus aroma.

So much had changed since I left that small logging town of Sidnaw. Many landmarks and favorite spots have disappeared. Some friends sleep in the cemetery at the edge of town.

I was afraid my memory of arbutus was a figment of childhood imagination, blown out of proportion through the years. But I was wrong. Some dreams remain real.

The Sidnaw kids usually picked arbutus for May Day baskets. It was always there for Mother's Day, and I knew the best site to gather it. My mother always knew she could expect arbutus from me on her special day.

I have written before about her, especially on Mother's Day. Those who wonder why I didn't write a Mother's Day column last week will understand when they read this.

This year, I went north for Mother's Day. On a pilgrimage, for a special reason.

My mother died in her thirties. Death took from us what nothing else could. She had lived through homesteading days in Wisconsin and Michigan, knew hardship and lifelong illness. She gave birth to five children at home, and buried her only son.

But she was a fighter. My mother never lost her faith, her spirit and zest for life. I still don't know how she accomplished that.

And so, I did something different for Mother's Day. It was time to fulfill a promise. Time does not stretch out for me as it did before. One grows older. Promises made and broken many times become habit.

My mother always said she wanted to return to the northwoods, to the place she love best, where she spent her childhood and where her children were born.

She felt trapped by fences and cornfields. She yearned for the coolness of the woods, the clear, unpolluted rivers, the Norway pines.

She missed the wild flowers, the buttercups, Indian Paintbrush, the magnificent violets that grow seven inches tall. She often spoke of the sun on shimmering birch bark after a soft spring rain. And the arbutus.

I used to wonder if she dwelled on the thought that none of the hardships of the Depression years nor the harshness of the north winters had taken a child from her. Even without doctors nearby to help her through scarlet fever, whooping cough and the like. But nothing in the Lower Peninsula, not hospitals, doctors, milder climates helped keep her small boy.

She said, hesitantly as I recall, knowing the truth of the inevitable, that she would like to be buried in Sidnaw. She wanted to return to the soil she loved. There was no money to grant her last request for the long trip north after her death. I have agonized about that for years.

I could do something. I could walk the pathways of the place she and I loved best. And I did.

This year, I retraced a spring yesterday. My mother's yesterday. My yesterday.

When I searched the long ago places of my childhood and found the arbutus, I smiled.

They say wild arbutus cannot be transplanted. I have been told all the reasons why, heard all the forest management and horticulturists insist it will grow only in its native area.

No matter. Triumphs have to be believed in to happen. I picked a sprig of arbutus for my mother's gravesite. She understands.

Man of the Depression Times

May 25, 1985

He was not a man of the world. Nor learned. Nor sophisticated. He was, however, a good man of solid Irish background who fathered 12 children, steered them on the right path in life, and treated his wife right.

His world was work. Work to keep the kids in shoes and clothes, the mouths fed, the bills paid. There was a no-nonsense trait about him, and he understood that living was hard in the Depression years – and a man's time was best used to make ends meet.

But there was the poet in him that cried to escape, to put down his worries, his dreams and his thoughts about his world.

His name sounded distinguished: Findlay Nelson McKay. And he would spend his lifetime searching for answers and chronicling his beliefs after he spent a long day toiling on the loading docks in Sault St. Marie. When that shift ended he worked as a part time farmer to support his growing family.

His granddaughter, Linda Painter, Sturgis, never knew him, but she knows his worth as a man. And what his poet words mean.

While McKay's words were not fancy, he captured the misery, sorrow, strengths and triumphs of mankind during a difficult era of history.

After his supper meal was finished, he crept away to write down his words of those years and what the events meant to him. He called his writings "After Dinner Mints."

There are better writers. And certainly better poets. But Findlay McKay, in simple sayings and unpolished words, told the stories of the Depression. And in his writings came forth the woes of the struggling farmers caught in the mesh of crop failures and bank fore-closures. From his scribbling came rallying calls, messages of urgency and hope for the laborers he identified with. It was McKay's cry to the world – and those of his counterparts.

His words bear repeating, especially when history so often repeats itself. McKay could have written these words today:

"The times today are on the blink, it makes us scratch our heads and think. How we can earn some honest cash, when most all jobs have gone to smash."

"The most of use are honest, too. We know to steal would never do. But how, I ask, can we get through, without no cash?"

"The country's good, we must admit. They're willing for to do their bit. But a man has pride within his head. He wants a chance to earn his bread.

"So give us work, then we won't holler. We want a chance to earn a dollar. Then times will mend, and you and me, won't have to ask for charity."

One can easily imagine the bone-tired McKay going to a seclud-ed shed on his farm and pouring out his feelings on paper about the times that changed men and women. Times that tested their endur-ance, hope, weakness and their courage. That generation of people never forgot those days. As McKay said:

"The farmer today is a patient man, he tries to do the best he can. But times like this, he's almost beat, for he must scratch if he makes ends meet.

"Some folks may laugh this off and say, Oh, the farmer has it all his way. Cause for food his money he don't need to spend it. He had his home and is independent.

"He has his food and his home, that's true, but it takes cash to keep that too. 'So how independent, I'd like to know, if he makes no profit on what he grows.

"He's no different than you, who work out by the day. When your wages won't keep you, you can't pay your way. So the same with the farmer, though he raises tons of stuff. If he can't make a profit, he has to give up."

Maybe Longfellow would wince, but those who remember the Depression years and feel the same threat now, understand what McKay meant.

McKay's character and courage are in every word he wrote, a testament to the years that sorely tried a nation's people.

We could use people like McKay today, who faced the same problems, but mange the strength to dream, believe, go on.

McKay's poems last far longer than his short lifetime. He died at the age of 56 on that loading dock in Sault Ste. Marie, still working – and believing in that elusive dream.

Andrea: A life to Celebrate

July 6, 1985

They had come to celebrate the life – and death – of Andrea Olney of Sturgis. The church was crowded as muffled weeping surfaced from mourners.

But when the paper was unfolded and Andrea's words were read, a powerful, warm feeling swept over the people who had come together in grief. It was an appreciation of the human spirit – and life.

"Dear Frank (her brother*): There are no words to describe the love I feel for you. You brought me up when I was rock bottom and told me I was special – and made me believe I was. . .*"

She was a pretty girl, her family said. And even though she was special to them, Andrea's relatives knew she gave more to life than it gave back. She was that type of girl.

Her mother, Christine, finds the family's loss overpowering, but remembers the firstborn child she adored.

"She always smiled. She was a gregarious, personable girl, always interested in people. She was sensitive to their needs. Too sensitive, probably, but she cared so much about others."

But there was an undercurrent that tugged at Andrea's life for years. She was diagnosed as asthmatic at the age of 18 months. Emergency trips to hospitals became a familiar routine. The family nearly lost her once when her dad, Dr. Frank Olney, was in Vietnam. Her allergies, respiratory history became life-threatening when instant asthma attacks came.

"Dear Megan (a sister): You have such a good head on your shoulders. You are special. Follow your dreams and ambitions for they will be yours for the *asking. . . I love you.*"

Andrea wanted to join the school band and basketball team, but the asthma prevented enough lung capability. Undaunted, Andrea turned to cheerleading. She was enthusiastic and earned many awards.

Andrea wanted to be a nurse, to give back some of the healing and care she had received. She entered Nazareth College in Kalamazoo, planning a health care career.

She worked while going to college, "because she wanted to be contributor, accept responsibility," her mother said. "We admired her determination, but worried whether she had the stamina for it."

"Dear NaNa (another sister): You are a very sweet girl. Your personality is warm, giving and kind. I have so much faith in you. I am so proud of *you. . .*"

Andrea nearly died after dissecting a cat during nurses training. She suffered an asthma attack and went into cardiac arrest. Her life was saved by a senior nurse.

But Andrea moved on in life. She was determined to complete her medical studies.

But something unspoken troubled her. It surfaced last February when her roommate heard her crying in the night.

The friend questioned her. Tearful, Andrea said she was frightened. She was afraid she was going to die.

The fear of leaving special words unsaid led Andrea to sit down in the early morning hours that day and write a letter to her family. She encouraged her family with thoughts of their successes in the years to come.

She left the letter with her roommate with the instructions that if she died, it should be given to her parents.

"Dear Jill (her youngest sister): you have always been my baby. You are turning into such a lovely young lady. I remember the emotions I felt the day you were born. I love you with all my *heart. . .*"

Andrea came home for the summer. In June, while working at the Three Rivers telephone office, she suffered an attack. CPR was given and she was rushed to the hospital. Efforts to sustain life were futile. Asthma, the nemesis that hounded Andrea so many years, claimed her life at the age of 20.

"Dear Mom and Dad, my best friends: You gave me life. Not only that, but a life worth living. I only hope you know how much I have appreciated you. I can't understand why this is happening, but I want you to know that I have come to terms with God and *myself. . . Mom, you are a model of what all mothers and women should be. Daddy, I am so grateful for the relationship we had. You could always tell when I needed you and were always there for me. . .*"

When Andrea's letter was given to her parents after her death, they realized the full measure of their daughter's courage. In her darkest hour, when a premonition of death came, Andrea found the strength to write loving, caring words of hope to her family.

"To all of you: Remember that love endures all *things. . .*"

It was Andrea Olney's final gift of love to her family – and a world she desperately wanted to live in.

WW II: A Time We'll Never Forget

July 22, 1985

I was a few days short of 11 years old when World War II began. I remember that day. I had gone to the barn to chop a hole in the ice in the horse trough so the cattle could drink.

When I walked back to the house, my father was sitting on the back porch without his coat. I thought that was odd, because it was a cold December day. He was weeping. Large tears rolled down his face. I had never seen my father cry.

"Pearl Harbor was attacked," he said between sobs. I wondered who Pearl was. I didn't know her.

But I learned what Pearl Harbor was — and what it meant — in those long years before the war ended, as I grew from childhood to a teenager. The details were etched in my mind by Edward R. Murrow in his dramatic newscasts from London. I remember Gabriel Heator saying "There is no good news tonight," in many of his nightly news programs that came over the old Airline radio. I read the words of Ernie Pyle, the beloved buddy of the ground troops, whose poignant columns told what our fighting men were suffering.

I remember newspaper stories and pictures, and the

announcements that said area boys had been wounded, missing in action, or dead.

I have not forgotten. Nor will I.

Some people say World War II was the last patriotic war. Perhaps they are right. It was a terrible war, but America joined its allies in a struggle to win freedom for a war-torn world.

We were a nation asleep when the Japanese bombed Pearl Harbor. The Great Depression had ended. Americans were on the brink of prosperity. Our serenity was shattered when Pearl Harbor was attacked.

But from that spot in the South Pacific our courageous fighting men and women fought at Bataan, Coral Sea and Normandy. Our hearts and minds were turned to far-off places: Ardennes, Guadalcanal, North Atlantic, Battle of the Bulge, Iwo Jima, Okinawa, Berlin and Tinian.

We rallied to war bond efforts, scrap drives, cookie baking, knitting and sewing sessions. We collected milkweed for use in pilots' flak jackets.

Women played a key role in the homefront defense effort as Rosie the Riveter led others to factory and assembly lines. Women would never again be simply homemakers.

Those who waited witnessed a steady stream of messages from the war fronts. There were no military representatives to break the news. It came by Western Union – yellow pieces of paper that shattered families' lives.

There was an indelible stain from that war, something this nation did of its accord. Without proof or substantiation, this nation in its hysteria and prejudice rounded up thousands of Japanese-Americans and interned them. It is a shameful memory.

But we wept, cheered and celebrated when the war ended. We understood the price paid for victory.

For those of us who remember, that time is as close as yesterday. No person who lived those years of World War II will never forget. Two more wars did not dim the memories.

It has been 40 years since World War II ended. It is time to remind other generations what it was like and how well this nation handled itself in those difficult years.

The words of those who served say it best. We present this series of stories commemorating the 40th anniversary of the war's end in gratitude and memory of those who served on all fronts. The Journal welcomes your comments.

A Knock Brought Christmas

December 21, 1985

The knock on the door came early Christmas Eve. There was reluctance to answer it. Mother, the one who kept the family held together by a precarious thread of determination and courage, was in the hospital. There was no car, so we couldn't visit her.

It didn't seem like Christmas. Besides, Christmas was my birthday and I knew there wouldn't be gifts.

If you have lived on the thin edge of poverty, you will understand all this.

There were four girls in my family that long ago holiday. The only boy had died. We didn't have much. Didn't expect much. When you pray for a change that doesn't come, you accept reality.

I had sneaked out earlier in the evening. I loved the winter. The snow lay deep and untouched in the streetlight's soft glow. No cars were on the road. I was alone. Everyone was gathered at family events, rejoicing in Christmas traditions.

I walked to the home of my closest friend, and looked in the window. The Shinglers, father, mother and daughters, were there. By town standards, they were affluent, but didn't carry on airs.

They were gathered around a large tree. In the blaze of multi-colored tree lights, I watched them opening presents. I turned away and went home.

I didn't cry. I'd learned long before that self-pity can be a heavy burden and doesn't dry tears.

My father tried to bolster our spirits. It must have bothered him a lot, not being able to buy special things for his kids. He was ill most of his life. Looking back, I imagine it was difficult for him at Christmas.

Still, we tried to act like Mother was home. We played games, sang some songs. Dad popped corn.

So, when the knock came, there was hesitation to answer it. We didn't want company. Trying to conceal our feelings had taken most of our spirit.

But the insistent rapping continued. Dad opened the door. All I could see was grocery sacks with huge arms wrapped around them.

"Well, for heaven's sake, lend me a hand," the man bellowed, struggling with the heavy load.

It was the tavern owner, Mike Syneck. Mike always seemed to turn up at our house when he was most needed. He was a gorilla of a man, with massive hands, wide shoulders and thick neck. And a heart as big as the rest of him.

"I've got this stuff here that I can't use," he said. "It'll go to waste."

Even I wasn't that dumb, to know some of the items wouldn't spoil. But I had enough greed not to argue about it.

There was a bit of everything in those bags. Fruit, meat, canned goods, bakery items, candy.

I didn't see Mike leave. I was too deep in sacks, checking out the contents.

Later that night, sitting in the living room while the lights shone from our Christmas tree, we listened to holiday music on our Airline radio. And ate candy until we were stuffed.

I didn't know until a few months ago that the family I spied on that Christmas Eve also had stepped in to help. Between Mike Syneck and the Shinglers, a Christmas offering was gathered to help a family they cared about.

I always knew about Mike's help. But Keith Shingler died before I learned the whole story and could thank him. But remembering that good man, I know he didn't need thank yous. He was the kind of man who cared enough to share his good fortune and make someone else's Christmas special.

You Never Really Forget the Farm

April 5, 1986

When I hear about farmers losing their land, an emotion deep within me surfaces. I have tied to hide it these many years, but it returns unbidden, like a ghost that takes glee in its haunting.

My people on my father's side, down into my generations, came from this land.

Conrad Hagemeyer, my grandfather seven generations back, took issue to the dictates of land barons in Germany. He stenciled the family name on a trunk and sailed for America. It was 1741 and he was 16.

Settling in Hagerstown, Md., Conrad planted his first farm crop. And later helped plant the seeds of freedom, heading a Committee of Safety, the organization that spurred patriotism in the Revolutionary War.

Conrad instilled the value of land in his children. In wills he left instructions on limiting timber use, how orchards should be planted, how often the land should lie fallow, and not to pollute rivers.

I came to respect Grandfather Conrad's ties with the land. So did other descendants. Although some of them were city dwellers, there was an unbroken line that remained with the land.

Conrad deeded land to his son, Jonas, a surveyor, farmer and land dealer. Jonas owned thousands of acres of fertile land in Maryland, Virginia, Pennsylvania and New York.

One of Jonas' sons, Samuel, was given land near Avon, N.Y. But Samuel, as happens with sons who do not listen well, was a scoundrel. He did not respect, nor nurture his land. In time he lost most of it.

But the family genes held true in Samuel's children. One of his sons, Andrew, continued the farm heritage. When Michigan's territory opened for sale in the early 1800s, Andrew bought property near Burr Oak.

Andrew, his wife and two teenage children died several years later of typhoid, leaving six other children homeless. Family took them in and the children grew up on farms. The land provided for them.

Andrew's youngest son, Earnest, was a farmer part of his life. So was Earnest's son, Ralph, and his son, Neil, my father. In turn, I spent part of my life on a farm.

But there came a day when my grandparents' homestead was sold. Not because they declared bankruptcy, but because my parents had died and my grandparents were in failing health. The grandchildren were unable to continue the farming tradition.

I walked the acreage that day, knowing that the centuries-old, unbroken family ownership of farm land was ending. I sat for a time by the spring in the pasture, thinking about it.

It was not a large farm, but living there had given me an appreciation of what my grandfather felt. Here a husband and wife raised a family. There had been good times, and here they had known tragedy, eventually burying all three sons. But they drew comfort from the land. Farm life has a way of culling out the weeds of malcontent, of drawing the true spirit and nurturing it.

I knew that day what losing the farm meant. Here the seasons of change had come full circle to mesh lives and land – and now would separate them.

I have not lived on a farm since. My children and grandchildren don't know the richness of farm life.

So when I read about farm problems across the nation, how families are forced to leave homesteads, I understand their anguish.

I know because I wept that day when I realized a way of life was being taken from me and I couldn't prevent it. My tears mingled with the waters of the spring. I watched them flow away, gone forever from the scene, but held through time in bittersweet memory.

Death was such a Futile Gesture

December 27, 1986

He was a good friend, full of laughter and warmth. A family man and teacher.

He had imperfections, of course. He was blunt in his words and sometimes reacted too quickly to criticism. Maybe it was simply that he was a man who spoke his piece with little tact.

What stood out most about him was his passion for coaching sports. And he loved kids and the outdoors. He often tramped the fields and woods, dragging along an assortment of neighborhood kids and dogs.

If there was an important school responsibility to assign, he didn't pick the obvious leaders. He chose youths who needed to be showed that they could be trusted and were important. It molded character in a lot of kids on the difficult path to adulthood.

He taught kids more than academics. Nature, he claimed, was one of the greatest healers of hurts. He gently led kids on walks down lanes, quiet moments beside streams, watched geese in formation, mended a bird's wing.

As a coach, he bristled at the confining binds of school dictates and community Saturday morning quarterbacks. He sometimes lost his composure – but admitted his shortcomings.

Mostly he was gentle and understanding, and instinctively knew when a kid or friend needed encouragement. He championed the underdog.

He was still in love with his wife after a 20-year marriage, and tremendously proud of his children. There would be a grandchild soon, and he was excited about that.

But on a day when brilliant leaves covered hills and woodlots, without a word to anyone, he killed himself.

His pain ended; ours began.

He left behind shocked friends and family who agonized for years about what went wrong, why we didn't see it coming, what we might have done to help.

There still is no answer. Time doesn't diminish the search for a truth that does not come. We can only guess at the reason why our friend chose to leave life.

We do know that whatever demons swirled inside him, unknown to even his closest friends, he quieted his torture.

It still hurts to remember the phone call in the night that told of his death. Lying in bed, it seemed the shadows would suffocate me. Pain was an anxious intruder, demanding to stay. I could not think of him gone – or why – let alone deal with it.

There is a difference between shock and surprise, but both came full circle that night.

I recall praying in those first hours that God wouldn't hold it against him for his action. He was too good a man in life; his death should be no different.

But part of me raged that he left us so much pain at his going.

It was hard to imagine that a person of such strong character, who loved life so much, had chosen death to quench his life's candle before it burnt its brightest.

Here was a man who loved to sit in back yards reminiscing. His was the voice that laughed the loudest at jokes, who swung the neighbor's kid the highest, who gently helped his daughter put on her ballerina shoes.

It was this man who drove 90 miles to invite a boy he considered a surrogate son to a father-son banquet. He had no sons of his own, but didn't whine about it; he reached out to others.

And that was why his death shocked us. He gave no hint of despair, no warning of trouble. We assumed his life stretched out in an infinite rainbow of experiences.

It took a long time for the pain from that friend's suicide to ease.

It was no one else's fault; we know that. But we still mourn the loss of that warm, sweet spirit, and miss the valued friend who was so much a part of our lives.

The irony is that he could help so many others, but not himself. And the worst pain is that we don't know why he ended his life or why he never reached out to us for help.

Louie: A Man of Good Purpose

February 21, 1987

He was the kind of man you wanted to call dad or grandpa. He was also the fellow you instinctively knew would remain a good friend and ally.

Mostly, he was a gentleman. So mannerly and proper that the last time I saw him, he tried to get out of his chair when I walked into the room.

He had become frail in body, but not in mind and attitude. He believed in the Old World custom of standing up in a woman's presence.

He, of course, was Louie Loetz, a rare human being who encompassed honesty, integrity, gentleness and warmth. We lost him the other day.

I met Louie a long time ago, but only saw him occasionally. At that first meeting he struck me as being a person of character, someone to draw wisdom and advice from, a man of commitment.

He never changed. Not once did I hear him raise his voice in anger. I don't know if it was simply because it was something he wouldn't allow himself to do, or if he had no such shortcoming in his nature. I thing it was the latter.

Anyone who knew Louie will remember him as always being nattily dressed, usually with a tie and suitcoat. And always, there was that familiar hat.

It was his eyes that first drew my attention. They were penetrating, but kind. There was directness about his gaze that said he was a man who had an open mind.

There was something else. Louie viewed the world with compassion. He accepted the frailties of weaker people, but did not condemn. He found instead a measure of strength.

Perhaps it was simply that Louie was a man who could not find it in his heart to hurt another human being. He simply could not force himself to that kind of pettiness.

He called me once in awhile. Sometimes months would go by before I'd hear from him. He always apologized for interrupting my day. How little he knew. That soft voice would take away my depression, stress, the daily inadequacies that sometimes threatened to defeat me.

Sometimes a note would come, brief in its message, but important to me. Maybe it was an article he had liked, or a suggestion about someone else I could write about. Louie wanted people's good doings highlighted, to be known to the world. He seldom thought of himself.

But the community thought about him. Few men accomplished so much in a lifetime as quietly as Louie did.

He came out of World War I with a purpose and meaning of what life should be. And this gentle, unassuming man spent the rest of his life doing good deeds.

There are so many titles he had, so many proud endeavors. Like serving the Sturgis First Presbyterian Church as an elder. Being a founder of the Sturgis Exchange Club, an organization Louie loved without reservations. He was a 60-year member and darned proud of it.

His deeds were so well-known that the Exchange Club established the Louie E. Loetz Scholarship to help others.

Then there was the Republican Party. He was a die-hard Republican and the closest you could get Louie into an argument was to say something bad about Republicans.

He gave freely and generously to the political, public and civic worlds. He was a city commissioner, served on the Oak Lawn Cemetery Board, was a county supervisor. There was tenure on the county jury board and the Maple Towers unit.

He was the epitome of what a good man should be, and he seemed to do it so effortlessly. He wore that deserved mantle as though he was the mold for it.

I'm not sure what the world will be like without Louie Loetz. Much the less, I imagine. I have no doubt that his sleep is restful, but I will forever miss that soft voice, beautiful manners and sweet smile.

Momentos are the Threads of Life

February 28, 1987

I'm a saver of old things. Maybe it's a carryover from childhood when there were few belongings.

I save newspaper clippings, pictures, momentos.

Now and then I get the urge to clean closets and the basement. But in the middle of sorting, I realize that most items mean something in my life, perhaps sentimental, a milestone, or just a keepsake.

What do I keep that's so important?

- My kid's first valentines to me, crudely cut out and pasted up, with terms of endearment printed on them. Can I throw away these personal touches of children's love? Hardly.

- A letter from an aunt that tells about early years and what it meant to be homesteaders in the harsh northern woods. Can I toss that missive in the wastebasket–those pages of family history that tell about survival and determination? Never.

- Notes from an uncle's World War II bride in England, the young woman he never brought home because of his failure to believe in himself. Her words stir my heart each time I read the letters. Should I send them to the incinerator just to conceal a relative's failings? Not likely. One accepts family frailties. We need those teachings of life.

- A picture of a small boy, dead before my time. My only brother. The picture is the only tangible tie to him, a tentative link with a child I never knew, but with whom I feel kinship. What will I do with it? Tuck it carefully away and understand the pain my parents felt when they lost him. It is all that remains of Richard. I can't destroy his short birthright. It would deny his existence.

- Another picture. Me at 16. Was I ever that young, with long, black hair? Was I that slim girl laughing at the antics of a classmate? Can I let this remembrance go? Not by a long shot, if only to prove to my kids that I really was thin once.

- A communication from the Mister, when he was stationed with the Army Fifth Corps in Germany. We were young then, our love new. It was sent when our second child was born–the daughter he didn't meet until she was seven months old. I can't discard that special letter.

- Scattered among the boxes are locks of my children's hair, clipped when they were tots. And added recently is one from Grandson Josh, who mailed me the "tail" he wore proudly for so long–from a haircut I disliked. His compromise in sending it to me is a warm reminder of his wit.

- Prom dance booklet. They are important because the people of those days were cherished friends. I need only look at it and recall those days of innocence before adulthood beckoned. So many friends have died, but this small item from our shared school days remains part of my life.

There is a new generation to consider now, and I keep the

writings, notes, school happenings of grandchildren. It is another link in the family chain, a continuing tie to happenings.

So that explains why few items of this nature are thrown out. Maybe some distant day another generation will look at them and discover the same closeness.

The simple truth is, one doesn't throw away the heartstrings of life.

Food Habits Hard to Change

March 21, 1987

How come they don't have Three Musketeer candy bars that have three bars like they used to years ago?

Doesn't anyone eat Bit-O-Honey and Walnettos anymore?

What's wrong with oatmeal, rhubarb, mincemeat, parsnips and cranberries?

Maybe what's wrong is me. I like everything others don't seem to like.

I even think a liverwurst sandwich is fantastic.

I do have dislikes. I hate lima beans; fresh liver looks like it could be left in the field to rot.

I got to like a lot of food in my young years, mainly because most of it was homegrown. The garden, orchard, pig pen and cow lot provided what we needed.

But I also can't handle spinach and radishes. Radishes taste awful going down and awful coming back up.

I guess we get our likes and dislikes from environment. But if that's true, how come I like so many foods now that I couldn't stand as a kid.

Maybe it's because I don't have to eat them now. I can pick and choose. A simple choice of mind over Mother. When I was young, she gave the orders.

I like liverwurst so much that I've taken it to work for lunch. But when I opened that sandwich package, the newspeople scattered. A city editor who used to work here turned pale when he saw liverwurst.

I'm a decent enough baker, but my cooking is questionable. Anyone who has eaten at my table knows my meatloaf never taste the same twice. Darned if I know what happens; I just throw in the ingredients.

But I do the same with apple pie, and nobody turns it down.

I admit I've had some boo-boos in my baking career. I've made pineapple upside down cake – and forgot the pineapple. I've made scalloped potatoes – and forgot the seasoning. I've made cherry pie – and forgot the sugar.

I don't know why that should be held against me; just a small lapse of memory.

The biggest problem for me is macaroni and cheese. I used to cook for six when the kids were at home. There was always a friend or two they'd invite to supper. Sometimes it was six or seven friends.

The other day, I made macaroni and cheese. Boiled enough macaroni for two large bowls, two left over. Gave another dish to my daughter's family and the birds got the rest.

The Mister, who clips coupons and is a careful shopper, was disgusted. I think my macaroni supper wiped out a month's coupon savings.

I never said I was a good cook when I got into this marriage. I never bragged about my finesse in the kitchen. I don't even own an apron.

Maybe there's something to using prepared food that comes in cans, boxes and in the frozen food section of the store.

But me, I still like to try my luck at upside down cake – with or without pineapple.

A Special Mother's Day Gift

May 9, 1987

My sisters and I gave our mother a special Mother's Day gift this year. It's something she desperately wanted most of her life.

She had talked about it for years and her thoughts were ingrained in our lives.

Mother died 39 years ago this August. She was also 39 when death took from us what poverty, illness and hardship could not.

There are four girls in out family. The only boy, Richard, died at the age of six months.

There is little to show of Richard's existence. No more than four pictures; his birth and death certificates.

I search old newspapers for something about Richard, but only short notations are there.

One reads simply: "The small son of Neil and Alma Hogmire is very ill."

Another article a few days later is more specific: "Richard Lee Hogmire, young son of Neil Hogmire, died of heart trouble at his Noble Township home."

Even then, the death announcement was partially correct. Richard, or "Dickie," as Mother called him, died of complications from whooping cough.

He was the second child in our family. A girl was born before him, and three more after his death.

I never knew Richard, other than from Mother's memories. Richard's death so pained my father that he never talked about him. That made it difficult, because without being able to talk about Richard, we couldn't acknowledge his life.

Mother took her grief within herself. Once, when I heard someone in the attic, I went upstairs to look. As the sunlight from a window streamed through the open attic door, I saw my mother on her knees, bending over a trunk. She swayed gently from side to side, head bent and arms clasping something to her breast.

I realized it was Richard's baby clothes, which she had packed away years before.

I crept quietly downstairs. Mother's anguish was too private to intrude.

My mother was only 18 when her small son died, but she mourned his loss until the end of her life.

Part of the reason for my Dad's grief was evident: With Richard went the last chance to continue the family name. There were no more boys, not even in the first and second cousin direct family lineage. With Richard's death went the name of the Hogmire (Hagemeyer) family that emigrated from Germany in 1740 to make a new home in America.

My mother's grief was far more personal. It wasn't only Richard's death that haunted her. Our family was poor – so poor that when Richard died, there could be no tombstone erected over his grave.

Richard is buried in the family plot in Fry Cemetery, just across the Branch County line. Beside him sleeps our parents, paternal grandparents and two uncles who also died young.

As fate willed it, my grandparents eventually buried all their sons; so it was that my parents buried their only son.

Each time we visited the cemetery, Mother's anguished words were heard: "Someday, this little boy must have a gravestone."

But it was not to be; family finances prevented it. Mother was a realist; she wouldn't deny her living children what they needed simply to ease her sorrow for a dead child.

But the message was clear, even if the promise was never issued: Richard must have a tombstone.

That thought grew more insistent after a Palm Sunday tornado several years ago destroyed Fry Cemetery records. Documents could no longer prove where my brother's grave was located.

But I knew. And so, this Mother's Day, I decided it was time. My sisters concurred. The tombstone was ordered. On it will be words I believe should be there: my brother's name, his full date of birth and death, and whose child he was.

Richard died 60 years ago on May 17, 1927. But the unspoken promise his sisters carried with us these many years has been fulfilled: Richard will have a tombstone above his grave on Memorial Day.

I think someone besides us rests more easy now.

'Taps' is a Special Memorial

May 23, 1987

He remembers the white crosses for the U.S. military dead on Saipan during World War II. The memory is indelibly etched in his mind.

Wallace Walter of Sturgis and his father both served in World War II and Wally's memories of wartime duties remain vivid.

But there are other memories that stir him each Memorial Day when he pays homage to fallen vets. And he doesn't forget those in veteran's hospitals "for whom the wars never end," he says.

Wally believes respect and appreciation should be extended to those who serve their country; he knows they earned it.

Wally has a special kinship with "Taps," the refrain played at funerals of veterans and a Memorial Day observances at cemeteries.

"After World War II ended, I was the bugler for the Sturgis American Legion Post 73 Firing Squad," he explains.

The legion was the only local veterans' organization with a firing squad and color guard at that time, Wally says. It was a busy – and sad – time.

Bodies of World War II dead were being shipped home form overseas. Many military funerals were conducted in Sturgis and area towns. The burials continued for several years.

Veterans' funerals have a profound effect on Wally, but several stand out in his recollections.

There was the funeral in Three Rivers when "the weather was so cold my trumpet froze. I thawed it out at the last minute with the hot exhaust from a car," he says.

But the one that bothered Wally the most was the funeral that no one attended.

It seems a veteran residing at the County Farm on U.S. 12 had died.

"It was in the summer. The only people at the funeral were Lou Moon (owner of Moon Funeral Home in Sturgis); the Legion Firing Squad/Color Guard; the minister; and me, the bugler," Wally recalls.

The firing squad stacked their rifles, carried the vet's casket to the hearse, and repeated the ritual at the cemetery.

"Even though no one else was there, the man was afforded proper honor; he was a veteran."

Playing "Taps" at military funerals is important, Wally believes, because he knows the meaning behind the use of "Taps" as the final farewell to warriors.

That's why Wally questioned, in his sensitive, but eloquent letter to me, if the public knows why "Taps" is played at military funerals, and also at day's end.

The first use of a version of a "Taps" was the French "L'Extinction des Feux," meaning Lights Out.

Napoleon might have liked it, but Civil War Union Gen. David Butterfield didn't. He was a Medal of Honor winner and sensed that something more personal was needed to comfort the men in his command.

Morale had reached bottom during the fighting at Richmond, Va. The troops had learned that relief forces weren't coming. They couldn't return home soon to wives and families. Despondent, the men dug in to await the onslaught of rebel forces.

Butterfield worked into the night to write down words for a special "Taps." The next morning he summoned a brigade bugler. After Butterfield hummed the tune a couple of times, the bugler tried his luck at playing it. That night was the first time "Taps" was officially played at an army field post to signify the end of the day's military duties.

When other units heard the plaintive notes ringing out over the countryside, they asked about it. Soon, "Taps" was played at other units.

And then a soldier from Capt. John D. Tidball's Battery A of the 2nd Artillery was killed.

It was unwise to fire the traditional three volleys over the grave, because of the close proximity of the Southern Army.

So "Taps" was played, beginning a custom at military funerals of the Army of the Potomac – and moving into a place in America's history.

The army officially adopted "Taps" in 1874, and by 1900 other services had followed suit.

They still fire three volleys over the graves of dead soldiers to end the funeral ceremonies. That custom was started by the Romans, who threw dirt over coffins three times to bid a warrior goodbye three times.

But it is "Taps" that stirs the emotions and best signifies the last farewell to veterans.

Wally Walter, the bugle boy from Sturgis' American Legion Color Guard, played that refrain many times. He never forgot its meaning – and never will.

Tillie Holds the High Ground

June 1987

Tillie came to Burr Oak last summer, wearing her gray and white finery. A bit shy, she strutted down Main Street like she owned it. She let everyone know right up front that she intended to put her mark on the village.

She has. Marked it up quite a bit, in fact.

Tillie is a dove.

No one knows where Tillie came from, although speculation and bets range loudly about her origin.

What is known about Tillie (assuming it's a she– and there is debate on that, too), is that she wears a band on one leg. Someone apparently, kept her caged at one time or another. But it's clear they didn't own her. Not if you consider Tillie's thoughts on ownership.

Tillie was simply there one day when business people opened their stores. Perched on a window ledge on a second story building, she looked the street over a long time.

And decided to stay. And made her mark, dotting the sidewalk with new spots. But no one cares. Tillie has come to town.

She flew from one window ledge to another the first months, while onlookers coaxed away. Tillie was friendly enough, but something from her past kept her from being caught or held. While she'd come close if you acted friendly, she still held back.

Tillie knew freedom once she experienced it. And wasn't about to lose it.

Where Tillie got her daily rations those first days, no one knows, but some venture to guess that she flew to nearby King Farms to fetch a few free morsels of corn.

But Tillie refused to take refuge or join a flock of doves that hang around the old depot building. After all, Tillie considered herself a lady. And a lady doesn't join a gang of gamey street doves that flit all over town.

But Tillie was responsive to humans. She continued her self-imposed squatters' right on her window ledges, alternating from the Burr Oak Hardware building to the Starlight 2 Restaurant and Foster Dry Cleaners.

For good reason. People in those establishments kind of adopted Tillie. Morsels began to appear on the sidewalk. Tillie knew a hand-out when she saw it and responded.

There was one fellow who figured that if enough care and attention was offered to Tillie, she'd respond more warmly. That fellow was an unlikely candidate of the village talkers, who offered ideas on what to do with Tillie. Jerry Foster, he of the gruff quick-lib and ever-present cane, decided to befriend Tillie.

They make an interesting pair, this cynical man and the elusive Lady Tillie. He sits on the edge of the curb, his dog nearby, and feeds Tillie. She saunters up to the food and takes her time eating. Why not? She considers that part of Main Street her domain.

So, Burr Oak has Tillie, whether it made the choice, or she did. She sleeps out in the weather, living as she wants to, unwilling to leave.

In the face of that determination, no one in town dares lay a hand on Tillie. For one thing, they are wary of Jerry's temper and his cane. Besides, they admire Tillie.

Some people might laugh and ask who would want to live in Burr Oak. Other people know why. So does Tillie.

So, all you visitors, be aware that you will be in harm's way if you disrupt or try to catch Tillie. It wouldn't be the smartest thing you could do in Burr Oak. But it might be the last.

There is one thing more to consider. Don't walk too close to downtown window ledges unless you want to be baptized from above. Tillie, you know.

Root Cellars and Family Roots

June 13, 1987

The road from the woods to the small clearing in the distance was barely visible. Time, the insistent healer, helped cover the tracks where oxen and heavy logging carts had pulled timber from the forests.

But sparse threads of snake grass clung stubbornly to the grainy white sand, seeking a place to put down roots. Like a wild rose springing to life in a mint marsh, the grass seemed out of place.

I walked a few roads, but with the spring rains, it would take a four-wheeler to reach the homestead.

They called the settlement Kentuckyville. Once, in this wilderness of jack pines and birches, where wild spearmint and arbutus waft their fragrant aromas, there had been people.

Most of those hardy souls had came from the hill country of Kentucky to homestead, first in Wisconsin and later in the Upper Peninsula of Michigan.

They were proud, independent people. During the time white pine was king and mining was a way of life, my great-grandparents and grandparents had settled a few miles from Sidnaw. My mother spent her childhood learning the meaning of hard work. But she also was a free spirit who ran barefoot in the sunny meadows she was fortunate enough to discover. Nearby was Markey Lake where she joined her siblings in summer swims.

It is quiet now, a home for beaver, otter, deer, and occasional bear, and sometimes a lazy porcupine. Life has come full circle.

But once, near Markey Lake and Kentuckyville, there had been a schoolhouse, homes and outbuildings. Most families had cleared the token government acres to file a homestead claim and raise families. They had trapped the rivers and streams, hunted the forests and made a living of sorts.

Standing there that quiet spring afternoon, I wondered why they had moved so far from town.

The meandering, tree-shadowed road led to Sidnaw – the nearest point of civilization, unless you counted a nearby railroad line.

That line is still used. Upper Peninsula people know the value of railroad transportation. Funds are being pumped into railroad maintenance to provide a means to move lumber and other commodities.

A childhood playmate from the 1930s, Fred McIntyre, accompanied me to the old homestead road. He knows the woods around Sidnaw well. Fred was a favorite hunting companion of my uncle and aunt, Floyd and Minnie Green, who now sleep an earned rest in a graveyard in the Lower Peninsula.

For a long while we sat in the car, trying to imagine what life had been in that 1885-1920 era. No doctors were present for birthing. Illnesses were treated as best they could. When a loved one died, the loss was mourned, accepted, and life went on. There was no room for softness; life in the northwoods was harsh.

We sat there as the afternoon sun filtered like waves of quicksilver through the woods, forming patterns on the pine bark. The wind played a crisp melody among the birch and poplar leaves.

Fred said trains used to stop at the crossing in the woods, blow the whistle, and unload supplies from town. One old-timer in Sidnaw said moonshine was sometimes delivered to Detroit and Chicago. Even if it wasn't Prohibition, folks won't say much more.

The railroad also provided unique transportation for Uncle Floyd, a gifted musician. Besides farming, he was employed as a band player. Sidnaw folks say he'd put a hand car on the tracks and "pump" his way to Sidnaw. There, he changed tracks and continued on to Ottawa Lodge, where he played for dances on Saturday nights.

When his band duties ended, Uncle Floyd pumped his way back home – at least 20 miles round trip.

There's not much left at the old homestead. Just a crumpled foundation and a demolished root cellar. Fred says he heard my Grandfather Powell caved in the roof of the root cellar when he moved to Markey Lake. Grandpa didn't leave anything for vandals.

I'm going back again. Maybe something remains; a small cooking pot, a kettle – a keepsake to prove that people I loved lived there.

Some folks say to leave yesteryear behind, a silent witness to another time. But something draws me back to that town I left as a child, even if I never lived on the homestead.

Perhaps I am like that snake grass, seeking a place to grab hold. Maybe it is not so much a search of an old root cellar, as it is a search for my roots and who I am.

A Mother's Touch, Unbroken by Death, Remembered

August 25, 1987

I will retreat a bit from everything today. My children have always sensed it and if they do not fully understand the reasons, they at least allow me the privilege of my moments and thoughts.

I am grateful for that. Selfish perhaps, too. But there is something in me at this time that is mine alone. My family cannot help me. It is a wondering backward in time to a place they have not known.

Most mothers say, if they are asked for their choice of a day to live over, it would be a time when their child is small again.

I would not. If I had that decision granted to me, I would be selfish. I would ask that I be allowed to spend one day as child myself again.

One day as my mother's child.

The veil of memory is a fragile one, only casting a shadow to disguise, if need be. Lifted from the recess of the mind, in warm recollections, it casts light on days from yesterday.

I would have it no other way.

It is 30 years ago today that my mother died. Strange, that I did not miss her this much in the beginning. But, as we grow older, as we seek the immortal in ourselves–perhaps in our own children–then we tend to seek another time.

Lesson Learned

Those of us who have lost our mothers young, learned a lesson early. A bittersweet truth. Much of what we experience as a parent ourselves needs the patience, strength and counsel our own mother could have given us.

Her name was Alma Powell Hogmire. She came from Irish and English background, with a bit of the German thrown in through the generations.

She had dark eyes and hair. Those eyes stare out at me in bronze-toned, faded photographs. Brooding eyes. Searching looks that seek answers that did not come.

Around her in those pictures are her many sisters and brother. Laughing, posing for the camera, it is she alone who has a look of innocence and, somehow, maturity. Only she looked beyond the camera's eye.

There is a look there, a haunting quality that leaves an unsettling feeling. What did she look for? Was it life she questioned?

Homesteaders

Her parents were homesteaders in the harsh Wisconsin and Michigan northwoods. It was work that aged one early; bone-tiring labor that took bits of childhood away in much too early responsibilities.

She learned early how to swing an ax, haul logs from the woods into the clearing.

She was a bright girl, but her schooling was soon halted. Work was necessary, family obligations many. She could bake a pie at the age of seven, her sisters tell me. They offer me rare glimpses of the young girl I never knew. They fill in gaps left when she died so young.

She married at 15 and was a mother at 16. There was no real childhood. Responsibility was the only thing she understood.

It was a stormy marriage. My father, an articulate man with a quick mind, also was young. Too young to know how hard life would be for him.

He left school before the 11th grade. I don't know the circumstances, only that it was to work on the family farm. I do know there was an edge of bitterness that did not leave him,

He was not a man of the land, though he loved it. His soul sought places beyond the farm. But a wife and too soon, more children, curbed his dreams.

But there was love. It was their caring that nurtured a young marriage and helped them through the years when their health failed early.

There were four girls in our family and one small boy. That child died at the age of seven months and it was a loss my father never mentioned. I did not question the reason; death had ingrained in him a sorrow that simply could not surface to be healed in sharing it with others.

Tenderness Recalled

But there was a tenderness in my mother. I remember finding her kneeling before a large trunk. Carefully, she sorted out items. It was apparent she had hidden something away from the prying eyes of those who did not understand.

The summer sunlight caught her face as she carefully picked up the little blue sweater and booties. She ran her fingers lovingly over them. Lifting her hands slowly, she raised them until the softness of the booties touched her cheek.

Slowly, silently, she rocked sideways. Her grief over a lost child sent me back down the stairs so I would not interrupt her privacy.

But there were other sides to my mother. Some portion of her character kept a bit of what the child in her had not been free to do. She could, in my early years, run barefoot with me through the golden dandelions until we were exhausted.

There was exuberance in seeking out fireflies at night. Or listening to the train whistle from under the coverlet where she would let me creep in the bed shared with my father.

Moments that do not fade from memory. Like sitting on the slate porch and listening to an owl hoot his loneliness at dusk. Having her hold my hand when I shivered at the sound.

Making sugar cookies at the spur of the moment. I remember how she always smelled of cinnamon and vanilla. After she died I found one of her aprons hanging on the pantry door. It still smelled of vanilla and cinnamon.

Blood Disease

Strange that I remember so much of these things about my mother. She was ill all her adult life and hospitalized often. She had eight operations, all serious, and suffered a blood disease that took her life in her thirties.

But she was not a complainer. There was not time. Maybe she also sensed there was no future ahead. I do know she had a compelling desire to live to see all her children grown and through school.

It was a wish death robbed from her.

I remember other things. Like the many times she paddled me for misbehaving. I also remember when I had whooping cough and she stayed with me nights when my body was raked from the ceaseless coughing. Her touch calmed me.

She was a strict disciplinarian. Maybe too strict. But I realize now much of the measure of her caring was knowledge she would not be around to guide us. And she put as much drive and character as she could into her children in the short time she had left.

She could compromise, however. Like the time when I 'borrowed' a neighbor's flowers to make up a May basked for her. She opened her mouth to lecture me—and then saw something on my face that changed her mind. She said nothing.

But the message remained clear, and I apologized to the neighbor. My mother was unbending when it came to integrity. Nothing was as important. She would consider nothing less—not from herself—or us.

Bond of Love

I know there is little sense in looking backward to what was—or could have been. But the bond of love that did not fade when she dies is left intact through a web of remembrance.

So it is a different time for me today. And I do not offer any apologies. I am too old to change habits that have become ingrained and easier to live with.

I am not always a creature of habit. I do not always journey to graveyards on Memorial Day. Oh, there is a tugging sometimes, and I go to the small country cemetery where she has lain these 30 years.

I do not find her there.

I prefer other unscheduled visits, when the first daffodil pokes its brilliant head to meet the world, or when fall leaves waft lazily into backyards.

I know, as surely as anything that is certain in this world today, that my mother understands and would not question.

Beally's Wake was some Party

September 12, 1987

They laid Beally out in his World War II Royal Air Force uniform. He'd have liked that. Beally was a patriot.

His fine kids – Tim, Teresa, Pat and Jamie – did the funeral plans up right, followed Beally's orders right down the line. Did it because they loved their Dad and because they knew that Beally believed in an after life and would have raised the dickens if they didn't.

Beally (a lot of Harry's close friends called him by his last name) seldom put on pretenses.

But he sure loved a party. And valued his friends.

Beally had a lot of them.

Judging from the folks who turned out for Beally's wake the other day, they come from all walks of life, all ages. There were civic leaders, factory workers, fishermen, neighbors and a cross-section of humanity. All there for one purpose: to say goodbye to Beally and to celebrate his life.

But how do you say goodbye to a fellow whose spirit transcends death?

Beally was the guy who came out of Canada some years back to set up the production lines at Rubber Products in Burr Oak. He had been a teacher at one time and was a gifted chemist.

He also was gifted with a strong vocabulary. He could be gentle, his words like amber honey; smooth, rich and tasteful. And he could be caustic. When Beally's fuse ran short, he'd mix colorful curses with Hail Marys and whatever it is that good Catholics refer to when they know they should repent.

My first glimpse of Beally was when I arrived early for my first day of work. The building was empty. And then I heard a loud clanging and followed the sound. There Beally was, his legs sticking out from under a vat of melted rubber, working on the equipment. He pounded away, the hammer not quite as loud as his raving.

Moments later he emerged, white dress shirt streaked with black rubber. He pushed his hair back off his forehead, grinned, grabbed my hand and nearly shook it off.

"Welcome!" he said.

Through the years I was privileged to call him friend. I watched his marriage to delightful Alex unfold. Beally didn't win many rounds. She kept him in line. Every once in a while she'd remind Beally that he'd been her teacher when she was in school. It was true. It always stopped Beally short and made him laugh.

They raised four good kids who did their folks proud. The only sorrow Beally knew was when he lost Alex to cancer several years ago. But he went on with life and finished raising young Jamie.

A couple of years ago, Beally decided to move to Arizona. In typical Beally style, he decided to throw a party for his friends. The invitation said he would be moving to Arizona to play golf, drink margueritas and chase women – and he wasn't promising in what order.

I still laugh about it.

Beally had some good months before he developed cancer. And he lived every moment, his children said. Even joked during the last days when Teresa chided him about ringing a miniature bell so often for assistance. It was the kind of banter Beally loved, especially after it became difficult for him to talk.

He even cooperated in the last hours. Waited until son Tim got home from overseas military duty so he could say goodbye.

Beally always was an accommodating sort.

And that's why there was a special gathering after the funeral service the other day. It included the food that the good church ladies always are so kind to cook. But more than that, Beally had instructed his kids that they were to "throw a party somewhere for my friends."

There weren't many tears at that gathering – not even for Beally. He wanted it to be a happy time. And so it turned out to be a celebration of Harry Beally's life. Of the good times, remembering the Beally who waved his arms wildly while talking, his favorite stories, the remembrances that cemented friendships.

Even a healthy swig and toasts of the harder stuff was encouraged. Beally always believed that his God was more understanding than critical.

I couldn't make the party, but I'm sure I'd have enjoyed it. Knowing good friend Beally, I wouldn't have dared do otherwise.

I'm going to miss that man.

Memories to Last
Past September

September, 1987

Sometime, when the leaves begin to turn, clouds hang low and smoke from bonfires wafts lazy into backyards, the melancholy will find you , too.

I have survived September. What it means at least, and I tell myself it will be easier next year. Why should this September be different than ones of other years.

This year it came so quickly I was unprepared. So many other Septembers had came unhurried, careful. This September was the first time I did not send a child off to school. True, the youngest is going to college, but it is different. There is no trying to say it is the same.

When the school newsletter came early, I quickly scanned through it. My first thought was to remind the boy to get his athletic physical, to pick up his schoolbooks.

Then I was struck by the fact it no longer was necessary. I had told myself other years that it would be rather nice when those busy, involved years would ease. I have found out– more harshly than expected –in reality it does not turn out that way.

A Look Backward

I will miss the annual trips to town to buy clothes –the never ending hassle about what is proper and what is right–the last minute hemming of skirts, the shirt that has to be the right color.

Do others remember children who had to have crayons that first day of school? There was always competition to see who had the biggest box, the most colors. Pity the child who came to class with any other brand than Crayola!

I welcomed (with some reservations) the day when my children entered school. It had been a marvelous experience for me and I had enjoyed school. I did not want to heed their progress, but still there was the numb, unspoken question when one left a child at the door. To trust them to a person you had known on a different basis.

Why did one look at that teacher as though she was a stranger? Did one feel her guidance would help the child grow into a person who would be unrecognizable? Was it simply we could not quite accept the fact that it would be a different world–and child–who would live in our house?

There are so many times that will not come again. Remember how we trudged the woods and fields gathering leaves to be used for science lessons? And how we listened with concealed amusement to a little girl who had to have "just the right color blue" for her gym bloomers?

And the smell of the hallways and desks. When did they change from our own schooldays? When did they start using wax instead of oil? Has it gone forever?

Times To Forget

There are some things better forgotten quickly, if possible. In nearly every child's life there will be teachers who have shown extraordinary guidance and understanding, who will remain in children's esteem forever. And, too, there will probably be in every child's life, a time when a teacher will break their faith and trust.

No one is perfect. And one must assure the child that even if he is treated shabbily, there is reason to trust again; there will be other teachers for whom only respect is gained.

The ballgames. Daughters with cold cheeks and hot hands from leading cheers for the team. Nights of sitting in ice and rain, watching defeats—and victories.

Washing grimy, smelly, uniforms. Working a half hour to remove grass stains from the pants and having them brought back the next day in the same condition. But so thankful that the children were participating in events that would mold them into men and women.

Youths who ran onto fields and courts wearing school colors. Watching as they learned discipline. Hoping emotions do not show and you will not embarrass them when they have been injured. After all, one must never run out to comfort them. They would never forgive you, you know—even if they did need you. Sharing the proudness in their courage when they swallowed defeat, sometimes not so bravely, but usually with a measure of honor. Knowing their joy when they won a victory that seemed unattainable.

The finality of truth when names were called the first game this year and youths ran out on the field. Knowing your own would never again be there. The suffocating tightness of throat at the knowledge you had not realized you would feel this way.

Small Secrets

Notes found tucked away in pockets on washdays. Some better

left unread and usually not mentioned. Just left in a place they can find them and not be embarrassed.

Field trips, hayrides, class papers and projects. Times to remember and some to place among keepsakes. Remember the first valentine and its crudely printed words "I love You"? The garish Christmas and Mother's Day gifts that defied one to know sometimes what they were–and cherished beyond question?

Proms. Shy, uneasy boys who knocked hesitantly at the door, clutching a corsage box. Nervously straightening ties. Sometimes driving around the block several times before courage welled to push them towards the door. And young girls just as nervous, waiting for their arrival, who cast furtive glances at the clock– and us. Reading in those glances that one should retreat to another room.

Watching young sons comb hair over and over, also checking watches, knowing they, too, must perform the same ritual–at her house! Seeing the warm look on their faces when they escorted the young lady of their choice to their own home so we, too, could share in the moment. Watching a girl holding tightly to our son's coat-sleeve as they came up the walk. Were we ever that young too?

Memories of other things. Report cards that boasted of study. Honor Society inductions. And other reports that meant a bit of shame and words of admonishment.

Parents Needed, Too

Helping pick out dresses and shirts. And learning they were changed for jeans and sweatshirts after one left for work. One had to be "the same," you know.

Times riding in buses, supposed to be chaperones. But in reality happy to have the chance to share memories those youths did not realize are just that. Memories. Events that they, too, will someday view in the same manner as I do now.

Long telephone conversations and whispered confidences. Smiles and tear-stained pillows. Hair that would not curl right. The first sign of acne. Jeans that had to be washed many times until they were faded and wrinkled.

Plays, musicals, award dinners. Seeing the faces of their friends, who were part of their young life and hopefully, their future.

Watching my children as they accepted their diplomas with assurance tomorrow meant a new world for them. Seeing, too, a bit of hesitancy that tugged at their feelings, hinting to them they were leaving behind a precious part of their lives.

Smiling thought tears at their accomplishment in attaining that diploma—and knowledge that life will not be as ready to forgive their mistakes as it was during youth.

Oh, yes, I survived this September, but I have been wounded and it will take a long time to heal. It is a loss of a part of my children, of yesterday, innocence, childhood and family control.

It is foolish to say I will not miss it, for I do already.

Tomorrow will bring new ideas, new challenges. If I am fortunate, I will be allowed to share them. It is something to cling to.

But this September was different and I still hurt.

That Fifth Kid was a Humdinger

March 19, 1988

Five kids grew up at our house. That may come as a surprise to some people. They remember only Barb, Kathy, Mark and Tim.

The fifth one?

That kid was named "Not-me."

And that youngster was more trouble than the rest put together. Seems like everytime something got broke or went wrong, that poor kid's name was mentioned.

If I asked who broke the picture frame glass and then put it back on the dresser – where I realized six months later that the glass was missing – I got the standard answer.

"Not-me."

When I was hoeing the flower bed and discovered the paddle that was used on the misbehaviors frequently, and which someone had conveniently buried, the answer was the same.

"Not-me."

That kid showed up at mealtime, when misdeeds were committed at school, on vacations, at bedtime.

When I questioned my sons as to who was too lazy to come

downstairs to use the bathroom – and who did their duty through the upstairs screen window – that guilty name came up again.

"Not-me."

And of course that imp was around when I found all the empty milk and pop bottles in the refrigerator and I loudly complained. When I rounded up all four of the older children, the answer was a familiar one.

"Not-me."

There was the incident when a red mark appeared on the kitchen ceiling, a mark that wouldn't wash off and which remains to this day. I knew who the naughty one was, even if the mark wasn't explained until 25 years later when I learned that it came from a red-handled broom batted against the ceiling. And who had been blamed all those years?

"Not-me."

When I came in from mowing the lawn, tired and worn, but knowing that at least there was a beautiful pie baked for supper, I was so pleased. But lo and behold, there were new designs in the top – with some of the underlying filling missing. I found the guilty one, alright.

"Not-me."

And there was the occasion when we still had the old washing machine. Clothes had to be washed, rinsed twice in clear water and once in bluing, then starched and hung proudly on the line. I was always a bit arrogant on how nice my wash hung in the sunshine for all the world to see, each item lined up according to size and color.

An hour later I went back outside and nearly fainted from shock. There were perfectly formed handprints on the middle of the white sheets and shirts. Muddy handprints. Oh yes, the troublemaker did it.

"Not-me."

So, there was much relief when the kids grew up and moved away. But I learned something surprising. I kind of missed "Not-me."

Eventually, the grandkids arrived. The other day two of the boys were at the house. They had a grand time. But when I asked who tracked in the mud – all across the kitchen carpet – I learned that the fifth kid never really left home.

You guessed it.

"Not-me" did it.

Brown's the Color
of Complaint

April 2, 1988

The Department of Natural Resources came up red-faced the other day. Kind of smudged its reputation, in fact.

Seems that an overworked DNR employee gave a pollution alert hotline operator a false name.

The false name was to be used when people called for help from the DNR on the PEAS hotline, which stands for Pollution Emergency Alerting System.

The way the employee worked it, the initials should have stood for Pass Excuses Around Some.

Old Fred's name was on the call system and the public thought he was a real fella. Not so. It was a grand move to keep the nosy public off the disgruntled employee's back.

DNR officials are quick to inform that once they learned about the errant employee, he was strongly disciplined (he should have been fired). They also said that the public had nothing to fear, because the employee's real name was recorded on the official log and appropriate follow up was made to each inquiry from the public.

Oh yeah?

If we didn't – and the DNR didn't – know about Old Fred, how are we to be sure he got his hands slapped?

How this all worked was simple. An answering system is contracted by the DNR (according to their official newsletter) to man the 24-hour-a-day hotline. When a call comes to the operator, he contacts the DNR office in the area where the problem is.

The DNR district office gives the PEAS operator his or her name and records the information. An investigation into the problem begins.

But when the one employee got tired of taking complaints, he used the name Fred Johnson.

When callers tried to locate Old Fred, they couldn't. Simple enough; there was no Fred.

Think of how this scenario might have worked in the recent Muskegon incident, in which a cracked pipe allowed thousands of gallons of raw sewage to escape into local waterways.

"Hello, PEAS?"

"You have the right number. What is your problem?"

"There's this strange odor wafting down our way."

"What kind of odor?"

"Let's just say it stinks."

"Can you be more specific than that?"

"Well, it's like manure, or waste products, something like that."

"Specifics, please. We deal in specifics. What color and odor is it like?"

"Well if you must know, it's brown and smells like ... "

"I understand. My goodness, you do need help. Who do you want to talk to?"

"How about Fred Johnson. He's the one that's supposed to take these calls."

"Let me see if I can locate him."

"I'll wait."

"Ah, I'm having trouble finding Mr. Johnson. You said his name is Fred?"

"That's what the other operator told me earlier."

"Well, he's not here. Can you call back?"

"Sure, but the sewage is pouring out into the lake."

"Hello, this PEAS. How may I help you?"

"I want to speak to Fred Johnson. Remember that sewage problem? Well, all the fish are dead and the lake waters are kind of muddy, kind of thick. . ."

"Let me get Fred."

"OK."

"I'm sorry, but I can't seem to locate Fred."

"Do you know Fred?"

"Come to thing of it, I guess I've never met him."

"I'll call back."

"Hello, this is PEAS. We are here to serve your needs."

"Give old Fred a message. Tell him my lake is gone, I've got several million flies and I can walk on top of the lake surface now. But the smell is horrifying. By the way, do you need fertilizer for your gardens?"

"Oh yes, we certainly do. All of us."

"Well, you've got several truckloads on the way."

"Thank you for calling. I'll tell Fred."

A Matter of Character…
and Search to Find Self

April 19, 1988

He was head of his high school class, considered the perfect student. He went away to college, buoyed by his teachers' praise and support from family and friends.

Everyone expected he would excel. The young man with the brilliant mind and bright promise would shake the world. People would notice his achievements.

Instead, he contemplated suicide.

He goes away to college. This is where his 'perfect' life ends. Is that all there is? There has to be something else. He has no desire to get a job, retire at 65 and simply die. It's getting darker. The light is society and it's fading. A few more steps and he'll be swept away in a swirling pool of total darkness. He's at a standstill. When he moves again, which direction will he choose?"

It isn't important what his name is, only that others understand the emotional whirlwinds that engulfed him, and how close he came to leaving a bright world for permanent darkness.

At college, away from hometown peers and pressure, the young man became his own person. When he returned home that first year, his parents found a stranger. There was concern because he had turned his back on the high road to success. There were confrontations, angry words.

The truth was shattering. The young man realized that much of the reason why he had been a high achiever most of his life was because other people expected, wanted him to be. And he had come to believe that was what he had to do. By doing well, he was making everyone else happy. But he was miserable.

His father recalls that turbulent time. "We thought he was throwing away all his promise, wasting his life. We were discouraged. We didn't understand."

His mother also remembers. "As parents, we try to protect our children from a life of pain, but I know now that isn't reality. They have to experience pain and make their own mistakes."

The 18-yr.-old was confused, afraid no one would understand his feelings. And so, in his despair, he considered something that would end his torment. Suicide became a flickering candle that lit his dark tunnel of despair.

But then, as if some unknown force reached deep within him and pushed a button, releasing the emotion so long held in bondage, he discovered new strength. In that quiet, but significant moment, he found the courage that prevented him from taking his life.

He chooses to simply live. No goals, no pre-planned destination. He chooses life over death at 18.

His parents had always been proud and supportive of their son.

They expected that he would have a brilliant career.

But they also learned a difficult truth. And they want to tell other high school graduates and their parents that too much pressure to excel can be dangerous. Life should have its balances.

What is failure? So many people out there struggling, scratching, fighting. For what? Achievement? To become happy? He's happy and he's achieved nothing. Is it possible that he's achieved everything and no one can see it?

Somehow, struggling to understand their troubled child, his parents found the key to the communication door. They reached out in love to their tormented son, willing him to understand that they had accepted his choice of goals. It was not easy, because they realized his achievement potential.

The turning point came when they understood that throughout their son's life there had been too much emphasis on success and too little on individuality.

"It had come from us, from his teachers, from society," his mother said. "And finally, we learned that we should give suggestions, not opinions. We realized that we had to talk more to our son, to find out what he wanted from life. It is so important that parents listen to what a child is saying and try to determine what he feels."

Mostly, the mother and father want to tell other parents that they "should not assume everything is well with their children. Sometimes it isn't. Listen beyond what they say. Always be there for them. Understand that young people face so much more competition in their world today than we did. Each person is special in their character and gift to the world."

"We must guide them, not push them," the mother said. "Let them go their way without the guilt of having to try to be what someone else thinks they should be."

"There are many young people out there competing, trying to be something they aren't. And they should be appreciated for just being themselves. We hope other parents don't make the same mistakes. And now, when so many youths are graduating and going off to college, it is important that other parents realize the stress these young people face and what can happen," the father said.

The parents understand now what courage it took for their son to find his way. "He is a very special young man and his mother and I are very proud of him," his father said.

"Society can't begin to comprehend what or who he is. Society does not even try. It merely chastises. It unmercifully attempts to destroy those that do not conform. He is one of those non-conformers. But he will not be destroyed."

Today the young man is happily married, works full time and is pursuing college courses. He has the assurance that he has earned the respect and support of his family, that he is appreciated for his own thoughts and opinion.

And he has achieved something far more valuable. He has learned who he is, his own worth. He has met his personal tiger and defeated him. That tiger was a battle for personality, inner character; his very soul. He has turned back his wall of darkness and found a valuable human being, capable of contributing his own character mold for the world.

People say he is wasting his life. He merely smiles; he's happy. He thinks of asking everyone what they've done with their lives. Is existing happily not enough? Life is wonderful. I am he.

It was a Thump and Bump Trip

July 2, 1988

I'm a glutton for a lot of things, but I didn't realize punishment was included.

Bowing to the Mister's suggestion to ride a train, we recently bought tickets on Amtrak. And tarnished the love affair I've had with railroads for 50 years.

We journeyed to Little Rock, Ark., so I could pick up a journalism award. The real award should have been for getting on that choo-choo.

The train was an hour late leaving Kalamazoo. I was already simmering over a $7 cab charge from our son's house. I reached the boiling stage when I realized that we might miss our Chicago train connection.

In Chicago we trotted a quarter-mile and managed to climb aboard the train. Actually, I dragged aboard. Took an hour to get my breathing and heart rate back to normal.

And then I leaned back to enjoy myself – and the foot rests wouldn't work. My temper edged higher.

It was soon obvious that the newer Amtrak coaches didn't ride as easy as the old New York Central ones did. Made of lighter material, a sympathetic conductor said.

For a large person, my fanny didn't stay in one place on that seat 30 seconds.

"Oh, they're repairing the tracks," the trainman said in answer to my perplexed look.

"How far?" I asked.

"To St. Louis," he said calmly. I entertained the notion to hit him.

That train humped, bumped and thumped all the way to St. Louis. In the midst of my misery, the Mister excitedly said: "Oh, there's the Arch!"

I could have cared less about the St. Louis Arch. All I wanted was to arch my back comfortably.

The Mister was engrossed in the scenery. I was engrossed in surviving.

We finally got to the Little Rock hotel and argued over first use of the shower. And then, exhausted, we took a nap – and woke up four hours later.

We left Little Rock for home the next day at an ungodly hour: 11:32 at night. And let me tell you, that train station wasn't the delightful depot of yesteryear. It was dirty, the overhead pipes leaked, and the wiring was exposed. I prayed to get out alive.

On the trip home, we realized that extended families – parents, kids, aunts, uncles, gramps and grammas – were aboard. They arrived loaded to the hilt – and that meant suitcases, food (fried chicken for breakfast) and belongings. Sometimes it was alcohol. One fellow wandered up and down the aisle all night, saying "I don't know where I belong." I considered helping him walk off the steps between the coaches.

He was the only person on the train who wasn't bothered by the coach's weaving. His dazed movements were perfectly synchronized with the train.

We had a three-hour wait in Chicago where there was standing room only and the air conditioning was on the brink. Finally, the call came and we started another long walk to our train.

A Red Cap said he would get us to the right train. Sure. They had changed the trains and ours was ready to pull out.

Another long, winded run and we found that they had hooked two trains together.

Off we went. For a half mile. Seems they put the wrong engine on the train. Started out again and then stopped in the rail yard. Turned out that they had forgotten to load water aboard.

Speaking of plumbing, I should comment on the toilets. Being a large lady, I discovered the toilets are built for people 18 inches wide. The Mister said the train's weaving didn't help him one bit, either.

We settled down to a long night in the coach, which had turned chilly. Across the aisle a young couple covered up with a blanket, the back of their seats laid down so they could stretch out.

I'd like to track that couple down in a few months to see what happened, because they certainly were active.

So, with me complaining, my body bruised and aching, my ankles resembling elephant feet, the night crawled on.

The Mister, realizing it was too dark to view the countryside, laid his head back on the skimpy pillow the porter had provided.

I could have swatted him, lying there so serene. There I was, unable to sleep, disgusted with myself for even getting aboard. I stared into the dimness of the coach as those around me slept.

And then the train lurched sideways. A suitcase on the rack

above a couple four seats ahead tumbled off and struck the man in the head. He bellered in pain. His profanity was startling.

"I told you not to put that suitcase up there," his lady said.

"Oh, shut up," he responded.

For the first time, I found enjoyment in the trip. I had live entertainment.

Wanting to share it, I turned to the Mister.

He snored on.

A time and way to Celebrate Life

November 12, 1988

Julia and Norman Giggy's world shattered Oct. 17, 1985 when their son, Brice, 18, died in an automobile accident on his way home from football practice.

"We had four boys. Like all parents, we looked forward to their growing up, having families and being with us until the end of our lives," Julia says.

"But our family suffered a terrible loss that night," the Howe, Ind., resident says, still trying to come to terms with the tragedy.

Brice was a popular teenager at Lakeland High School, where he excelled in football and also wrestled. He enjoyed the usual sibling rivalry and fun with his brothers: his twin, Brent, and Bradd and Brian.

When Brice died, his family knew that there was no choice for them; life would have to go on without him.

Shortly afterward, Julia learned about a support group in Bronson, Mich., organized to help people who had suffered loss of loved ones.

"I went to the meetings. Those people helped me get through some rough times. Some of them had lost children, so they know what my family felt, "Julia says. "With their understanding and help, plus that from family and friends at our church, we were able to look ahead."

But Brice's loss was difficult to accept. Julia and Norman struggled for a way to express their grief in a meaningful way. And in time, and idea from the Bronson group, "New Beginnings," emerged.

"The Bronson people had started a project whereby they used a Christmas tree and allowed others in the community to place a memorial ornament on it. The first year they used a cut tree, but the second year they planted a live one so that the memorial tree would be a permanent expression of remembrance," Julia says.

And that started Julia to thinking. Couldn't a similar project be started in Howe? Wouldn't it help others to remember their loved ones in a symbolic expression?

And so the Living Memorial Tree project was started in Howe. With help from Sharon Peachey, Martha Cox, Sue Hasbrouck and Rev. Michael Wilson of the Howe United Methodist Church, the church committee announced its plans. Approval also came from town officials.

Because Christmas is a time when families come together in warmth and love, and because it also is when the loss of loved ones is difficult to handle, the holiday season was chosen for the public project.

The tree will be decorated with ornaments of four shapes: angel, heart, bell and star. On each ornament will be the name of someone's deceased loved one. Those placing an ornament on the tree will make a donation that not only covers the cost of the ornament, but will help beautify Howe Park, where the tree will be located. Playground equipment for children also will be purchased from the donations, Julia says.

A brief memorial service is planned for 7:30 p.m., Saturday, Dec. 3, in the park. A list of ornament names will be read and the tree lights will be turned on. The lights will remain on until Jan. 1, when the ornaments may be picked up by the donors until next year. The tree will be removed Jan. 15.

Next year, the Howe residents will plant a live tree. As it grows and more ornaments are placed on it, Julia is confident that personal losses will be shared by the community.

"We feel that this is a way for us to come together, to share our grief and to remember those we loved in a positive way," Julia says.

People wishing to have the ornament of their choice placed on the tree have until Nov. 15 to make a donation. Checks should be payable to Howe Memorial Tree Fund, C/O Howe United Methodist Church, P.O. Box 206, Howe, IN 46746, or call 562-2182, 562-2161, 562-2172, 562-3944 or 562-2250. Choice of ornament shape – bell, star, angel or heart – should be noted, as well as the name of the person the ornament is in memory of.

Julia says her family will always miss Brice. But she and Norman take comfort in the sons they still have. Brian is in the Army in Texas; Brent is attending college, and Bradd is a junior in high school.

"In joining others who suffered loss of loved ones, we found that we can share our feelings, can give and receive strength to go on without the one we lost," Julia says.

And Julia knows that remembering Brice in a positive way is not a revival of sorrow, but a celebration of his life.

Hunting Season was Great Time

November 26, 1988

Deer hunting season always draws me back to the Upper Peninsula and Sidnaw, if only in memories.

That time of year was a highlight when I was young because at least 15 Lower Peninsula and out-state hunters converged on our home each year.

How we made room for all those guys amazed me, seeing as how there already were two adults and four kids in that house. But make do we did, because most were our friends. It also brought needed income into the house.

It meant work for my mother. She was the one who got up before dawn to get the old wood-burning stove ready for the breakfast meal.

And a meal it was, because the men spent most of the day in the woods on hunting excursions. And they needed a warm, full belly to brave the elements.

The weather was bitter cold and a fellow had to know his way around the woods to be a successful hunter – or to survive if he got lost. The northwoods can be cruel and unforgiving.

Mother usually fixed sidepork, eggs, coffee, hash, potatoes. And then there were pancakes and French toast with hot syrup. We never had cold syrup on our table.

I remember the mountain of pancakes mother made on a long, black griddle atop the cookstove. Then she'd pile the pancakes on a platter and store them in the warming oven until the hunters were ready to eat.

She had cooked most of the night, preparing pasties for the hunters to take to the woods in case they didn't come in for dinner.

Dinner was known as the noon meal in those days. No fancy thing such as lunch. And so pasties were a mainstay.

Mother made pasties with beef, onions, potatoes, carrots, turnips, celery and other items. She usually added a bit of gravy before sealing the ingredients inside rolled-out crust. You've never eaten good pasties unless they were homemade. I've tried all the store-bought and café ones and they aren't fit to be called pasties.

Rolled up in a newspaper and then re-rolled in a towel, the pasties stayed hot for hours.

Supper was a big event, with the hunters re-living their tales from the day's events. And then it was down to the business of eating. Meat (venison, pork, beef or ham), potatoes, vegetables, goulash, soup, parsnips, scalloped corn, baked beans homemade bread. And topped off with home-canned cranberries, blueberries, strawberries or raspberries.

And then there were cakes, pies, cobbler and cookies. The aroma wafted throughout the house.

But my favorite happening took place in mother's white-painted wash room. That's where the hunters gathered for the card games. Booze was purchased by the hunters and tossed in a washtub. Ice was handy; just went to the nearby lake and cut a chunk.

I was the "runner-after" person for those card games. I uncorked the bottles and kept a careful eye on the money that inevitably rolled off the table. Sometimes, the hunters would tell me to keep the coins – and for a kid who couldn't afford a 10-cent movie admission, it was fat pickings.

It was in those times that lifetime friendships were made with people like Miles and Clint Burnside. Berwyn Flach and D.B. Royer. Lynn Hull and Walter "Doc" Smith. And dozens of other people who enriched my life.

The only thing I held against those hunters was that they helped my parents move us to the Lower Peninsula on their trip home in 1940. I didn't want to leave the North.

Some people relocate without problems. Others take a long time to adjust to new surroundings. I'm a bit of a stubborn purist. I believe that hearts should remain true. And that's why hunting season turns my thoughts North to Sidnaw.

Canyon/Caniff were Well-Loved

December 3, 1988

Whatever will I do now that "Steve Canyon" is gone? Will the comic strip sections of newspapers ever be the same?

Back during the 1940s, the Sturgis Journal announced that it might not renew several of its longtime syndicated comic strips. Readers were asked to comment on which comics they wanted to keep.

I was young then and hostile to any attempt to discontinue Steve Canyon in the newspaper.

I still have a copy of the letter I wrote to the editor – my first and last, by the way.

A lot of other folks also didn't like the idea of losing Steve Canyon. The publisher of the paper renewed the comic strip, which was published for many more years.

Steve Canyon's creator, Milton Caniff, died April 3 at the age of 81. Although he had completed enough drawings to continue the strip for several months, King Features, the syndication company, decided it was time to end the story line.

It was a popular strip, as was its predecessor, "Terry and the Pirates." Caniff created Terry and the Pirates in 1934, situating the strip's adventures in the Far East. The popular strip was carried in hundreds of papers before Caniff walked away from it 12 years later when the syndicate refused to grant him ownership rights.

He got even by creating Steve Canyon. That new strip closely followed the Terry and the Pirates theme. In time, Steve Canyon was published in 500 newspapers throughout the world.

Canyon was ahead of his time, but several of his comic strip story lines did not become outdated. We can find a lot of Terry and the Pirates in the movie, "Raiders of the Lost Ark."

Caniff was born in Hillsboro, Ohio in 1907 and began his career in 1932 with his creations "Dickie Dare" and "The Gay Thirties," both for Associated Press.

They were popular strips, but it was Terry and the Pirates and Steve Canyon that brought maturity to serial comics. Caniff used what other cartoonists later described as bold use of different angles and dramatic silhouettes.

Caniff brought realism to his dialogues, something most of the other comic strip artists were unable or unwilling to attempt.

Caniff was ahead of his time, especially in the description of Far East events. He accepted the possibility of World War II sooner than politicians and statesmen.

And when war came, the role of Steve Canyon and his friends changed to reflect the men and women in uniform. Just as the 1930s Buck Rogers' adventures seemed possible in the future (many of the incidents came true with the rocketry and astronaut age), so too, did the Steve Canyon episodes.

When Milton Caniff died, King Features said the decision to discontinue the strip was testimony to the cartoonist's singular abilities.

I believe that. So did 23 artist colleagues of Milton Caniff, who created an editorial cartoon for their friend. The cartoon shows Steve Canyon putting a soldier's helmet with the name Caniff on it atop and artist's pen – a tribute to a fallen comrade.

The creators of such comic strips as Peanuts, Mother Goose, Prince Valiant, Gasoline Alley, Doonesbury and Beetle Bailey signed the memory drawing.

You can have your Alley Oop, Dick Tracy and all the rest of the comic strips. For me, a chapter of my life closed when Milt Caniff – and Steve Canyon – died last April.

Coal Search taught a Lesson

December 17, 1988

There are many reactions to dealing with poverty. One of the most important is the outlook of people who have experienced it.

My family was poorer than the well-known church mouse. We couldn't even boast of having one.

We got along pretty well during the warm months, but in the Upper Peninsula town of Sidnaw, winter came early. The bitter cold increased the worry of how the budget would stretch to include fuel.

We had a wood-burning stove for warmth, but couldn't afford to buy any. And even with all the wood available in the forests, my father was too ill to do that duty.

Ingenuity, guts and determination was how many families endured those times.

We had food because we planted a large garden each year. My mother canned everything in sight. She wouldn't leave a tomato on the vine. If she had to, she'd make tomato juice.

Fresh meat was sometimes difficult to come by, but my dad did what every other father in the same position did: we had venison even when it wasn't hunting season. The game wardens looked the other way for humanitarian reasons.

But fuel remained a problem. Few homes had insulation and

rooms were drafty. We'd awake in the morning to find snow had sifted in through the window frames.

We used soapstones for bed warmth. My parents would put them in the oven to heat, and then warp them in a towel. Inserted under the bed covers, the heat kept us warm all night. It did me, at least, because as soon as sister Mary Jeanne fell asleep, I'd move the soapstone over to my side of the bed.

I always knew my dad had some sort of secret means to obtain coal. And it involved the railroad.

We lived directly across from the railroad coal tower, where there was ample coal supplies. My father was no angel, but he wouldn't steal coal. He had another plan, which I learned as his accomplice at the age of seven.

My dad had one big imperfection in his character. Pride was his buffer zone against the inadequacies of life. I had a clear understanding of that one morning about 5 a.m. when he rousted me out of bed.

He was waiting in the kitchen with a gunny sack. I knew my time had come; I had arrived at the age of coal hunting time.

Now my father wasn't about to let any town resident catch him picking up coal that had fallen along the railroad tracks. His pride dictated that we do the necessary chore in the darkness, away from prying eyes.

Whispering, we walked to the railroad and started searching for coal in the darkness. We worked quickly and quietly.

And then, our job completed, we sat down on the tracks for a moment. Breathing heavily, the frost from our breath formed small clouds in the thin air. I knew my father was satisfied that we had managed to get the uncomfortable deed done.

And then, as the early morning sky started to lighten, we heard scuffling sounds down the tracks.

"Hush!" my father warned as we sat there.

As morning dawned, we saw our neighbor and friend, Gus Rappi, with one of his kids. Gathering coal.

My father sat for a long moment, frozen in stillness to that railroad track. And then he rolled backward in the snow, his laughter carrying down the tracks and alerting Gus, who took stock of the situation and sat down and joined in the not-so-private revelation.

I think I respected my father as much for that moment as for anything he ever did in his life. His pride had been vanquished, but not his understanding of the complexities in life and the humor necessary to endure them.

I grew up a bit that morning of my childhood when I realized that laughter can make the human spirit triumph – if we try hard enough to forget our pride.

Battlefield Christmas Recalled

December 24, 1988

It was Christmas Eve 1914 and the Great War was only a few months old.

The British and Germans faced each other over miles-long, deeply-dug trenches in France's farmland. They had been fighting each other for weeks. Neither side planned to retreat.

There would be no rear line dinner on Christmas. No furloughs or letters from loved ones. It was so different from happy Christmases that soldiers on both sides remembered from their brief lives. And certainly not the manner in which they wanted to observe a holiday.

But battle orders were clear. Hold the front lines at all costs. In the morning, the carnage would begin again. Machine guns and mortars were primed for action.

And so the men huddled in the trenches that cold December night. Morale was low for the soldiers forced to remain on a battle-field far from their families and homelands.

Despair mounting, the men looked at their bleak surroundings. Death was a few feet away at the top of the trenches. They huddled in earth-carved holes filled with snow and water. Rats shared their food supplies.

Counterattacks and gunfire were expected in the morning, the day when mankind traditionally paused to remember the King of Kings on his birthday. But war and killing did not stop for a holiday, no matter its significance.

On the German side, the exhausted men read Christmas messages from the Kaiser. In the British trenches a scant few hundred yards away, troops read greetings from their King.

It was a terrible time for the soldiers, who only prayed that the fighting would stop, that they would survive and return home to their loved ones.

Late Christmas Eve, a British sentry guarding the lines of the Fifth Scottish Rifles heard a poignant sound. Across the barren ground between the rows of trenches, across the area where no soldier dared cross the field known as no-man's land, a song was heard.

"Stille nacht, heilige nacht."

It was incredulous, but true. A German soldier, forgetting the danger to his life, trying to capture a bit of Christmas spirit he remembered from another time, was singing a beloved Christmas carol.

The British soldier could not resist. Eyes brimming, voice husky, he began to hum along. And then his restraint broke. He began to sing the English words of the song, buoyed by his heart's message.

"Silent night, holy night."

The soldier from England joined in a duet with the young soldier from Germany, their voices revealing their homesickness.

"Heilage nacht, holy night," the duet continued.

And then, caution thrown aside, a second and third British soldier joined in. other sentries followed suit. Another Christmas song followed. Soon, the words were picked up in German from enemy lines.

A short time later, the British saw that the Germans had put a ragged evergreen tree with lighted candles atop their trench.

In the early dawn of Christmas, another sight gladdened the hearts of the British infantrymen and the lonesome German platoons. There, offering messages to each other, were "Merry Christmas" signs.

It was too much to ignore. A gentlemen's truce, unspoken but understood, was declared. Disregarding the danger, a few soldiers on each side laid down their rifles and crept beneath the barbed wire. Scores of British and Germans followed the first brave souls.

They met in no-man's land, a place where none had dared to venture before because of certain death.

Photographs of families were shown. Gifts of candy and cigarettes exchanged. A soccer ball was offered and the soldiers played a brief game on a site that was not pocked with mortar holes.

And then their commanders arrived on the scene. Horrified, the German and British officers ordered their men back to the trenches. Firing resumed. The Fifth Scottish Rifles command issued the order that "We are here to fight, not to fraternize."

History recorded that bittersweet chapter of World War I. Most of the young men involved in that skirmish died there or at later battlefields.

But enough soldiers survived to tell the world that for one brief moment in a cruel and insensitive war, there were men who remembered the true meaning of Christmas. The story would be recounted and published many times in the years to follow.

For a few hours on a bitter cold Christmas in 1914, brave souls proved that there was only one master – neither King nor Kaiser – but the Prince of Peace.

Let's Light Up the Capitol Dome

December 31, 1988

Bet you don't know that Michigan's Capitol building in Lansing will be 110 years old Jan. 1.

And did anyone tell you that a Detroit native is collecting signatures to light the dome of the Capitol on its birthday each year – and special occasions such as Flag Day, Fourth of July and Veteran's Day.

The colored lights, of course, would be red, white and blue.

If successful in his efforts, Andrew Anthos would make Michigan a chapter of the history books, because Lansing would then be the first state capital in the nation to honor the colors of the American Flag.

Our Capitol building was modeled after the one built in Washington. It cost $1.5 million and was dedicated Jan. 1, 1879.

An extensive refurbishing of the Lansing structure already is planned, and with the colored lights used on legal holidays, the Capitol dome would be a sign of Michigan pride.

Governor James Blanchard signed the petition for the dome's lighting. So did Lt. Gov. Martha Griffiths and 18 other high ranking state government people.

And if you think the petition is geared only for Michigan, be advised that people from 28 nations and 28 states have joined in.

Michigan became a state on Jan. 26, 1837, and our capital centerpiece is a proud symbol to citizens. So why not dress it up at special times?

Cost of preliminary lighting installation would be about $50,000, which includes labor, insurance and other items.

The actual cost to turn the light on each special day would be $7 for the hours 6 p.m. to midnight. That's not bad for a government project.

So would Anthos be there if the project is approved and when the light switch is thrown?

No.

Instead, he wants the governor to do the honors. And have the governor include a child, a homeless person, a handicapped citizen, a student, a senior citizen and a Native American to demonstrate statewide support of a cross section of its citizenry.

Anthos believes that the colors would signify and honor the sacrifices and gallantry of our Michigan sons and daughters who served in all wars, and those serving in law enforcement agencies to protect us.

So why do we need red, white and blue lights in the Capitol dome on special occasions?

Why not?

Wouldn't it be nice to have people – not the government – provide the funding to complete the project? It would be a sign of unity and pride.

I think citizens should handle this project so that they'll feel it is truly theirs.

We could let the Government pick up the $7 light bill tab the few times the dome would be lit. Government officials shouldn't holler about that; they feel free to do what they want with our money anyway.

Family doesn't Share
Taste Buds

January 7, 1989

I hate liver. I detest lima beans. I can't stand them at the same table where I'm sitting.

I'd just as soon pick soybeans and cook them, as try eat lima beans.

To me, liver in a butcher's meatcase looks like it's still alive and could wiggle its way out the door.

I have never considered putting those two items on my dinner table since I was married. And there is no chance I ever will.

If the Mister wants lima beans, he can go to someone else's house. But I doubt if he'll do that for liver; he shares my feeling for it.

Experts who study the human race claim families eventually tend to think alike and cater to the same food habits.

Hogwash. They've never interviewed my family.

I happen to love parsnips, cranberries, rhubarb and mincemeat. The Mister says they are foreign substances and won't touch any of them. He'd have to be interned in a concentration camp and starving to even consider one of them, and I'm not sure if that would do it.

That fellow I married so long ago is a bit strange. He likes sweet rolls and doughnuts dry. I like them doughy. He'd rather eat a hard cookie than a soft one. I opt for moist, tender cookies.

He wants his meat cooked long enough to bounce it off the floor. I like mine medium done. I've heard him wail like a banshee when a waitress dares to bring him steak that shows a hint of light pink in the middle.

My children also are weird. The youngest son loves raisins, but won't eat them in cupcakes, cake or other mixes. The same for nuts.

The older son won't tolerate onions. He believes God put them on earth as punishment for human frailties. But then, this kid is the one who puts mayonnaise on French fries.

My daughters aren't nearly as particular in their food habits, and that makes me wonder if I raised them right and the boys wrong, or is the female gender more sensible?

Men are different in their outlook and attitudes, I think. The Mister took a stab at cooking a couple of years ago and found he did pretty well. But we disagree on the ingredients, of course.

He believes in exact measurements. A teaspoon is a measured teaspoon. I just grab a regular spoon and toss it an educated guess, which he says with disdain has nothing to do with being educated.

I never measure sugar or other ingredients for fruit pies. I just put in what looks right. As far as I know, the Mister hasn't turned down any pie.

But I admit to errors in some areas of the culinary field. Having cooked for six people for years, it was difficult to cut back as the kids left home.

Consider macaroni and cheese. I bake it with different cheese flavors. But I never measure the macaroni before boiling it. One holiday the kids begged for some, so I boiled a batch. Turns out I had enough for two large baking bowls, enough to send home with all the kid's families, and leftovers for my grandkids' dog and the neighborhood birds.

I still don't understand why that incident was so funny and why it's brought up at nearly every family gathering since.

And beans. Good old baked beans are a mainstay at most homes. But I don't like those liver-colored attempts at baked beans. Any baked beans worth eating should have brown sugar, onions, smoked barbecue sauce and sausage in them. And they shouldn't be runny or watery. (The family doesn't turn away from those either, except for that kid who doesn't like onions – and he doesn't know that I use onion flakes).

I think cooking for families is strange. How can two grandchildren in the same family unit hate salad dressing – when both their parents love it? Have you ever realized that American eating habits revolve around salad dressing? I can't imagine two kids not ever eating potato salad just because it has salad dressing in it. Such a waste of taste buds.

Back when my kids were small, they ate what was on the table. They didn't have much choice in what was served. And there were no snacks and microwave-quick foods to make up the difference.

They ought to thank me for all those years of standing over a hot stove and developing their culinary tastes.

They really ought to appreciate that I never served a couple of foods. Not one of my grandkids has ever asked for lima beans or liver.

Judge a Town by its Memories

January 14, 1989

A woman called me awhile back and accused me of lying.

"I've read your columns about Sidnaw, in the Upper Peninsula, and it's nothing like you said! I purposely stopped there and I couldn't find any of those places you described!"

Hardly. The memories I wrote about occurred in the late 1930s.

Which tells me some people have a hard time deciphering what they read in a newspaper. You can tell by my photo in the column that those wrinkles aren't smile ones. And I've mentioned many times that those happenings were from a long time ago.

So, one last time. It's no secret: I turned 58 Christmas Day.

I keep telling myself that I shouldn't write about Sidnaw, located about 60 miles west of Marquette. But then readers ask for more of those memories, which for one reason or another, they tend to identify with, even if the locales are different.

I can't explain that attachment, except that people must have fond memories of their childhood, just as I do.

I get postcards mailed by strangers who stopped off in Sidnaw just to see what I found so wonderful.

And sometimes I get notes from people disappointed to learn that their search for the Sidnaw train depot was in vain.

One time I got a pointed missive from a gentleman (I'll allow him that much) who exclaimed: "I can't believe that a coal tower was located just across the road from your home!"

The heck you say, mister. It was my favorite playing spot.

I laughed when I received a letter mailed from a city in Georgia a couple of years back. How anyone got my column there I don't know.

"Just where is that CCC camp you wrote about?" the woman asked.

Gone with the time, sad to say. I'd even like to know what happened to all those homesick CCC boys who considered my mother's kitchen a gathering place.

"And don't tell me you had a town pump to fetch water!" she intoned.

Shame, doubtful one! We had two town pumps.

Why do people believe everything they read in a news story and doubt some poor old columnist?

I'm just someone who knows my place, respects my beginnings and isn't afraid to say how it was in that innocent time before World War II.

It never bothers me to write about the times I took pieces of cardboard to school each day to cover holes in my shoes.

And what's so bad about not having store-bought underpants until high school? My mother and her sewing machine handled those needs. I admit it was difficult when war came and elastic was hard to come by. My mother just improvised; she made under britches with ties on each side. For obvious reasons, I always tied mine in a knot.

Sidnaw was a kid's dream. There was a creek with brook trout.

Kids were free to roam the woods and fields. There were logging camps and hobo jungles to explore.

Wild cranberries, blueberries, strawberries and red raspberries were abundant in areas crowded with deer, beaver, otter and bear.

The railroad water tower allowed for impromptu showers in the summer and there always was Steve Martino to fly in once a month for rides in that old Waco airplane.

To this day, there are no strangers in Sidnaw. Residents remain the close-knit neighbors they were so many years ago. And they welcome visitors. The town gas station has an old sofa so folks can sit down and be comfortable.

I know that some people regard Sidnaw as a backwards town – but not in my earshot. We always had good people there. Excellent teachers, a top-notch school system, grocery stores, saloons, dry goods merchandise, and garages.

So we didn't have a public library, a fire department or the like. We did have the Oldfellows Hall, where movies were shown. We had two train lines with fellows who'd choose a library book at a city library up the line and return it for me after I read it. Talk about free delivery service – and with smiles.

I know people who stop in Sidnaw now may think there's nothing much there.

Of course there is. Why, right down that street is where my best friend, Karoll Shingler lived. And a block away is where Tom Dentel and I doused each other every time we hauled water from the pump.

And the building that housed the old Episcopal Church remains. It was a mainstay in my childhood.

I have only to think of those days and Sidnaw remains unchanged in my mind.

The trouble with too many folks is they never learn to hold anything dear. All you have to do is cherish a town and memories remain bright forever.

A Character we called Hoot

January 21, 1989

I thought I heard him calling just after supper, when evening shadows moved through the pine trees in the park across the street.

But it was only memory – and wishful thinking – that stirred my heart.

I nurtured five kids. The most loving of them was the one I lost.

He came to us one cold spring day, wrapped in the oldest boy's coat. When I peeked inside, two large eyes stared back.

And then he snapped his bill in defiance.

"Hoot" had arrived. And our home – and hearts – would never be the same.

In terms of description, he was a Barred Owl, named because of bar-like stripes on the feathers. But the common moniker was hoot owl, hence his name.

He grew up on a diet of raw chicken necks and hamburger. Plus a few mice that neighbor kids supplied.

We laughed when a guest, unfamiliar with owls, shrieked one day that "Hoot just threw up!"

Actually, all Hoot did was upchuck the bones and material that his stomach couldn't digest – a common owl trait.

He loved water. Let a rainstorm come and he'd be out under the

455

downspout, holding out his wings with glee and rolling back one pair of eyelids (owls have two).

We watched Hoot chase a lawn sprinkler for a couple of hours one hot summer afternoon. The sprinkler moved back and forth in long, lazy swings. Hoot would chase it and stand underneath, only to find the water had moved on. Finally, he trotted up to the sprinkler, hopped aboard and rode it for hours.

Hoot never learned to fly. We tried launching him one day and he flapped into the side of the neighbor's house. He never tried it again.

No need. He had the fastest legs on the block and used them frequently, chasing away cats, squirrels, dogs, a horse a friend was riding, and a meter man.

But he loved our dog. The admiration was mutual, but the dog refused to sleep in the same quarters with Hoot. So, my Mister spent weeks building Hoot a grand, elevated house with steps to climb up. Hoot inspected, then rejected it. The dog got a new house.

Hoot relished car rides. If he heard the car leaving without him, he'd come trotting behind. It was a ridiculous sight, his legs in pursuit, wings outstretched. And hooting in anger at being forgotten.

We'd put a blanket in the car's back window and he'd sit there for hours. He created quite a stir when we stopped at grocery stores or the laundromat.

The only time Hoot left the car was to attempt a swim in a lake during a family outing. He only floated, with his wings outspread. A small child spied him and hollered "vulture!" The beach emptied.

Hoot disgustedly waddled back to our car (he knew which one it was), jumped up on the back seat and into his window seat.

Sometimes he misbehaved. He'd wandered over to a neighbor's

house. When I'd call him to come home, he'd click his bill and ignore me.

But let me start after him and he'd make a hasty retreat for home, usually detouring around a nearby house. And then sulk like a spoiled child when I chastised him.

Most of all, Hoot loved to ride the handlebars of our kids' bikes, going to area haunts and ballgames. He even knew when Mark came up to bat and sounded that familiar eight-hoot cry that delighted the crowd and made Mark flush in embarrassment.

We knew we'd lose Hoot some day. When he developed encephalitis, we realized that it was only a matter of time.

He died quietly one summer day, tucking his head under my arm and giving a soft hoot in farewell.

That night I waited until Mark was in bed before I attempted to bury Hoot, hoping to spare my son the pain. But then I heard his voice in the darkness.

"I'll do it," Mark said.

And then, stomping on the shovel in hurt and anger, he said: "I knew I shouldn't have loved him so much."

A young boy left childhood behind that night when he lost a treasured friend. It would be years before he could speak openly of Hoot.

Now and then, when darkness falls and a stillness moves over the yard, we hear an owl in a nearby tree.

It is not our beloved Hoot, but we like to think it is his spirit, returning to the family he loved.

I Shed No Tears for Ted Bundy

January 28, 1989

I doubt if it was remorse that Ted Bundy felt shortly before he died in the electric chair Tuesday. Most likely it was fear of what his Maker would say.

He had reason to fear. He maintained his smug silence for years about the deaths of young women he was suspected or convicted of killing. Not once in that agonizing time did he say he was sorry.

Bundy, who eluded the electric chair several times, reveled in his courtroom theatrics. It was disgusting to watch.

And in the end, his mother had to hear from the media that her son had given deathwatch confessions of some of the murders.

In a reign of terror over several states Bundy roamed college campuses, ski resorts and shopping malls, willfully stalking his prey.

Bundy's victims had no hint that evil lay behind that easy smile. Young women apparently trusted him. A few tried to help Bundy when he feigned a broken arm. He even used crutches to avoid suspicion.

Court records show Bundy wasn't insane, just an evil sociopath. That's a character trait, whereby a person commits unjust, sometimes terrible things, and then lies about them.

It should be remembered that Bundy was deliberate and scheming. Court psychiatrists testified that he enjoyed the thrill of stalking victims, the lure of the chase and the sexual frenzy in killing helpless people.

Bundy once teased investigators, theorizing how some of the murders "might" have happened. He didn't confess, but officials gained insight into the final moments of the victims.

In one case, two women were kidnapped the same day. In "supposing" the crime, Bundy described how one woman was raped and killed while the other victim was forced to watch.

Even then, Bundy scorned the judicial system. While awaiting trial for one murder, he escaped and killed three more women.

Bundy had years to tell investigators where some bodies were so that families could bury loved ones. Mind you, Bundy lived 11 years beyond his death sentence – one year less than the time his last victim, a 12-year-old girl, had on earth.

Weep for Bundy?

Not me. I weep for the victims' families. Can you imagine their torment, wondering about their children's last moments? The cries of lost daughters will haunt their moments. They question if their children suffered before they died.

Of course they did. The rape and torture, the certainty of their fate was unspeakable torture.

Pathologists know that terror can shut down the body's digestive process. Depending on time elements, the process can stop hours before death. Autopsy reports reveal it happened in many of Bundy's victims.

Pray for Bundy's soul?

That's difficult, even if he expressed remorse at the end. Bundy's cruelty was horrendous.

But I pray for a family in Florida. Think what their child suffered.

Before death mercifully ended her torture, Bundy ravaged and mutilated her. And then left her body in a pigsty, thrown away like yesterday's trash.

I know the Bible says we should forgive those who are repentant for their sins. I think repentance and sin have their degrees.

In Bundy's case, I find forgiveness impossible. I remember the years of appeals, his courtroom smirks, his denial of guilt.

I believe Bundy felt sorry only for his miserable self when he knew that execution stays were exhausted and society demanded payment.

I have sympathy only for his own family and the survivors of the young people whose life candles were snuffed out for no reason other than to gratify a depraved monster's desires. And I am angry because one man's evil could be perpetuated upon the innocent because he thumbed his nose at society and relished it.

Bundy enjoyed killing. I can't feel much of anything for him. His existence was a blight upon humanity, his life a mockery of everything good and decent.

Bundy blamed pornography. I don't discount that tie, but more likely it was self-indulgence and lack of moral conscience.

I can't say that I approve of capital punishment or the macabre actions of people who gleefully waited outside the prison gates before the execution. But if justice came Tuesday morning when the first jolt of electricity was turned on, I hope Bundy felt mental as well as physical pain.

Had Bundy sought therapy in his early life, or years ago admitted the crimes and offered information about the cases, perhaps I could muster some semblance of pity for his wretched soul.

But not now. His only contribution to the world was pain.

Display the U.S. Flag Properly

February 4, 1989

The flag of the United States is important to us. But even in our reverence and respect for the flag, we continue to improperly display it.

I've viewed this problem several times – even in Sturgis – and sometimes found the flag displayed wrong on a speaker dais, or flown incorrectly on staffs.

While Flag Day is June 14, many Americans choose to display our flag year round. It's a way of showing patriotism and support of our Republic.

The Flag Code is an important document, drafted by the 77th Congress of the United States' Second Session and known as Public Law 623. The code has been amended since then and adopted by at least 45 organizations, including the American Legion, Veterans of Foreign Wars, scouts and others.

Here are excerpts of the Flag Code, which should familiarize citizens, businesses and organizations how to correctly display our Flag.

- Display it from sunset to sundown on buildings or stationary flagstaffs. If flown 24 hours a day, however, it should be illuminated at night. Never should it be in darkness.
- The Flag should always be on the observers left (the flag's own right).
- When carried in a procession, the flag should be either on the

marching right of the other flags, or in the front of the center of that line.

- When a flag is displayed from a staff projecting horizontally or at an angle from the window sill, balcony or front of a building, the Flag's union (the star area) should at the peak of the staff unless the flag is at half-staff. And when the Flag is put at half-staff, it is first raised to the peak and then lowered. When it is taken down, it should again be taken to the peak and then lowered.

- When suspended over a sidewalk from a rope, the Flag should be hoisted out from the building toward the pole, union first.

- When the Flag is displayed over the center of a street, the flag should be suspended vertically, with the union to the north in an east-West Street, or to the east in a north-south street.

- When used on a speaker's platform, the flag, if displayed flat, should be above and behind the speaker. When displayed in a church or public auditorium, the Flag should hold the superior position at the speaker's or clergyman's right as he faces the audience. Any other flag is displayed to the left of the clergyman or speaker as he faces the audience.

- When flags of states or cities, or other pennants are flown from the same halyard with the American Flag, the Flag of the United States should always be at the peak. When flown from adjacent staffs, our Flag should be hoisted first and lowered last. No other flag or pennant should be placed to the right of the American Flag (to the observer's left).

- When flags of two nations are displayed they should be flown from separate staffs at the same height and should be approximately equal in size. International usage forbids the display of the flag of one nation above that of another in the time of peace.

- Our Flag represents the living country and is considered a living thing. The union of the Flag is considered the honor point. The right arm is the sword arm and therefore the point of danger. Hence the place of honor goes back to heraldry rules.
- When used to cover a casket, the Flag should be placed so the union is at the head and over the left shoulder.
- When the Flag is no longer in condition to display, it should not be cast aside, but destroyed in a dignified way, such as burning, observing the proper rules.

Certainly all of us revere the Flag and enjoy seeing it. But it is meaningless to display it if we ignore the Flag Code. If we remember that our Flag is considered a living thing and observe the proper rules, we will honor it with pride and respect.

The Message in Lisa's Death

February 11, 1989

A citizens' jury has spoken. It's called justice and we're expected to live with it.

Joel Steinerg, a disbarred New York lawyer, was recently found guilty of manslaughter in the death of his illegally-adopted daughter, Lisa. He faces up to 15 years in jail, but good behavior will probably get him out in six.

He should make it. There aren't any six-year-old kids in prison for him to abuse.

Think of it. One year in prison for each year of Lisa's young life. I call that unfair. His future will continue. Lisa has no tomorrows.

I'm angry with Steinberg and his common-law wife, Hedda Nussbaum. Such flimsy excuses for their actions: they couldn't cope with life, wouldn't accept the responsibility of rearing children, took their rage out on a defenseless baby.

That kind of behavior is unacceptable by man's and God's rules.

But I'm a lot angrier at neighbors, family and friends of Steinberg and Nussbaum. What excuse do these seemingly clear-headed, socially-adjusted people have for not stepping in and doing something.

I've heard it all, from the "I didn't feel I should interfere in another family's problems" to "I didn't know where to go to get help."

Hogwash.

I'm also not convinced that social services in New York did so hot in their investigations of the Steinberg home before Lisa's death. The Big Apple ought to polish up its act, beginning with humanity and conscience.

Lisa was abused for years, according to court testimony. And we know that in her last hours she was beaten unconscious.

So what did the people who were supposed to love her do?

They boozed a bit, snorted some cocaine and went to bed – while their daughter lay in a coma a few feet away on the bathroom floor.

Nussbaum wasn't capable of nurturing a child. Although she had been a talented illustrator of children's books – ironic considering what happened to Lisa – she was unable to escape the mental and physical abuse suffered at her husband's hands.

Police records show that Steinberg beat Nussbaum for years. She appeared in court with a gangrenous leg and broken bones.

Nussbaum should have done something about her predicament years before. After you're broken in body and spirit it's difficult to walk away. Experts in the criminal and psychiatric fields know that some individuals are incapable of defending themselves. But standing by while a helpless child is killed is inexcusable.

I even wonder about the jurors who decided Steinberg's fate. They could have found him guilty of murder instead of manslaughter.

I know something about the judicial system's crime and punishment categories. We are so careful to protect the rights of the accused. And then we bargain on a price tag for a child's death.

I'm sorry for Nussbaum, who was beaten to a pulp, but unable to fully convince the jury what her husband did. But she will recover.

I weep for a child who wasn't even protected by the judicial system when Steinberg illegally adopted her. Who's to blame for that mistake? And why?

I can't bear to dwell on what Lisa thought about her family. Did she question if other children had loving parents? A part of me prays she didn't know that, callous as it sounds, because it would have made her pain worse.

There are people who say that Lisa Steinberg is better off dead than to live in a house like that (I can't even call it a home). They say she's at peace and can't be hurt again.

I think that's a copout. It's an excuse to ease consciences. Suffering shouldn't be exchanged for death. By the grace of God, why should we even consider it?

It's time we did something about the senseless slaughter of children. We must insist that investigators work harder, that law enforcement not become hardened to this cruelty. And we must demand, not ask, our legislative and judicial officials to enact and levy the king of punishment that fits such heinous crimes.

But we have to start with ourselves. Law and society can only do so much.

Until we value our children, until we resolve that the world we bring them into is a better place because we set good examples, then there will be more Lisas. Not just in New York, but in our town, our neighborhoods, our homes.

I think what bothers me the most is that a little girl died and the message of her passing won't be heard.

Just Call it Ketchup, Please

February 18, 1989

For years I rallied – and wailed – because food companies refused to spell catsup like it sounds. You remember that better-known word, ketchup, don't you?

For the life of me, I never understood why they called it catsup. When I was a young kid, I thought it was something for cats and that we had it on our table at supper because we were poor.

That's stretching things a bit, of course, but anything as familiar as ketchup – an American mainstay – should be spelled like it is pronounced.

No wonder so many kids think the English language is difficult to learn, let alone spell.

And now, just when I figured that I was the only person left on this planet who was holding out for a decent spelling of the tomato-based condiment, I hear of a major breakthrough.

Seems that Del Monte Foods USA, a leading manufacturer of the product since 1916, has finally thrown in the towel. They announced last November that they will market their product as ketchup instead of catsup.

I've got one question.

How come it took the company 72 years to make up its mind?

Boy, do they have holdouts in that firm.

If you don't believe that other people besides me wondered about the spelling of ketchup, be advised that 80 percent of all U.S. households purchased ketchup last year. And it isn't even native to this country.

We can thank English seamen from the 17th century. Seems ketchup has its roots in Malaysia, where the sea-faring fellows cultivated a taste for a salty, spiced sauce prepared from the brine of pickled fish.

The early American version was made from oysters, blueberries and other fruit.

Today, ketchup must contain tomatoes to carry the name. Some companies use more than 4.5 pounds of tomatoes as part of their secret concoction. Other ingredients are salt, onions, vinegar and spices.

So there, I've just given you a history and chef lesson, all in one.

The only thing I ever had against ketchup was that it sure could stain clothes, tablecloths and carpets.

I've had my share of it. Four kids who devoured ketchup (when their mother didn't get to it first) could paint a house red with that delicacy.

The Mister thinks we are all crazy to put ketchup on meat. Spoils the taste, he says. Wonder if he's just complaining because he was probably last in his large brood of siblings to get ahold of the ketchup bottle.

And, speaking of ketchup spills, they've now come up with plastic squeeze bottles. Unbreakable of course.

That boggles my mind.

How in the world will these moms of today ever know what homemaking really was like in the bad old days?

Just think. We had to use old scrub boards and then the loud washing machines to get our kid's clothes clean from ketchup stains. Today's moms have automatic washers to use.

Worse yet, they have those plastic ketchup bottles that don't break.

We're never going to convince the next generation that home-making was a fulltime job.

Flu isn't Bad; Callers are Worse

February 25, 1989

It doesn't pay to take a day off work when you're ill.

I admit it was self-defense to stay home. If the flu bug stopped with me, then I wouldn't get it again when it made its return trip through my co-workers.

This is the first time in years that I've had flu shot, so I didn't expect to get sick. But there I was, wrapped in a comforter – that not being the Mister, who kept his distance from any chance to inherit the flu by osmosis or invitation.

The Journal people were told not to expect me and I dozed back to sleep, hoping my stomach would hold horizontal stability. Catching some well-appreciated sleep, I was awakened by the phone.

"Answer it," I told the Mister, and then remembered that he had left on an errand.

So, waddling to the phone, I said hello.

"We want to keep you as a subscriber to our magazine," the woman gushed. "Surely you want to renew."

Fat chance that I would in my condition, when dying seemed closer than living.

Back to the couch and rest.

The phone buzzed again. I ignored it. Finally it stopped.

"Ha!" I reasoned. "All one has to do is forget it."

Wrong. It rang again.

Thinking that maybe it might be a family emergency, I staggered over to answer it.

"We just know that you forgot to answer our last inquiry about signing up for our frozen food offer," the lady said.

Food was the last thing I wanted to talk about, seeing as how it and my stomach had not cooperated the past 12 hours.

I turned down the offer as nicely as I could, seeing as how putting my body on a vertical level was starting a new inner tidal wave.

I returned to the couch and oblivion – this time with the portable phone beside me.

The blasted phone rang again.

I picked it up after the second ring. No one was on the line.

Now some of you are wondering why I didn't leave the telephone off the hook so it wouldn't disturb me. Couldn't do that because the Mister is a volunteer firefighter and when emergencies occur, the calls ring in at our home.

The incessant ringing returned a half hour later and I rose to meet the challenge.

"We'd like to have you as our product customer," the fellow said. "How are you today?"

I described my ailment in graphic terms. With a tone of embarrassment, he said: "Well, I don't imagine you feel up to talking today."

At last, a smart caller.

Finally, I settled down to a decent nap, praying that my stomach contents would do the same.

The phone rang.

"We used to have you as a customer for our newspaper delivery," the eager voice said. "Would you consider signing up again?

God forbid that it had been a caller from the newspaper where I work. As it was, it crossed my mind to tell the caller what she could do with that paper besides using it on the bottom of a bird cage.

My temper had been held in check too long.

Seething, muttering to the only thing that was close enough to listen, I told my hanging plant that there are a lot of idiots out there.

And before my body touched the sofa, the last call came.

"Betty?" the woman said.

"I'm not Betty," I replied.

"Oops, wrong number," the woman said and hung up without an apology.

I headed for the bathroom, finally giving up the flu holdout. I tell you, it's less stress and trouble to suffer illness at the workplace.

From the High Seas
to Michigan

March 4, 1989

Some folks are fortunate to have famous ancestors. It's a nice historical footnote to pass on to later generations.

Victor Palmer of Sturgis claims Nathaniel Brown Palmer, whose likeness graces a U.S. commemorative stamp issued last September.

Nathaniel was a well-traveled fellow on the high seas. Born in 1799 in Stonington, Conn., he was trained in his father's shipyard at Stoningham. He went to sea young, as a blockade runner in the War of 1812.

In 1813, he was crossing oceans, and by 1818 was second mate on the sloop "Galina," sailing to the South Seas. The next year he was named Captain of the "Hero," and made a second voyage to the South Seas, where he discovered an island at latitude 67°, longitude 70°, later named Palmer's Island.

He next commanded the "James Monroe" on an expedition to the South Shetland Islands and later captained the "Cadet" on voyages to Cartagena and the Spanish Main. While there, he was employed by the Columbian government to transport a portion of General Bolivar's army to the River Charges.

Word of his seamanship eventually got him assigned to the brig "Francis" and the "Anawan" on voyages of discovery east of Cape Horn. When he went ashore later at Juan Fernandes Island, he was captured by Chilian convicts. Only his identity as a Mason saved his life.

He continued his sea duties, commanding such packet ships as "Huntsville," "Hibernia" and the "Paul Jones," which he sailed to China.

He was captain of the "United States" steamer when it made a journey to Germany in 1848.

Palmer retired from sea duty in 1849 and was a charter member of the New York Yacht Club.

But he is best known for two other reasons. He is believed to be the discoverer of Antarctica (National Geographic 1971) although two British mariners were there earlier, as were two Russian exploring ships.

In the southern summer season of 1820-21, his ship was serving as scout for a squadron of Stonington ships looking for seal grounds.

Palmer was only 21 when he captained the "Hero" on that historic journey and discovered the area called Palmer Land in his honor.

His second claim to fame came for designing clipper ships named "Samuel Russell," "Contest," "David Brown," "Oriental" and "N.B. Palmer." He also designed pleasure boats and once held the record for sea voyages: to Hong Kong – 84 days – and to Liverpool, England – 15 days.

Palmer's feats are documented in several publications, including "The Discovery of Antarctica," "National Cyclopaedia of American

Biography," "Captain Nathaniel Brown Palmer, An Oldtime Sailor of the Sea," and "Stonington by the Sea."

The old salt died at San Francisco June 15, 1877 and was buried in Stoningham. Most of his brothers and sisters remained in the East, but branches of the family moved westward to California and Oregon. At least four branches settled in Michigan.

Although the land he is credited with discovering is now known as Antarctic, The National Science Foundation's Palmer Base Research Center is located on the Antarctica Peninsula. Twenty-six scientists and staff members handle research there.

Vic Palmer is proud of his heritage. Even if the Michigan Palmer branch he springs from is many miles from the seas his ancestor sailed.

And he treasures the U.S. stamp issued last September, which carries a picture of ancestor Nathaniel Brown Palmer on it.

Misery Loves Company; Ask Me

March 11, 1989

If anyone wants directions to Pain City, I know the route well. And I'm willing to share it with friends or foe. Doesn't make a bit of difference in my state of mind.

Two years ago I was surprised with what doctors call a "frozen" shoulder. After therapy treatments, whereby pain was a closer companion than even the Mister, I was "put under" and a specialist worked the shoulder free.

When I woke up I figured the shoulder would be sore, but usable, and I'd be back on the track again.

Wrong.

It was merely loosened a bit so that physical therapist could have another go at it.

If you've never had the attention-getting experience of having cortisone shot into a shoulder socket via a needle that's big enough to frighten an elephant, take my honorable word that it hurts.

To make a long story short, after nine months the shoulder finally worked – with about 20 percent less stretch than it had, which was blamed on my age (they really know how to double hurt you).

476

So much for misery.

Happily content that I could at least use my arm and shoulder without pain taking away my breath, I continued life as before. Wasn't worried about the problem, although no one knew why the shoulder had locked. No injury, no arthritis, no calcium deposits, no bursitis. I told good friend Dr. Hugh McCullough that maybe it was because I was weird. He didn't argue the point.

Last Christmas I got an unasked present. The other shoulder started to act up.

Naw, I reasoned. No one could have two shoulders lock up.

Ignoring the obvious symptoms for awhile, the discomfort coaxed me into doing the therapy exercise at home that I had done for the other shoulder, I wasn't about to get another locked shoulder. I figured I'd just offset it by doing the pulley treatment, the broom handle exercises, the ice packs.

Surprise. The left shoulder locked up as neatly as the other one did.

So, here I am, back in Pain City, undergoing therapy at Sturgis Hospital. You remember that I wrote before about how Dirty Dennis, the therapist, showed me what true pain was. I swear Dennis can find places in a body that hurt beyond description.

Poor Fred, the other therapist, just looks sideways at me when I come in. I think he's half afraid to work on my shoulder for fear of getting his name in this column. Fred doesn't understand that misery loves company – and he got here anyway.

If you've never been inside a physical therapy unit, be advised that interesting conversations float through the curtained compartments.

"That's all. No more. They ain't a'gonna touch me again," a man's voice said one day.

Through the nearby curtain drifted, "Is my toenail still there?" in reference to electrical stimulation on a fellow's legs. "I think the callouses on my feet just disappeared," he intoned.

I understood.

Down the way another poor soul was undergoing another exercise. "Oh Lord! Oh, dear! I just can't handle this," came the plaintive cry.

I smiled. If I was in pain, everyone should be in pain.

I can tell you about ultra sound treatment (it's comforting and nice); electrical stimulant (it feels like a wire brush is scraping off your skin); ice packs (your face become red from pain, but the rest of your body is a large-size ice cube); wrist weights (I'm convinced that if they'd make me wear one of them while eating, I'd be the thinnest gal around).

I asked Dennis what a shoulder socket contains. When he told me, I realized why it hurts so much. Try and cram that much bone, muscle, nerves, fiber, tendons or whatever else is around into that small space and something is bound to go wrong.

Seriously, Sturgis Hospital has a great physical therapy department. And I overheard the therapists say that they'll be starting a special back therapy program soon. People should take advantage of it before they get in any condition – feeble and complaining.

I'm resigned to the fact that it will be a long time before this darned shoulder is pain free. Worse yet, I don't like having people do things for me simply because I can't reach around my back.

The Mister has to help me get dressed. And he's broadcasting all over town that he's getting in more bra time than when we were young. I can't win.

Nurturing is Necessary to Kids

March 18, 1989

One wonders why some kids go wrong. The best of families can rear youngsters right, give them the love and attention they deserve, and then one strays. It happens for no specific reason.

Few people possess the answer to why this occurs. But in some cases, it can be traced back to small things.

Like school events. Kids who aren't having trouble in school will have their parents in attendance at parent-teacher conferences. Yet students who need parental support, moms and dads who should hear what teachers are saying, won't bother to make appointments to help their youngsters.

Does the seed of rebellion and resentment take root at that point in those young people lives? Do they begin to question if they are important in their parents' world?

Does the seed germinate when families ignore the obvious – or sometimes subtle – behavior of their children? The younger generation, especially those of early grade school age, are so open to the world around them. They are so vulnerable that they are easily wounded. If their needs go unanswered, the fertilizer called resignation is heaped on the path to failure.

And when the seed sprouts in the teen years, do parents recognize that youths need space to grow, but with discipline and firm hands to help along the way? Or do parents react angrily or display indifference? Do they provide the climate that allows the sprout to lean the wrong way?

It is the formulative years that count the most. How many parents are too busy, too unconcerned to attend Honor Society initiations? How about athletic games and band concerts? There isn't a youth around who doesn't take satisfaction in knowing that mom and dad, grandma and grandpa, are in the audience, looking on with pride.

Just watch youth's faces as they scan the crowd. Those who don't see parents there, who feel abandoned, have more reason to become disillusioned. The seed of youth has grown into a sprout ready to flower or wither, waiting to decide what harvest route to take.

Certainly there are reasons why parents can't satisfy all their children's wants and needs. Most kids understand that and will adjust well if they realize that they are loved and supported.

For the most part, it is not society's blame when kids go wrong. It may be indirectly related to how society has changed, but that is not a valid excuse. It starts – and often ends – in the home.

Society can change, but the basic rules can't. Parenting is still what it always has been: sweat, worry, financial headaches, time-consuming. And it must be balanced by understanding, communication, empathy and all the love one can muster.

But look at the rewards. Watch that youngster's face when he realizes mom and dad are there for him. It is proof of responsibility and caring. Seeds that are nurtured will germinate favorably.

But the key to all of it is not the planting, but the care taken to protect and sustain something of value. There must be no lapse in the nurturing. It requires the understanding tears of setbacks and the healing growth that comes from smiles of pride. And then comes the reward – or disappointment – of the harvest parents create.

Phyllis: Symbol of Volunteerism

March 26, 1989

Phyllis Ayres has touched the lives of many people in her volunteer work through the years. But ask her about 1,200 youngsters and she will rattle off their names, their duties and how proud she is of their efforts.

Phyllis, a longtime Sturgis resident, has been a volunteer Safety Patrol supervisor at Congress School for 34 years.

Think of it. Thirty-four years of rounding up kids to be leaders, who accept responsibility, who give freely of their time to ensure the safety of their friends and classmates.

Along the way, Phyllis racked up some impressive awards for her untiring efforts to make Sturgis a better place to live. She earned the Citizen of the Year award in 1974. Former Gov. William Milliken saluted her work. The state presented Phyllis with an award for a bicycle safety program she coordinated.

And her guardianship of the Congress School Safety program has not gone unnoticed at the national level. Several of her patrol captains received all-expense-paid trips from AAA to Washington, D.C., as reward for helping others. Congress patrols were twice selected as a nationally recognized safety patrol.

And now Phyllis has been selected as a finalist for an adult-elementary award from The National School Volunteer Program's Outstanding School Volunteer, sponsored by Kraft, Inc., and Walt Disney World.

A winner and runner-up will be named in seven different categories on March 29, and winners will be notified in early April.

A few years back, a celebration was held to recognize Phyllis' 25 years of Safety Patrol involvement. Several hundred former patrollers were present to explain that Phyllis guided them to further responsibility and honor status while in high school.

Dr. Larry McConnell, superintendent of Sturgis Schools, praises Phyllis' work.

"The Sturgis Public Schools are deeply appreciative of Mrs. Ayres' long years of dedicated service to students. She is a model for our many volunteers," he said.

Cindy Sprowl, a teacher at Congress School, says that "Phyllis Ayres is truly the best example of volunteerism that I know."

Roy Peterson, Congress School principal, says "Mrs. Ayres has high expectations for the safety patrollers she tutors. They know what a tradition of excellence means and they consistently maintain those high standards. I have seen many leaders develop as a result of the responsibility required to be a Congress Safety Patrol."

Gene Melchi, a parent, agrees. "She is committed and dedicated to helping students. She is a caring person and an excellent role model for our children."

Leading a Safety Patrol program takes time – about 10 hours a week. Students receive on-the-job training starting in the spring of third grade to prepare them for the beginning of the fall school year. All the time volunteered by students is after school hours. There are monthly meetings, training sessions and honoring of individual patrols for outstanding service.

And don't think it ends there for Phyllis. She spends many hours each week spot checking the performance of her patrols and discussing problems and responsibilities with patrol officers.

Phyllis demands excellence from her young people. That makes sense, because each patrol member holds the safety of other students in his or her hands. Phyllis is committed to the program. Her perception of its need and importance has not changed in the 34 years she's been associated with the Congress School program.

Sturgis residents hope Phyllis will emerge a top winner in the group of 140 semi-finalists for the esteemed volunteer award. They'd like to see her duly honored and sent on a week's trip to Walt Disney World to attend the award ceremony at the Land Pavilion, sponsored by Kraft, Inc., at Epcot Center May 22.

Sturgis folks know how important the National School Volunteer Program is. They also know that they already have a winner in Phyllis Ayres, who has worked tirelessly for 34 years to help make schools a safer place. They appreciate her efforts to develop leadership characters in her young charges.

The award committee does not directly inform finalists of their nomination for the coveted volunteer awards. So here is Sturgis residents' chance to send Phyllis a note, call congratulations, and tell a wonderful woman how much she has been appreciated these 34 years. And don't forget to mention that she's a great role model of true volunteerism.

Tiny Kirtland Warbler
on way Back

April 1, 1989

Tragedy to triumph. Sometimes it works.

In the case of the Kirtland warbler, that tiny wisp of bird that nests only in one location in the world, there is a measure of success.

The Kirtland is making a comeback in the Northeastern portion of the Upper Peninsula, because it has more breeding habitat. Conservationists and biologists have worried for decades about the Kirtland warbler, which was well on its way to extinction. Only 167 of the singing male warblers were counted in 1987.

The problem lies in the fact that the warbler nests only in a five-county area in the Upper Peninsula. It migrates to the Bahamas in the winter.

It is a persistent and staunch defender of its nesting area, perhaps because it has never extended its habitat beyond its Michigan summer range.

But fate may have played a part in rescuing the tiny warbler from extinction.

A devastating 1980 forest fire that burned 20,000 acres, destroyed property and buildings and killed one person, may have saved the warbler species for future generations.

The warbler is a strange breeder. It is a ground-nester and will make its home only in Jack Pine tree areas.

Moreover, it will only breed and nest in certain Jack Pine ranges, where young trees are a specific density, height, and growing on specific soil.

Biologists have sought for years to determine why the Kirtland warbler is so particular in its nesting habits. If they could fully understand why, they could move the warblers to other areas in the hope that the species would continue. The Catch-22 of all this is that there are so few warblers to use that environmental experiment.

Biologists fear trying that tactic because it is known that the Kirtland has refused to establish new nesting sites.

The fire in northeastern upper Michigan created sprouting of new Jack Pines trees. Apparently the natural environmental changes helped the warbler to thrive because of ground clearing and new tree growth.

So important is the Kirtland warbler that the National Forest Service recently conducted a seminar in Lansing on the species. They know how close it is to extinction because of environment problems and because it is so selective in its choice of nesting territory.

Forest service workers last summer counted 207 male warblers, indicative that the forest fire may have turned out to be a blessing for the bird and animal world, which also shows signs of experiencing more successful habitats.

Anyone who has seen the yellow-breasted warbler and heard its beautiful song will appreciate its uniqueness.

We may help and sometimes succeed in making forced habitat

changes, but the Kirtland warbler remains an elusive species, willing to become extinct if its natural habitat is not maintained the way it wants it. The Kirtland warbler will die rather than change its habitat because of man's foolishness.

We could learn something from the Kirtland warbler, a bird native only to Michigan, and then only in one small area. We must work to preserve this wonderful species.

Peppy was an Extra Dividend

April 8, 1989

The sound didn't startle me. It was just a subtle reminder that Peppy wanted in. Peppy was our poodle dog, known in the neighborhood as a kid's best playmate.

She had been scolded for scratching on the front door, so she developed a habit of scratching on the porch window. It was a noise that alerted the family to open the door for her.

I got as far as the front door and then realized with a terrible sadness that it wasn't Peppy, of course. She died six years ago.

What I heard was the branch of a bush in front of the house rubbing against a window.

For a moment, I was lost in another time, when our household included a scrappy, friendly rag-muffed dog. It was a time of laughter and enjoyment, when a small animal captivated our days.

We always had a dog. Our kids never knew what it was like not to have one, along with a skunk, a squirrel, a hoot owl and any other animal or creature that crossed the yard.

According to the Mister, animals needing homes had a mysterious private grapeline to know where a home could be found. The only animal we didn't have was a cat, a token acknowledgement that the Mister had some household rights, seeing as how he hated cats.

When we went to pick out a dog, the youngsters had chosen one they thought was best suited for use. And then a feisty, little ball of fur crawled out from under the owner's davenport and entered our lives.

She trotted over to me, grabbed my pant leg and tugged away. The kids laughed, then nodded their heads.

It was decided as simply as that. This puppy would fit right in our hectic household.

She was something. Her preferred lap was our oldest son's, but it was the other three children who cared for her needs. She had a sense of loyalty – to a point.

The youngest daughter couldn't understand it.

"I'm the one who's given her so much love. And yet, when she sees Mark coming home from school, guess who she runs to first," Kathy remarked. She was right.

The dog was contrary to what poodle experts say the breed is. She wasn't a one-family dog. If we weren't outside to play, she'd head for the nearest neighbor to find a kid and romp.

And we'd find piles of small toys in our yard after Peppy had swiped them and brought them home. We'd have to make trips around the neighborhood to give them back.

Sometimes a youngster knocked on the door and we thought they wanted one of our kids to play. Wrong.

"Can Peppy come out and play?" they'd ask.

Peppy liked school, too. There were times she'd sit patiently on the sidewalk, watching the kids walk the three blocks to classes. When they were out of sight she'd hightail after them. She wasn't breaking the rules and following them; just making her own route.

Occasionally, a teacher would let her visit for the day.

Peppy also had favorite stopping places uptown, especially the grocery store, where the owner tossed her bones. She was known by name at the post office, the garage, the pool hall, the restaurant, the beer joint, the library. Peppy was popular, it seemed.

I suppose one becomes so used to a family pet, loves it so much, that the possibility of death is pushed aside. I always thought we'd lose Peppy to the wheels of a car, seeing as how she considered the road part of her regular playground, often tossing a rubber ball in the air and catching it. If she couldn't find a playmate, she played by herself.

When the kids went off to college and married, Peppy was left with the Mister and me. She tolerated us pretty well, but kept her daily routine, seeking kids to liven up her time.

One fall evening, we noticed that she seemed quiet. But when we went outside, she sought out her ball and begged for it to be thrown.

Later on, she appeared to be breathing heavily and indicated that she wanted to go out. She sometimes chose to sleep outside in good weather, so we weren't too concerned.

I found her lying in front of the garage the next morning. Death had apparently come softly and easily in the night.

We buried her under the apple tree where she had spent many happy hours. Our youngest son refused to come home from college for a long time because he couldn't bear not to have her there to welcome him.

In time, we accepted her death, but we have not had a dog since Peppy died. I am not sure whether it is because of time constrictions, or simply that we are unable or unwilling to love so much again.

Hurt has a way of making one vulnerable.

But yet, when I misunderstand the sound of the bush against the window, I think it is Peppy asking to come in, and my heart gladdens. Love does that kind of thing to you.

Lions are Community Backbone

April 15, 1989

You'll see them if front of banks and other business establishments on May 10-12. You'll recognize their purpose when you see the White Canes.

They are members of the Sturgis Lions Club and they join their peers in doing what they can during White Cane Week April 28-May 6 to help those with eye and hearing problems.

So they'll be a couple of days late in appearing on the streets after White Cane Week. What matters is that they care.

And so should you.

The Lions have been active in Sturgis since Feb. 14, 1950, when the club was chartered. Robert Suits is the only charter member left and he remains enthused about club activities.

"We do a lot to help the community," he said, as his associates John Bordner and John Childs nodded.

Childs is a 30-year club member. Bordner joined the group 1 ½ years ago. He formerly belonged to the Burr Oak group, which has disbanded.

So what do Lions do? Consider these:

They contribute college scholarships to area students.

Assist in Little League activities.

Collect used eyeglasses and hearing aids to send to needy people in developing countries.

Support the Michigan Eye Bank in Ann Arbor.

Assist the Welcome Home for the Blind in Grand Rapids.

Contribute funds to help the Leader Dog School in Rochester, Mich.

Send funds to the Lions Club International Foundation to be used for crisis around the world.

Support Camp Chris, a Three Rivers summer camp for deaf youths. The need has grown and two camps sessions are now scheduled.

The Sightmobile.

Support the Child Quest project in which awareness of the danger of drugs and alcohol is relayed to students.

Contribute to the July 4 celebration in Sturgis.

Suits said that most of the club funds support local endeavors and that members are committed to community involvement.

"We have a long history in helping the community. That's what Lions Clubs are all about," he said.

The first Lions Club was founded in 1925-26 in Chicago, when insurance people and realtors recognized a need for a community-oriented organization. The next year, a club was chartered in Canada, making the organization international.

Membership now stands at 1,300,000 internationally, with representation in 58,000 geographical locations. There are six Lions Clubs in St. Joseph County.

The club maintains drop off sites for people to leave used eyeglasses and hearing aids. The locations are at New Vision, First National Bank, Banc One and optometrist offices.

Dick Frost is White Cane chairman this year, Bordner said. But he has able assistants to help the cause.

You'll find them at the banks and business establishments Friday and Saturday, May 10-12. Help them out – so they can help others.

A Search for John

April 29, 1989

They met in 1945. He was a small German boy born in 1939, a week before the war broke out in Europe. Young Horst Cunaus' first remembrances were hunger, war and fear.

But in 1945 his life changed. A few weeks before World War II ended, the Americans arrived in Hettstedt, Germany, Horst's hometown.

Horst, the adult, remembers what it was like. In a letter to Sturgis Mayor Donald Easterday, Horst tells his poignant tale:

"I will never forget that spring day... the small jeep at the top (leading) the many Americans panzer (tanks) and all the friendly American soldiers."

The Americans opened up Horst's world.

"One of the soldiers lived in our home for a short time. We called him John. Maybe John was not his real name; I am not sure. Very soon, our John was a good friend to all my family. Especially, John cared for me. Never have I forgotten him and his love for me," Horst wrote.

But soon John had to leave the five-year-old Horst for what is now known as West Germany. Russian troops occupied the part of Germany agreed to in a pact between the U.S. government and the

Soviet Union. It was a change that took the Cunaus family from the Hitler regime to a Communist lifestyle.

But through the years, Horst remembered his friend, John. He knew that John came from Sturgis, although he forgot his last name.

And now Horst wants to learn more about Sturgis – and try to locate John. Although he doesn't have a picture of John, he sent Mayor Easterday one of himself.

"I'm now 49, married and have two children." Horst wrote. "I am a mining engineer and work in the town's 800-year-old copper industry." He added that he likes football, woodworking and studying history of the 1,000-year-old town where he resides.

His wife, Brigitte, is 45 and teaches kindergarten. His daughters are 26 and 27.

"We have three grandsons," Horst wrote. He apparently dotes on seven-year-old Ulf, who lives nearby.

As a young child, Horst was awed by the kindness of the Americans. As an adult, he wants to learn more about life in Sturgis and America. He would enjoy having pen pals.

But more than that, the experiences a small boy cherished over 44 years have brought Horst to ask one small favor.

If there is anyone in Sturgis who recalls a spirited youngster who welcomed an American soldier into his home, Horst would appreciate the information.

Horst knows that John would not recognize him in the picture that he sent with his letter. But he hopes that somewhere in Sturgis a former GI will remember a time in war-torn Europe when an American soldier forgot that Germans were supposed to be the enemy. Horst has not forgotten that the American GI befriended a young boy and his family.

Mayor Easterday hopes that John can be located. And that's why he brought the picture and letter to the Journal.

If John is out there someplace, Horst wants to rekindle the friendship that sparked brightly during the war.

And for that reason – and because there might be folks in Sturgis who want to correspond with Horst and his family – I am including Horst's address.

Just write to Horst Cunaus, Willi-Kaczmarek-Str. 2, Hettstedt, 4270, German Democratic Republic.

And if John reads this and recalls young Horst, please call me at the Journal. I'd like to let people know how this story ends

The Bulbs of Love

May 6, 1989

The tulips in my yard poked their brilliant heads toward the sunlight early this year. And brought back memories.

I had a wonderful childhood, in spite of poverty. I look back and realize that those early years were precious, because we had my parents who lived only a few more years.

We had strict rules in our home. A couple carried over to adult-hood. We were taught not to lie or cheat. From my first awareness I knew that one's word meant honor. To forsake that was a sin.

There was another deadly sin – stealing. It wasn't that I was a good child. I knew what penalty would be assessed to my bottomside if I stole anything.

And for the first few years of my life the threat worked. The fear of a licking and the resulting shame prevented me from wrongdoing.

Oh, there were mild indiscretions, such as the time I peeked into Sister Alice's trunk and confiscated one of her Sonja Heine pictures from her movie clip collection. I think she had more information about Hollywood than the gossip columnists did.

And Sister Mary Jeanne had a beautiful doll. I was never known to play with dolls, but I loved the ribbons that adorned the dress of one doll – and I kinda set them aside.

Donna, the youngest sister, was safe. All she had were diapers and a bottle – and I certainly wanted neither.

And then came a terrible day.

My best childhood friend was Tom Dentel. We both were small, wiry, freckled kids. And we shared another trait: we were spirited daredevils. You name the mischief and we did it. People always came to us first even when we weren't guilty. We had the reputation.

One bright spring day, Tom and I ventured over to Mr. Prickett's house. He was the richest man in town, if not the only one. Made his money in mining ventures, I heard.

A crippled man, he'd sit near his front window and if kids strolled by, he'd motion them in. Those were the days when a man could offer you money for ice cream and not be accused of some terrible sexual perversion.

Mr. Prickett knew that most of the kids in town seldom had money. So he'd concoct a feeble excuse that because of his crippled leg, he didn't feel up to walking to the store for ice cream. He'd enlist us to get him a cone and one for ourself. That way, we didn't feel like we were accepting charity – and our parents couldn't accuse us of asking for money.

Tom and I were invited into the library where Mr. Prickett solemnly drew out three nickels from his pocket.

"Now, I'm mighty hungry for ice cream," he said. "Would you be kind enough to help me out – and for running the errand, I would like to pay you."

We did and were dutifully rewarded with ice cream.

Tom and I sat on the sidewalk in front of Mr. Prickett's office eating the ice cream. And then our eyes riveted on the beautiful tulips inside the iron fence.

We looked at each other and back at the tulips.

My parents were too poor to buy tulip bulbs. It was tough enough just to muster funds to keep the kids clothed and fed. I really liked Mr. Prickett's tulips.

And then, without a word, caution was thrown to the wind. Tom and I stuck our hands through the bars and picked tulips. I can't remember how many Tom took, but I know I swiped three.

We ran off to the railroad tracks where high piles of logs were stacked. We had our own little fort there.

What we thought we would do with the tulips, I don't know to this day. We couldn't take them home and so we just held them until the wilted. With guilty looks, we crept from out hiding place and went home.

At the supper table, my shame began to bother me. I couldn't eat. My parents asked if my stomach hurt.

Not likely. It was my conscience.

I never told anyone about stealing the tulips. But someone knew.

I stayed away from Mr. Prickett's house most of the summer, ashamed to tell him the terrible truth. But on a warm, fall day, I ventured past his window, hoping he'd ask me in to read one of his numerous books.

He did. And a couple of hours later, as he ushered me out of the door toward home, he spoke.

"Wait a moment. I have something for you," he said.

He limped to his study, where he kept his special treats. He handed me a brown paper bag, the kind you get from a grocery store.

I waited until I was outside to peek.

Inside the bag were three tulip bulbs.

Spring Prom Enriches the Winter of Lifetime

May 13, 1989

Dannet Smart stood in front of the mirror, staring at her reflection. Dressed in a T-length blue gown for her junior prom, the Burr Oak student wondered if her date would approve.

After all, the 17-year-old thought, some of her friends and classmates had wondered aloud about her choice of an "older fella" as her prom date.

She also realized that her date probably would enjoy dancing more than she did.

Dannet, an "A" student and gifted athlete, was more interested in school academics and athletics than dressing up and stepping out on a dance floor. But she had to consider her date, who had offered to be her escort months before.

Dannet knew her "best fella" was special. Who cared about his age? She knew from longtime acquaintance with him that he was trustworthy and proper. She didn't mind what her peers might say.

Down the road, her date was doing his own fussing. Decked out in formal attire and tails, he wondered if he could handle the evening affair. It had been a long time since he attended a prom, and this girl meant a lot to him.

And then, adjusting his tie with a nervous hand, Dannet's date nodded in satisfaction.

A few minutes later, he walked into Dannet's home.

Dannet's date – her grandfather – was ready to join the young prom generation.

Merlin Smart is 68, father of six, grandfather of 13, great-grandfather of one. He's known around Burr Oak as an outgoing and outspoken man.

But Merlin has a soft touch and it involves his family. He has always referred to his wife, Marie, as "my beautiful wife." He made that statement years ago when the two cut a cool figure on the dance floor. He says it today. Clearly his family and especially his grandchildren are valued treasures.

Dannet, who goes by the nickname "Fred," at school, is close to her grandfather.

"Back in December, I mentioned that I didn't have a date for the prom," Dannet said. "Grandpa said he'd take me. We kinda joked about it in the family, but Grandpa was serious."

"I got too busy to find a date and I decided that taking my grandfather wasn't such a bad idea. He isn't always going to be around, you know, he's getting older. I love him very much. I figured he'd be a pretty good date."

And Grandpa accepted her invitation.

Merlin, knowing that a date should be taken to dinner before the prom, dutifully escorted his granddaughter to John and Dot's restaurant near Sturgis.

Following tradition, he presented Dannet a corsage of white roses.

She gave him a boutonniere.

And then it was off to the prom at the Burr Oak gym.

Not to be outdone, Merlin danced the night away. It was soon evident that he was the hit of the evening, maybe overshadowing the crowning of the prom royalty.

Most youths who attended the dance thought inviting a grandfather was "pretty neat," Dannet reported. "I was worried that they might ridicule him or something, but they really enjoyed Grandpa."

Not as much as Merlin enjoyed his night out.

The traditional studio prom pictures were taken and Dannet's parents, Dan and Janice Smart, took their own snapshots for the family album.

"We are proud that Dannet thought enough of her grandfather to take him to the dance," Janice said. "She's always been a considerate girl and isn't afraid to buck tradition."

And Merlin?

He's bragged all over town about his special evening. And he's telling everyone about the grand march, which he insisted on participating in.

And he can tuck away another memory to enrich the winter of his life. He can boast of a granddaughter who cared enough about him to proudly take him to a junior prom.

Give Time to Child,
and see Difference

May 20, 1989

Dave Wing of Three Rivers wants to locate some Big Brothers and Big Sisters. And his heartfelt wish for all children is that they have special people who can spend time with them if there is a need in their young lives.

Wing, who is associated with the Big Brothers/Big Sisters of America, knows how much that means to youngsters.

"The need is so great that we've had to go from serving a three-county area to a 4-county one," he said. "As of May 15, we will cover LaGrange and Steuben counties in Indiana and Branch and St. Joseph in Michigan."

The organization has made strong inroads in Three Rivers and has begun to search for Big Brothers and Big Sisters in the Sturgis area.

"Volunteers willing to spend time with children and older youths should be able to devote 3-4 hours a week in a one-on-one situation," Wing said. "They should try to maintain the relationship for at least a year, if possible."

"It should be sharing everyday experiences, anything that an adult

504

might want to share with a youth. Hobbies, fishing, any routine that works out with the adult and child," Wing added.

It is the time spent that counts, Wing said.

Matching the right volunteer with the right child is stressed. Many children come from single parent families and are ages 6-17. Some are referred by social services departments.

Most children who join the program need to develop individual relationships with other adults. Children come from all areas of society, Wing said.

There are strict rules to ensure proper relationships, Wing said. For instance, there is a home orientation of the volunteer, two interviews in the office, a police check and three references required.

Three children are usually selected in each case, from which a volunteer can make a choice. At the present time there are 35 children waiting.

"We interview the parent or parents, the children and the prospective volunteers," Wing said. "We want to make sure that the match will work for both sides."

Wing stresses that Big Brothers/Big Sisters are not expected to be Santa Claus, transportation providers or babysitters. Volunteers are chosen to reinforce a child's emotional needs, to develop communication and social skills and provide a more stable environment.

Parents who have children involved in the program should not deny the Big Brother/Big Sister visits as a means of punishment if children misbehave in their own home.

"Our organization wants to maintain an open relationship with the children," Wing said. "And we do not allow volunteers to criticize a child's home life."

Beginning June 1, the Big Brother/Big Sister group will be available on a 40-hour week schedule for interviews to match participants.

Although the Sturgis Salvation Army is not associated with the program, it has allowed Big Brothers/Big Sisters use of office space at its complex on Monday and Thursday of each week, Wing said. Those wishing to volunteer or to find a Big Sister or Big Brother for their children may call 616-279-2732 or 1-517-278-2434. The Salvation Army also will refer calls, Wing said.

Wing knows the program's value, because he's served as a Big Brother several years. And he will work with local council members Tim Littman, Elisabeth Mason and Margaret Schultz to reach more youths.

The organization has a sole fundraiser – a Bowl for Kids Sake – in July. But right now they need adults to pair with youngsters who wait.

An Ode to George

May 27, 1989

George called the other day. He didn't see my Saturday column and wondered if it had been discontinued.

"I usually come in from the field on Saturdays and ask my wife what you had to say in the column," he said.

He'd better not read it today.

George isn't always keen on calling me because he's afraid he'll end up in the column like he did once before.

George is longtime friend George Mayer. I've known him since childhood and I can tell you that's a lot of years and changes – the biggest being my size. George remembers when I was a skinny kid attending Trayer School in Branch County.

Trayer is long gone, but not the memories and the many friends I found there. Next to Sidnaw in the Upper Peninsula, the Trayer/Honey Lake community is a favorite place.

Back when a kid knew what made life important. The special things were family, school, church and community. All were indelibly connected to the land that sustained us.

Most of us were rural kids who treasured the land that provided most of our necessities. We knew hardship, but were rich in family and friends.

George is a tad older than me and I like to chide him about it. He also ended up marrying one of my closest childhood friends, Myra Cary, so we go back to the days of planting gladiolas on our hands and knees in the scorching sun.

That was when I worked on the Russell Cary farm. He was the father of Howard Cary, who started the dynasty of gladiola growers in the area. I remember long days of hard work in the fields and the breaks when Russell treated us to cold Pokagon pop.

The last I knew, the Mayer families continued that tradition for their workers.

But back to George, he's the son of Irene Mayer, a well-loved lady in the Honey Lake community. She's also the lady who welcomed kids into the yard and provided Kool Aid. She also chose to ignore the fact that kids were swinging from ropes high in the hayloft.

I had a crush on George in those days and this is the first that he will know about it. George, of course, only had eyes for Myra, so I tormented him in other ways.

Like learning to play a passing game of baseball (although he could hit and slide into base far better than I could), and sneaking up on him when he didn't know I was around.

George tolerated me – for what reason I didn't know. Maybe he took pity on a freckled-faced kid. All I know is that I delighted in causing him problems.

And so the other day when George and I visited on the phone, we talked about memories and some of the latest things that had happened in our lives.

George said he had read the obituary of my husband's aunt, Regina Rasbaugh, in the Journal. George remarked that his mother was descended from the Rasbaugh family, but he was unsure of the connection.

That was a complete surprise to me and I grinned in delight. Old George is stuck with me after all, even if it's by marriage. Imagine that. Kissing cousins of a sort.

George had better not complain too much or I'll tell secrets from yesteryear. I know a lot more about George than he wants folks to hear.

I was one of the neighborhood girls who rousted George and other boys out of the swimming hole at the creek. They were skinny-dipping.

It's Really a Chaos Machine

June 3, 1989

They call it a computer. I call it chaos. I can do things on it – the wrong things – that defy explanations. The people teaching me this new contraption at the Journal keep asking me how certain stories I work on get in some parts of the system.

Well, I can't tell them. If I knew how they got there in the first place, I wouldn't have put them there.

They programmed an item into this gadget that's called a cursor. They named it right. The things I've called it couldn't be printed in this newspaper, let alone the National Enquirer.

They say you can't teach an old dog new tricks. I tend to agree with that adage. This thing has been giving me fits of temperament that I'm ashamed to admit.

Let me explain what is causing me to be so short on the phone when people call and interrupt while I'm trying to sort all this computer stuff out.

First of all, I am working in what they call three programs so I can type copy, edit copy and put headlines on it. I don't even understand the programs; let alone how to work them. I've been showed a half dozen times and the result ends up the same. Chaos.

I follow what I think are the proper directions and I lose the darned copy. Searching for it is a pain because I don't know how to search for it.

And then, I find the copy in some spot where it's not supposed to be. Joe Mielke, my city editor and a whiz at computers, looks at me like I've lost my berries. He's right.

I have the terrible feeling that something I lost will turn up in the middle of something I do months down the line. Wouldn't that be interesting?

Don't laugh. The first computer we had at the newspaper once hiccupped in the middle of one obituary and picked up in the middle of another one. Without a hitch, that computer never missed a comma and married the guy in the first obit to a woman in the next.

Ever try explaining that coincidence to the two families? To this day they avoid me on the street.

What really makes me angry is that this computer is smarter than I am. That does nothing for the ego and little more for the fragile confidence that I seem to have these days.

The computer has some interesting titles. It has File, Edit, Windows, Find, Font Size, Style, to name a few. Whatever do I want with windows anyway? Come to think of it, the computer's window is the only one I have in the cramped cubbyhole I call an office.

I sit here and talk to this machine and it talks back. When I err, it asks me a dumb question like "Do you really want to do this? Are you sure?

Why not?

It won't allow me room for error at all. At least the old computer would let me make a fool of myself anytime I chose. Not this machine. It thinks it knows everything and proceeds to tell me so.

I just know that someday I will lose something in it that seemed important and it will travel to netherland or whatever place you want to call it. I have an unprintable name for it.

There is one gadget that alarms me. Among its finer points, so they say, is a built-in dictionary. Woe, life has come full circle. I knew it would come to this. I have bemoaned the fact that so many people can't spell worth a darn today. Now this machine will make it easy for them.

I have no doubt that built-in dictionaries will become part of the regular schooling and that 20 years from now people won't spell much of anything.

If you don't believe me, you should try and work this dictionary. The other day I called up the correction format and it wouldn't accept words I've used all my life. Words that have been in every dictionary I've used since childhood. The darned computer won't even accept the word "Sturgis." That was bad enough. But things grew more ominous that that.

When I typed in the last line on one of my Heartlines columns, the darned computer refused to accept the name Ankney.

So much for egos.

A Look Back at Yesteryear

June 10, 1989

It baffles me why youngsters today have so many toys. Kids don't entertain themselves; they're entertained.

They have expensive gadgets that hook up to televisions and they match wits with them. I'd rather see a kid match his wits with the environment or with experiences and challenges of the real world.

I admit that some of my grandkids have such gadgets and some watch videos. And I mourn that they may not know the kind of memories kids from my generation stores away to gladden their later years. Like exploring neighborhoods, fields and making up fantasy worlds where creative thinking comes in.

Do kids today know what meadows are? Do they wander through them in search of wildlife and see rabbits, quail, pheasant and the like?

Do they still roam the tall grasses in search of butterflies and grasshopper, or stand entranced when an owl flies by?

I can't believe all that violence on TV and the movies is good for young children. It puzzles me why this world has come to the place where so many kids can't find thrills unless they witness violence.

Why not spend more time outside, sliding down hills in frosty weather or walking along icy streams where there are sights and smells to delight the senses?

The role nature plays out is more rewarding, more challenging than watching videos and soaking up so much violence against mankind.

Maybe I am being unrealistic. Perhaps that time I remember will not come again. There is a kind of innocence in the wonderful time called childhood. There was a time when young girls weren't expected to wear hose and beginner's bras, not at the age of nine and 10 anyway. And when boys of the same age spent more time avoiding girls than oogling them.

Have we omitted the time and term of childhood from our lives? I hope not.

I'd like to see more kids roller skating, lying on their bellies looking down through river waters to what lives below. I wish they could hear those lonesome train whistles, the kind that sent shivers up and down your spine. I'd like to see kids outside in early summer evenings, watching those miniature lanterns we call fireflies.

It isn't just today's kids' world that disappoints me. Adults have moved away from porches, those magical places where people could watch the world go by. Comfort took that away from us in the name of air conditioning, I guess.

Do people still call across yards at dusk, inviting friends to join them on porches for lemonade? Is the sound of wooden screen doors slamming lost in yesterday's memories? Do mothers still gather in backyards to snap beans while exchanging neighborhood gossip?

Are radios used for more than music and weather? But then, the Fred Allen show is gone with time. There is no Gangbusters show nor Inner Sanctum stories to stimulate our thinking process. Just about the worst we could expect then was that our imagination might be stimulated. A lot of people don't even listen to classical music anymore, and a lot of the country music sounds like rock.

Mosquitoes Rule the World

June 24, 1989

I hate them with a passion. Here we have a half-way decent summer as far as cool weather is concerned and we have an invasion of insects.

Last summer was the pits. I've never seen a summer of that kind of discontent. Having asthma, the humid, hot weather forced me to stay indoors. My freckles even stayed light for the first time in my life.

So I figured that there couldn't be two miserable summers in a row. Wrong again.

I love cool weather. Actually I love cold weather. I could easily go from Spring to Fall to Winter without harping. Anything warmer than 70 degrees puts my temper in the same climate.

So it seemed reasonable that this year might be a good time to get back outside and see what happens in a world without air conditioning.

My usual rotten luck happened again. With all the Spring rain, we have a record number of mosquitoes.

The Mister takes his shirt off and simply lets them bite. He says I make too much of all this. I disagree.

To begin with, I have had perfect strangers wave merrily back at me while passing by in vehicles. What they don't know is that I'm not waving at them. I'm batting at mosquitoes.

And then there's the convulsive manner in which I do all that. I suppose the neighbors think that I have palsy, especially when they see me gyrate in a form that seems impossible.

What I can't understand about mosquitoes is why they don't pick on my neighbor's dog, which simply snoozes away in the middle of the lawn. Even saw him with all paws to the sky the other day and I thought at first that maybe the mosquitoes have bitten him to death.

I try to outwit those miserable insects by going out one door, letting them find me and then hightailing it back inside. Then I trot out the door on the other side of the house. Unfortunately, all the mosquito relatives and extended families await me there.

I tried spraying the hose around me. I should have known better. After all, mosquitoes are hatched in water. They love it.

And those old standby insect repellants? This year, they appear to be on the mosquito menu. I have the proof.

Discovered something else. Folks who used to amble uptown at a leisurely pace now do it in double-time. Kind of interesting to watch the anatomy in all that.

I have calculated how fast it takes me to get from the door to the garage and into the car, but a block away I realize that a horde of mosquitoes have joined me on my journey. Ever try to drive and bat mosquitoes at the same time? They congregate at your ankles and chew away.

I've been observed standing inside our French doors while mosquitoes swarm around it, trying to get at me. Kind of fun to give them the raspberry, seeing as how I'm reasonably safe inside.

I don't intend to be food for anything as bothersome as mosquitoes, regardless of what the Mister says. He doesn't realize how fortunate he is. I've got a lot more body for mosquitoes to feed on. And I know that's what he's grinning about when he sees me taking aim at mosquitoes.

The village I live in – Burr Oak – sprays each year to rid the town of as many mosquitoes as possible. I usually help.

But this year was different. It only made the mosquitoes mad.

Jennifer: A Rich Legacy

July 1, 1989

The name raised a red flag in my mind when I heard it mentioned at the crash site, but it wasn't until I got back to the Journal Office and went over the details that I realized who the young victim was.

Jennifer Ware. Jenny.

Jenny impressed me when I met her five years ago. I was working on a series about county services for the mentally impaired. I had only intended to write about the statistics, the programs and services available in the area.

But when I met Jenny, I knew her story had to be told.

She was a youngster of 12 at the time. A beautiful child with huge eyes and long hair, there was something about Jenny that stood out.

I followed Jenny through a day in her life, including her schooling at the Pathfinder Center in Centreville, where extensive programs help the mentally and physically handicapped.

Jennifer was dressed in a fashionable dress that day, a blue one with lace trim. She was proud of it as I recall. She also showed me the anklets she wore, which had little designs on the overcuff.

I like kids. But Jenny was meeting me for the first time. I wondered if she would accept an outsider in her life.

There was no reason to doubt. She helped me understand the

activities at Pathfinder and instinctively sensed that I was there to help, not to sensationalize. I was amazed at her perception.

Driving home that night, I was filled with a sense of fulfillment that Jenny would succeed in life, regardless of the fact that she may have been given a bit less than others at the time of birth.

Her parents, Richard and Delores Ware, could have turned away from their child when they realized that there would be hurdles ahead for them and Jennifer. But the Wares accepted what God had destined to be Jenny.

Certainly it wasn't easy. But with faith and drawing strength from their family unit, Jenny was welcomed into the home.

My story about Jenny back then was not about her physical short-comings – the same a story about any other child would have been. Any why not? Jenny had the same hopes as any other child: dreams and a sense of purpose.

Always, Jenny had an optimistic nature, a compelling urge to test her skills, to attempt the impossible.

That she did. Having questioned many times why other children had gone through the communion process at her church, Jenny ventured a request to her parents.

And with the same purpose and determination, the Ware family gathered around Jenny and approached the priest at Holy Angels Catholic Church in Sturgis.

And so, after months of hard work, Jenny was able to do what every child in the Catholic Church does – participate in a First Communion.

It should be noted here that although some of the requirements were modified so that Jenny could handle the process, she had to work hard to reach her goal, the same as any other young child.

I remember how excited Jenny was in her plans back then and how much she put into life. Her parents always said that she was a joyful youngster and added richness to their lives. Friends said that Jenny also participated in Grange activities. Her Grandma Pokorny was a Grange member and sometimes the family participated, too.

And so, when the bus carrying Pathfinder students was involved in an accident, I followed the reports from the hospital. When one of the children was discharged, I hoped that Jenny would follow suit.

It was not to be. Her injuries were too serious. But Jenny struggled on for days, her valiant heart working to sustain the life that had already given so much to the world.

The news of Jenny's death was a shock.

She was 17, a pretty girl who was destined to add much to the lives of those she touched. But in a way, her spirit of sharing, her love of challenges, her strength of purpose did not die with her. It lives on in the many people who remember her courage, brightness and warmth.

I had forgotten that Jenny was mentally impaired. To me, Jenny was what everyone who knew and loved her thought: a lovely young lady. And she left us an important message: We should look beyond infirmities, and love individuals for what they are.

People like Jenny are only handicapped if we label them as such, if we refuse to allow them the chance to seek their full potential. Jenny's legacy, though short in life, is a rich one. She will be remembered with love, the kind she knew in life.

That Fly could be Trouble

July 15, 1989

I thought the kid had lost her mind – or if she forgot her gender. The only shocked person was me.

My granddaughter, Becky, is 15 and an avid fan of youth trends. Name a hairstyle and she'll try it. No matter that her long, dark locks disappeared in a quick swish to a short bob. It was the new style and she was prepared to try it.

Two years ago it was sneakers that came up the ankles. Can you imagine what that looked like when she wore a dress?

And then came plain old T-shirts, the kind most people wear as undershirts. Baggy, old plain T-shirts that we used to try and hide.

But nothing prepared me for the most recent clothes trend. She showed up on my doorstep wearing undershorts. Men's undershorts. The kind with polka dots. Stripes. Checks. Prints.

I gasped. I thought she had awakened in a fog and grabbed the wrong item of clothing from the clothes dryer.

Not so. She was wearing what the kids call the latest craze. I'll bet store owners are thrilled to death. Can you imagine what they tell salespeople when they order extra stock? Can you just see the look on the faces when they say to order a lot of them in popular patterns? For the girls?

I know there were fads when I was in my teens. I remember dragging out my dad's wool, red and black checkered shirts to parade around town in. And we'd roll our jean pant legs up to mid calf. Heaven forbid if we wore them rolled down to our ankles.

My daughters had their own clothes world, too. But they sure didn't run around in underwear!

I asked Becky if she had a hard time finding the shorts.

"Naw. They have a lot of them in the small size," she said.

I can just imagine the horror on salespeople's faces when she pawed through a stack of underclothing to find the right patterns she sought. That kid can shop for hours.

My next question to Becky was where in the public did she wear the undershorts.

"Why, everywhere," came the reply.

Everywhere? Places my friends went, where they could talk about it? Lordy, but life can be difficult.

Becky by nature is a bit quiet. She's been serious since the age of two and I keep waiting for her to go through those teen years when girls are all giggles and silly talk. Apparently, she skipped most of it.

But these shorts baffle me. Why in the world would pretty girls – and it's apparently the trend in the area – want to parade around in underpants? And men's underpants to boot.

I know a couple of things. There will be a lot of questions in laundromats when girls of 13 and 14 fold dozens of male shorts.

All I could tell Becky was to please sew the fly shut.

A Tombstone for Grandville

July 22, 1989

Grandville finally has his gravestone – 42 years late – but significant to folks who know and loved him.

I first wrote about Grandville Alvin Owens a year ago. He was the young fellow from the hill country of Arkansas. Grandville grew up in Friendship, Ark., and joined the Navy in 1942 at the age of 18.

Grandville served until 1945 and returned home to Friendship, expecting to take up the business of living in a peacetime situation.

During the war, Grandville had struck up a friendship with Vic Palmer of Sturgis. The two served at the Naval Air Station in Pruunene, Maui, Hawaii. Vic was later shipped out for air service rescue duty and the two lost touch of each other.

But Vic never forgot the young boy from Arkansas and for years wondered how Grandville's life turned out. But marriage, a family and other commitments prevented Vic from getting in touch with Grandville. But the dream remained; Someday Vic would go to Arkansas and see Grandville.

"Grandville was a quiet guy, a beautiful person," Vic told me a year ago. "He was open and honest, a boy who went off to war and just wanted to get back home. I really liked him."

And so it was that Vic finally made a trip to Friendship in 1988 to see Grandville again.

"No one knew where he lived," Vic said. "After searching and asking questions around town, I finally located a woman who knew about Grandville. In a small town of 150 people, I figured more folks should have known about Grandville or his family."

The reason few did soon was learned. Grandville had died in California in a traffic accident in 1957. He was only 23.

"I was shocked to learn about his death," Vic said. "All those years I assumed he was alive. I regretted so much that I had not contacted him. And to think his life ended so young. . ."

So Vic's journey turned bittersweet. He would go to the cemetery and pay his respects to his friend. But there was no tombstone, no marker on his grave.

"I was angry," Vic admitted. "Here was a young man who had gone off to war and fought for his country. I also knew that the government pays for a gravestone."

So Vic's odyssey turned elsewhere. He contacted members of Grandville's family, but none expressed a clear interest in obtaining the free grave marker.

"I damn sight knew I was going to get that gravestone for Grandville, one way or another," Vic said. "If the government wouldn't do it, I would. But it's the government's last duty to their veterans."

With the help of the treasurer of the cemetery governing board in Friendship, the work began to secure a marker. But even then, things stalled.

"I checked some months ago and the marker was sitting on the porch of one of Grandville's relatives a short distance from the cemetery," Vic said.

Vic persisted. And just before Memorial Day this year, Vic returned to Friendship to visit the cemetery.

"There it was," Vic said, his eyes misting at the memory.

"Grandville finally had his marker. I figured for a guy who had cared enough to serve his country, Grandville's last mission – and mine – had ended."

A Presidential Letter

July 29, 1989

Allen Anway didn't think he'd get a reply, but there it was: A letter, personally signed by George Bush. THE George Bush. President of the United States. "I thought, after several months, that the president simply didn't have time to answer my letter," Anway, a Sturgis resident, said.

But the president apparently has a great love for veterans. And Anway paid his dues to his country. He spent much of his adult life in that capacity. First it was the Army during the Korean War. Then it was the National Guard, where he eventually was promoted to commander of the Guard unit at Sturgis.

He holds the title of major in the Reserves, with "pocket orders" that would be activated during a national call to arms.

But back to the letter from the president.

Sometime back, while looking through his late brother, Donald Bartley Anway's wartime scrapbook, he discovered that Don, also of Sturgis, had served with George Bush on an aircraft carrier during World War II. He even found a picture of the pilots – one of them Bush – who flew missions off the carrier.

"I thought that the president might like to have the pictures that were taken back then," Anway said. "So, I packaged them up and sent them to the president, hoping he'd enjoy the items from his wartime experiences."

Apparently the president did – and said so in a recent letter to Anway.

Anway is a patriot and doesn't mind people knowing it. He believes service and duty to one's country is a privilege and honor. So did members of his family.

Besides Donald, another brother, Richard, served in the Navy. A brother, Robert, was a Marine during World War II. And yet another brother, Duane, worked for the U.S. Navy in Panama.

And then there is Anway's son, Steven, now a staff sergeant with the Army in Germany. And one has to count another son, Douglas, who saw Army duty.

Add Anway's step-son, James Bradford, who saw service in the National Guard, as did Al's son, Kenneth Anway. You might even total up the son-in-laws, too, for their National Guard and Army duty.

Anway thinks that President Bush should do fine as president. He supports many of the president's programs, although he's a bit reserved in his opinion of building bombers that might not be used much.

But he stands behind Bush on being militarily prepared.

"I saw what happened when I served in Korea, only five years after World War II. We weren't militarily prepared to do what we should have done in that war," Anway remembers.

So what's he going to do with his missive from the president?

"Well, I'll probably give the original letter to Don's widow. After all, it was Don who served with Bush. But you can bet I'll keep a copy of the letter," he said.

And Anway, nearing 60, said he would still return to duty in the case of national emergency. He holds his rank of major (retired) in pride. And isn't embarrassed to say that he appreciates a personal letter from his president.

A Package from 'Happy'

August 5, 1989

The package was thick and bulky. At first glance, I wondered what was in it.

And then I saw the return address. Angelo "Happy" Botzner. A friend who goes back to when I was nine years old and the new kid in the neighborhood.

We had just moved to the Honey Lake area in Branch County, where my grandparents settled many years before. After years in the Upper Peninsula, where he met and married my mother, my father decided to return home and live on his parents' farm.

It was December of 1940, that innocent time before World War II changed our lives. I was homesick for the northwoods and the lifestyle I had known. Fences and cornfields trapped me. I felt betrayed, lost and indifferent to everyone new I met.

But Happy was different. I loved him at first sight. He was plain folk, with no pretenses. A fellow whose word was trusted and friendship treasured.

Throughout my teen years, marriage and the years that followed, Happy remained close. Maybe I didn't see him often, but I heard about him – or heard from him.

After his beloved wife died of cancer, Happy moved to California

to be near his children. Folks who read this column will remember
that the Botzner kids are Clyde, Carol and Mary. Kids reared with
the words of the Bible, with the admonishment from their parents
to treat other people honestly and fairly. I've never heard anyone
contradict that the lessons passed on to the Botzner children weren't
well learned.

So, when the package came from Happy the other day, I was
delighted and anxious to see what was inside.

There were pictures of Happy and his children.

And a letter. A long letter. To be honest, it was 32 pages. Happy
writes like he talks. Spends a week writing a letter of this sort, but it
is sheer delight to people fortunate to receive one.

I will keep that letter to pass on to my own children, so they
will have a glimpse of another time, of what family, church, school,
friends and community mean.

In his long missive, Happy brought me up to date on his children,
including a descriptive explanation of the carrot farm where his son-
in-law, Marvin, works. It was fascinating to read.

I also learned about family history; found out that Happy's family
had once owned farmland next to my grandparents.

Happy even told me about his trip to Hawaii with his children. It
remains one of the highlights of Happy's life.

Along about the 16th or 17th page of the letter, Happy reminded
me that folks at the Burr Oak bank still send him a card each year
"and they all sign their names," he added.

And Happy mentioned again of when his mother died and his
father was returning to the Bronson area with his young children.

During the height on the long train trip, the children became fussy. An exasperated woman, unable to sleep in the commotion, complained to Happy's father.

"Where's the children's mother?" she angrily asked.

Happy's father quietly replied: "In the baggage car ahead."

Happy's father was taking his wife home for burial.

As it turned out, when the train passengers learned what had happened, they helped with the children, giving the father needed rest.

To make a short story short, a woman on the train later wrote a song of what happened on that train ride, titled "The Baggage Car Ahead."

Happy was adopted by his aunt and later told about the train event. For years he tried to locate the sheet music of the song. When I wrote a column about it, a Sturgis resident gave me a copy.

You can imagine how Happy felt when I sent him the music. Today, he still writes about his mother, his extended family and friends, and his belief in mankind.

The Mister says that kids and older people are drawn to me. I guess that's true. For years a former Sturgis resident named Lou Moon wrote to me. We had never met and he began his first letter with a proper "My dear Mrs. Carol Ankney, editor of the paper." In time, the greeting became shorter. Before his death, Lou wrote "My Dear Carol." I treasure those letters.

And now it is Happy who still writes. He's in his nineties and I know that someday I will answer the phone and hear words that will lessen my world.

But until then, I eagerly await the letters from a fellow named Happy.

A magic couple – and love

It was a rare love affair. I watched it, sometimes as an intruder, as it developed over 40 years. But the affair (actually, it was a marriage) was going full-bloom 10 years before that.

Their names were Leland and Hilda, he of the timeless grace and she of the ladylike ways.

They were like old wine, mellowed and warm, adding color with the years. I knew, even as a child, they were set apart from other couples.

I recall my dad once saying, "Leland is the best of what every man wants to be." My dad's words still fit the man Leland is today. Leland's many Sturgis and area friends will testify to it.

I loved Leland and Hilda as a child, but found it difficult to tell them. It seemed too forward, unneeded. It was as if their world was secure and already rich in love. I was too young then to understand that there are many kinds of love – and all are needed.

But once, just once, I was presumptuous enough to tell Leland and Hilda something. I felt no guilt in saying it.

I told that magic couple that if God had granted me seconds, I would have wished, after my own folks, that they were my parents.

Neither Hilda nor Leland reproached me. They knew there was no disrespect meant to the memory of my parents, who had died young.

Leland and Hilda moved through life with a tastefulness of another time. There was an old world aura surrounding them. They were content with what life brought them and cast no ill word about others.

Their lives were too appreciated to find – or make – problems.

They seemed the epitome of what parents should be – but had no children. I never learned why and certainly no family member ever talked about it. Whatever the reason, it was theirs, a private affair.

Hilda was a small lady, but a great wit. Her laughter and love of life was infectious. She radiated energy. Leland was tall and quiet, a balance of manners, integrity and graciousness. They were incomparable.

As many couples do who are childless, they built their lives mostly around each other. They were mirror images of thought, a happening that sometimes comes from sharing a half-century or more of another's life.

Through it all, they remained lovers and friends – and were not embarrassed for others to know it. They truly liked and loved each other.

They married in the spring of their lives and journeyed together through their summer and fall. In the winter of their lives, without warning, Leland lost Hilda.

He buried her on a day when crimson leaves carpeted the country hillside with a patchwork blanket. He hesitated a long moment before he left the gravesite, looking back over his shoulder a last time.

They gave each other a lifetime of rare happiness. Leland knows that and does not despair, though his days are lonely and less meaningful without her.

One sometimes wonders about love affairs like theirs, and if love should be of such magnitude that the loss brings great pain.

One might ask Leland Hogmire. He does not question. He has a lifetime of treasured memories. He loved a great lady. Leland knows what a rare gift from God means.

Bathtimes can bring Surprises

My grandson balked on taking his daily shower the other day. He's eight and being all-boy, water for body-cleaning purposes is kin to a dirty word in his opinion.

"But, I just took a bath yesterday," he wailed, indignation rising in his voice.

"I don't care. Take another one" I replied, knowing full well that he not only had romped in the black dirt in the park across the street, but had undoubtedly handled every dog and cat in the neighborhood, give or take a few toads along the way.

He gave me a reproachful look, the kind that's supposed to make grandmas feel guilty.

I pointed my finger at the bathroom.

Sulking, he stalked toward the bathroom. And then, flinging one last retort, he said: "I'll bet you didn't have to take a bath every day when you were a kid."

Touché.

A bath a day? With no bathroom? Only an outhouse?

Now, that's not to mean that my mother allowed dirty bodies.

"Poor we may be; dirty we are not," she drilled into us.

And that meant a ritual that today's kids will never know.

Back then, in the Upper Peninsula town of Sidnaw, we didn't have a pump nor running water on the premises. When we needed water, we did what the other citizens did – went to the town pump. There was one situated at each end of town.

We used a large milk can to haul the water in a wagon in summer. In the winter, a sled was necessary. Let me tell you, obtaining water and taking a bath was treacherous in those days.

To begin with, everyone had to try that touch-your-tongue-to-the-cold-pump in winter. Ever do that? Left half your tongue skin on the pump – if you were fortunate enough to get the tongue loose. I was a slow-learner; had mine caught three times before the age of 10. Never could turn down a dare.

And then, after struggling with that load of water all the way home, the water had to be put in a copper boiler on the stove and heated. The stove, of course, was wood-fed and that meant more work for a kid, hauling in wet wood for fuel.

We were allowed to use water from the rain barrel to wash our hair, but not for bathing. The hard water was bathing, drinking and washing clothes.

After the water heated, my mother scooped pans of it into a washtub sitting at the side of the stove.

And then she'd stand back and wait.

"Who's first?" she'd ask, seldom glancing at me. It was common knowledge that I was the last to hit the tub. My idea of a bath was to douse in the creek in the summer.

As always, my older sister, Alice, had demurely completed her bath away from the prying eyes of younger sisters. Mary Jeanne, my elder by 18 months, was the dutiful child, never having to be led to water.

And then there was Donna, my younger sister by six years. She was the blond cherub, the kid who could charm everyone. She loved baths because she could fit in the tub; the rest of us were a bit big for it.

I was always last, with Donna preceding me. It was a ritual – until a revealing day when Donna was three.

As usual, I was stalling to escape the weekly bath. Weekly is correct. You "washed up by hand" or "took a sponge bath" the other days. On Saturdays came the full immersion, the baptism of tub, so-to-speak.

There I was, finally forced to get in that washtub. I was sitting down, my bony legs hanging over the sides. Donna, wrapped in a large towel, wandered up to view the event.

"Guess what I did in the water," she said.

Bored and bothered with a constant hanging-on younger sister, I waved her away.

She persisted.

"Guess what I did," she intoned.

"Well, you're going to tell me, so go ahead," I said, not paying much attention.

"I went potty in the water," she said solemnly.

I was out of the tub in half a second. Staring incredulously at her, I hollered to my mother.

"She peed in the water," I screeched, close to hysteria. "And I took my bath after her!"

"You always take your bath when I get done," Donna reminded.

I had the distinct feeling looking at her innocent face that there was more.

"I ALWAYS go potty in the water," Donna said triumphantly,

staring at me with those big eyes.

I never took my Saturday bath after that kid again.

My grandson is fortunate. He doesn't have a younger sister who can make an impression in a big way.

Hospice: Help in the darkness

There are few things in life more terrible than a terminal illness. To those who know their death sentences, living out the remainder of their lives can be terrifying.

The fear, pain, questions, strain of family relationships, handling the emotions of knowing approximately how long one has to live is a world of uncertainty. There is a feeling of being alone, unable to look ahead and live the best measure of the time left.

But there is a group that can make those final weeks —or months— more comfortable, easier to bear. Not easy. Easier. And in the crushing truth of knowing life is limited, that beacon may be the one thing that helps.

Hospice Care, Inc., in Sturgis is one year old, but in terms of what it has meant to the people served, it is an era of timeless thankfulness.

Hospice is a group that offers special help during a person's terminal illness. The amount of help depends on the individuals. Hospice volunteers are trained to be available when they are needed, whatever the need is. For some clients it may be simply a voice to talk with. Or it can mean special help, such as transportation to doctors, medication dispensed under doctor supervision, or helping if a client is bedridden. The services are varied and open, with the first regard the particular needs of the client.

The foremost goal of hospice is to provide clients a means to live out their allotted life span to the fullest, with the concept that the family is the unit of care. It affords clients the assurance they can remain at home with their loved ones if they choose, with help from hospice teams a call away. Help also can be given to hospitalized clients.

In terms of the modern hospice, its birth took place in London in 1967 under the guidance of Dr. Dame Cecily Saunders.

The first hospice program in the United States was formulated in 1974 and units are established in 50 states. Nearly 1,000 hospices are caring for 19,000 terminally ill patients, according to the National Hospital Organization. Predictions are the units will number 4,500 by 1990 and 6,800 by 1994. Medicare has certified 119 units.

Hospice is a non-profit organization. Though, the Sturgis group was founded before 1984, it accepted its first client last February. Thirty-two referrals were made to the organization, and the unit served 26 families in 1984. Families were under hospice care a total of 1,099 days, hospice officials said.

Before service volunteers are accepted into the hospice program, they must attend training sessions. They must be prepared to deal with crises –physical, medical and emotional. Most of all they must be understanding, sensitive people who can relate to the individual needs of terminally ill clients. In addition, patient care coordinators keep close touch with volunteers and trainers.

Referrals to the hospice program come from many areas, such as doctors, hospitals, nursing homes or individuals. Not everyone facing a terminal illness wants to use hospice services. And hospice officials understand. They are ready and willing to help only if clients choose that route.

Brochures about the hospice program are on display at most area physicians' offices. In addition, hospice has several speakers who will address clubs and organizations to explain the hospice concept. A movie, "Day by Day," also is available for public or private viewing. All one needs to do is call 651-6255 to arrange speaking engagements.

There is much more one could write about hospice, about its funding, its goals, but the words of Elisabeth Kubler-Ross, in her book, "Death, The Final Stage of Growth," eloquently explains the meaning of hospice:

"Lord, make me an instrument of your health: where there is sickness, let me bring cure; where there is injury, aid; where there is suffering, ease; where there is sadness, comfort; where there is despair, hope; where there is death, acceptance and peace."

"Grant that I may not: so much seek to be justified, as to console; to be obeyed as to understand; to be honored, as to love, for it is in giving ourselves that we heal; it is in listening that we comfort, and in dying that we are born to eternal life."

Who Cared about Shaun?

His name was Shaun Gates. A Detroit newspaper reporter interviewed his aunt, who said he was "the sweetest boy you'd ever meet."

Someone didn't think so. They threw him out with the trash.

Detroit police say Shaun's battered body was found in a dumpster near Tiger Stadium. Shaun had met all his tigers earlier. Two-footed ones.

Death ended Shaun's agony, but a medical examiner said the final beating wasn't the first in the four-year-old's life.

One wonders what humanity did to that little boy, but Shaun is representative of what happens every day. If we can stand to, we should look at Shaun's life and learn what happens when innocent children fall between the cracks of justice.

Shaun's mother died when he was two, leaving eight children. Shaun's father couldn't – or wouldn't – take responsibility for the children. He asked the court to grant guardianship of them to others. The court, routinely, didn't check out the guardians. Shaun was shuttled to homes of friends and strangers.

The father, however, wouldn't stay away. Although he wouldn't take the child, he kept interfering. Guardians threw in the towel.

But statements from them tell the horror of what society allowed to happen to Shaun. One guardian said Shaun thought she and her husband were his mom and dad. Shaun's grandparents told him they weren't. But they offered no help. The guardian said Shaun was taken from her home and placed elsewhere by his father. He said "Shaun then thought he had two dads."

Shaun had proof that few people cared. He never had roots, never knew where he belonged. No one gave him the stability, nurturing and love he needed.

But at his last residence, police say, someone gave Shaun fear, beatings, broken bones and death. Police have charged the guardian, Shaun's father's friend, with involuntary manslaughter, and her husband with murder.

Neighbors now admit they saw Shaun often, bruised and with lumps on his body. They saw he seemed frightened. Of life? Of death? More likely, both.

Except for one person who called children protective services, no one acted. The complaint was checked, but nothing came of it. After Shaun died, the murder suspect's sister testified she saw the guardian slap Shaun in the face so hard it drew blood. Why? He wasn't eating fast enough. But the sister did nothing.

What have we come to, when innocent children are placed in homes where they aren't wanted and are mistreated. Did anyone care how Shaun lived? Or if he lived?

Don't say it isn't our problem. By the grace of God and all that is decent, it is.

The courts will deal with Shaun Gates' murderers. But that doesn't ease my anger. That boy's death could have been prevented.

I'm angry at courts that don't follow through and check on

children. I'm angry at friend of the court departments who become mired in so many cases they become immune to individual needs. I'm angry with a legislative and justice system that ties the hands of caring people and prevents them from doing more.

But I'm easy to make complaints about child neglect or abuse. It isn't easy to take children from parents or other individuals. But waiting can be too late. Who spoke for Shaun? No one spoke loud enough.

Don't think it happens in someone else's town. Child abuse and neglect happens here. Down our street. Ask law enforcement officers. Check the court records. And listen when children complain.

If we demand society use better rules, insist tougher laws be available to courts, provide resources so authorities can handle caseloads, then maybe somebody wouldn't look into a dumpster and find the battered remains of a Shaun again.

Shaun didn't have to be thrown out in the garbage like yesterday's trash. If we had the collective conscience to demand accountability, we could ensure that kids receive the care and love they deserve.

But I'm a realist. I know there are too many people who don't care enough, won't become involved or be responsible.

There will be more Shauns next week, if not tomorrow.

Who Spoke for Felicia's Life?

In the picture she smiles at the world with that mischievous look tots her age usually have. Most mothers love three-year-olds like Felicia Humphrey.

Felicia's mother didn't give a damn about her child. She killed her.

Detroit police say Felicia's mother admitted putting the youngster in a running washing machine as punishment for wetting her pants.

She purposely helped her child on her trip to death. The ride wasn't free; the price was Felicia's life.

Ironically, death meant peace for Felicia; life was the real torment.

Felicia's death was horrible. An autopsy showed she died from drowning and a swollen brain.

Felicia's mother told officers she beat the youngster with belts and a plastic baseball bat, locked her in a closet at night, and tied her in a high chair because she misbehaved.

Felicia also was forced to wear her soiled underpants over her head, and whipped for not following orders.

Worse yet, when Felicia's mother locked her in the closet, she gave the key to Felicia's uncle. He raped the tot.

All this to a little girl just beginning to view the world around her, to taste life.

Many people are coming forward to say they saw Felicia mistreated for a long time. They'll talk now, but it's too late for Felicia.

What I want to know is, did anyone care how Felicia lived? Or if she lived?

Cases like Felicia don't always happen in other cities. They happen in our town, down our street. Ask prosecutors and law enforcement officers. If you doubt it, ask the Friend of the Court, Protective Services and other officials who are there to help kids, but can't act if they don't know about the abuse.

We should be outraged. Don't say it isn't our business, our responsibility. By any measure of decency, it is.

The courts will rule on the crimes of Felicia's mother and uncle. But that won't stop the killing of other babies, the mental and physical abuse that blemishes the American scene.

Why are children treated so terrible? I've heard some reasons, such as children having children and being too immature to raise them. I've seen statistics that explain stress in lifestyles. I've examined documents that show courts and protective service departments' caseloads are crowded.

None of it washes, just as the brutal washing machine action didn't cleanse the so-called improprieties of an innocent child.

What makes me more angry is that so many people said nothing, wouldn't interfere. It can't be called interference when a child is beaten, raped and jammed into a washing machine and her cries for help ignored as she slowly drowns.

I hear the outcry about abortion, the crusade to prevent killing the unborn children. Can't we do more? Why is it too few people are willing to step in to save a child's life outside the womb?

Don't tell me it's someone else's problem. If a child can't depend on loving care by the people who should care the most – the parents– then others should do something about it.

Journalists can write words about it, hoping to stop the carnage. But I'm a realist. It will happen again next month, next week. Probably tomorrow.

Wake up, world.. Felicia isn't unique; there are many other children who suffer unspeakable abuse.

Common decency should prompt us to stop these things from happening. We must demand that courts change their rules, ask for more investigative money for protective service units.

And speak up. If we don't become involved, there will be more children who suffer Felicia's fate – kids thrown away like yesterday's trash.

CPSIA information can be obtained at www.ICGtesting.com
Printed in the USA
268350BV00005B/1/P